PRAISE FOR *AMAZON*

'If you believe in the philosophy of knowing your enemy then *Amazon* is a must-read for any omnichannel retailer.' **Tim Mason, CEO, Eagle Eye Solutions**

'Natalie Berg and Miya Knights have written one of the definitive accounts of the rise of Amazon and its dramatic impact on the world of retail. As a financial analyst that has followed Amazon for over two decades, I found this book to be chock-full of insights and datapoints. Berg and Knights' explanation for why Amazon "went physical" – developing Amazon Go Stores, acquiring Whole Foods – is particularly compelling. There are valuable lessons in this book for investors and for retailers, especially for companies looking to excel at WACD: What Amazon Can't Do. I highly recommend this book.' **Mark S Mahaney, Managing Director and Analyst, RBC Capital Markets**

'Amazon is a phenomenon – focused relentlessly on customers, reinvesting heavily to drive growth, not letting the here-and-now distract it from its long-term vision. For any e-commerce entrepreneur, Berg and Knight bring rich insight into how Amazon has become a 25-year overnight success. But as well as unpicking Amazon's growth, it's also a well-timed reminder about the seismic and exciting changes in customer behaviour that's helping new retailers like Missguided make an impact.' **Nitin Passi, CEO and Founder, Missguided**

'Berg and Knights' in-depth look at Amazon will be the go-to handbook for retailers looking to understand its impact. And because of their comprehensive, up-close-and-personal knowledge of that business, and its peers across US and Europe, it's rich with objective insight. But it's much more than a book about Amazon; it's a social commentary on the impact of higher-than-ever customer expectations supercharged by technology. Shoppers know what was impossible is now possible; what was unfeasible, feasible; what was a dream is now a reality. Berg and Knights remind us reinvention to serve this new customer is not optional for any retailer.' **Andy Bond, CEO, Pepkor Europe**

'As well as being a comprehensive and authoritative insight on how the Amazon model relentlessly evolved to create more Amazon, it's also an indispensable insight into the future of shopping and how retail must adapt to stay relevant to the "on-my-terms" customer.'
Robin Phillips, CEO, The Watch Shop

'Berg and Knights lay out in a comprehensive manner an essential primer on Amazon. This roadmap of history and progression of the online behemoth surgically explores key inflections and pivots that have led to the DNA of Amazon. Most importantly, the insights and implications presented will provoke anyone who participates in the "Industry of Everything" that Amazon competes in to reassess and evolve their own strategies. I know I will.'
Anh Nguyen Lue, North America Open Innovation and eCom Category Management Leader, P&G

Amazon

How the world's most relentless retailer
will continue to revolutionize commerce

Natalie Berg
Miya Knights

KoganPage

Publisher's note

Every possible effort has been made to ensure that the information contained in this book is accurate at the time of going to press, and the publisher and authors cannot accept responsibility for any errors or omissions, however caused. No responsibility for loss or damage occasioned to any person acting, or refraining from action, as a result of the material in this publication can be accepted by the editor, the publisher or any of the authors.

First published in Great Britain and the United States in 2019 by Kogan Page Limited

2nd Floor, 45 Gee Street	c/o Martin P Hill Consulting	4737/23 Ansari Road
London EC1V 3RS	122 W 27th St, 10th Floor	Daryaganj
United Kingdom	New York NY 10001	New Delhi 110002
www.koganpage.com	USA	India

© Natalie Berg, Miya Knights, 2019

ISBNs

Hardback	978 0 7494 9772 9
Paperback	978 0 7494 8279 4
Ebook	978 0 7494 8280 0

British Library Cataloguing-in-Publication Data

A CIP record for this book is available from the British Library.

Library of Congress Cataloging-in-Publication Data
Names: Berg, Natalie, author. | Knights, Miya, author.
Title: Amazon : how the world's most relentless retailer will continue to
    revolutionize commerce / Natalie Berg and Miya Knights.
Description: 1 Edition. | New York : Kogan Page Ltd, [2019] | Includes
    bibliographical references and index.
Identifiers: LCCN 2018049311 (print) | LCCN 2018051183 (ebook) | ISBN
    9780749482800 (ebook) | ISBN 9780749482794 (alk. paper) | ISBN 9780749482800
    (eISBN)
Subjects: LCSH: amazon.com (Firm)–History. | Electronic commerce. | Stores,
    Retail. | Selling.
Classification: LCC HF5548.32 (ebook) | LCC HF5548.32 .B457 2019 (print) |
    DDC 381/.142065–dc23
LC record available at https://lccn.loc.gov/2018049311

Typeset by Integra Software Services, Pondicherry
Print production managed by Jellyfish
Printed and bound by CPI Group (UK) Ltd, Croydon, CR0 4YY

CONTENTS

It's an Amazon world

Relevant 'rɛlǝv(ǝ)nt *appropriate to the current time, period, or circumstances; of contemporary interest.*

Retail is going through a transition. The naysayers will call it an apocalypse; to others, it's digital transformation. But one thing we can all agree on is that this is a period of profound structural change.

The rise of online shopping, combined with broader shifts in consumer values and spending habits, has exposed an overbuilt retail landscape. Stores are now closing at record rates and retail bankruptcies are at recessionary levels. Traditional business models are being displaced and everyone is scrambling for survival. The world's largest retailer has even changed its name: after nearly half a century as Wal-Mart Stores, in 2018 the retailer dropped Stores from its legal name to reflect the new digital era. This is retail Darwinism – evolve or die.

But there's one word that often gets overlooked in all this talk of an impending apocalypse – relevance. The most important rule in retail is being relevant to customers. If you can't deliver on the basic principles of giving customers what they want or standing out from the competition, then you don't stand a chance. For these retailers, yes, the Doomsday clock is ticking.

For those willing to embrace change, however, this is a fantastically exciting time to be in retail. The future is fewer, more impactful stores. The future is offering shoppers a more blended online and offline experience. And the future is excelling at WACD: What Amazon Can't Do.

The titan of 21st-century commerce, Amazon has grown from online bookseller to become one of the most valuable public companies in the world. At the time of writing, Amazon accounted for nearly half of US e-commerce sales.[1] In 2010, the retailer employed 30,000 people. By 2018, that figure rose to 560,000.[2] Amazon has become the undisputed market leader in everything from cloud computing to voice technology. It is the number one destination for product search ahead of Google[3] and, by the time you're reading this, Amazon will likely hold the title of largest US clothing retailer.[4] In 2018, at the time of writing, Amazon was worth the equivalent of Walmart, Home Depot, Costco, CVS, Walgreens, Target, Kroger, Best Buy, Kohl's, Macy's, Nordstrom, JC Penney and Sears combined.[5] Those cardboard boxes are certainly changing retail.

As if that's not enough, Amazon has been busy ramping up its global operations. In 2008, Amazon's international presence was limited to six markets: Canada, UK, Germany, France, Japan and China. A decade later, operations outside of the US accounted for one-third of retail sales, spanning 18 foreign markets from the bright lights of Mexico City to the remote hills of the Himalayas.[6]

Amazon more than doubled its square footage in just three years; by 2018, Amazon owned or leased more than 250 million square feet of space around the world.[7] Amazon has added more than 30 new product categories since its site was launched,[8] and now boasts over 100 million Prime members around the world willing to pay roughly $100 a year to shop with them.[9]

As with most disruptors, Amazon is an outsider. They are a tech company at heart, albeit a customer-obsessed one. They have relentlessly built out their retail offer, not just through category expansion – upending entire sectors in the process – but also by enhancing entertainment, fulfilment and technology capabilities to create a unique, frictionless and fully embedded experience for the customer.

One of the fundamental reasons for Amazon's success is its unwavering commitment to a vision laid out over two decades ago: to relentlessly innovate in a bid to create long-term value for customers. Amazon's success stems from its constant dissatisfaction with the status quo, its appetite for disruption, its desire to build lifelong loyalty among its shoppers. Amazon is full of surprises, but every action is ultimately guided by a vision that hasn't changed since its inception.

To competitors, Amazon is ruthless and fearsome. To customers, Amazon is effortless and, increasingly, indispensable. They have hit the ultimate shopper sweet spot by combining access to millions of products with ever faster delivery. And that's just the beginning. Capitalizing on the strength and trust of its brand, Amazon is now spreading its tentacles across entirely new industries. The mere whisper that Amazon might enter a sector is enough to send stocks tumbling. And it's getting clearer by the day that Amazon is not satisfied with just being the retailer; it also wants to be the infrastructure. We believe that, by 2021, the majority of Amazon's sales will be derived from services rather than products, as cloud computing, subscriptions, advertising and financial services grow in importance.

But Amazon is at an inflection point. The king of e-commerce has recognized that, for all its conveniences, online-only is no longer enough. The convergence of physical and digital retail is accelerating. If Amazon wants to crack the grocery and fashion sectors, it needs stores. If Amazon wants to offset rising shipping and customer acquisition costs, it needs stores. And if Amazon wants to further drive Prime membership, adoption of voice technology, and one-hour delivery, guess what? It needs stores.

By acquiring Whole Foods Market, Amazon sent a very clear signal that the future of retail is clicks and mortar. Amazon will redefine the supermarket for the 21st-century shopper – stripping out checkouts, making mobile a defining feature, utilizing stores for fast delivery and, crucially, engaging with shoppers in a way that they could never do online. The store of the future will become more experiential and service-led.

Grocery will unlock a very big piece of the puzzle for Amazon: frequency. As an ex-Whole Foods boss puts it, 'food is the platform for selling you everything else'.[10] This is why Amazon's move into groceries should worry all retailers, not just supermarkets. It's another step closer to achieving total retail dominance.

As we'll portray throughout this book, Amazon is, in many ways, uncatchable. They play by an entirely different set of rules with access to cheap capital and an entrenched ecosystem that is nearly impossible to replicate. But Amazon will be a force for good in that retail will raise its game. We'll see a bifurcation of the winners and losers. The undifferentiated and underperforming retailers will be weeded out, and the retailers left standing will be much stronger for having reinvented themselves – ensuring relevance, and ultimately, survival.

Notes

1 Vena, Danny (2018) Amazon dominated e-commerce sales in 2017, *The Motley Fool*, 12 January. Available from: https://www.fool.com/investing/2018/01/12/amazon-dominated-e-commerce-sales-in-2017.aspx [Last accessed 12/6/2018].

2 YouTube (2018) Jeff Bezos on breaking up and regulating Amazon (Online video). Available from: https://www.youtube.com/watch?time_continue=85&v=xVzkOWxd7uQ [Last accessed 12/6/2018].

3 Nickelsburg, Monica (2017) Chart: Amazon is the most popular destination for shoppers searching for products online, *Geekwire*, 6 July. Available from: https://www.geekwire.com/2017/chart-amazon-popular-destination-shoppers-searching-products-online/ [Last accessed 12/6/2018].

4 Thomas, Lauren (2018) Amazon's 100 million Prime members will help it become the No. 1 apparel retailer in the US, *CNBC*, 19 April. Available from: https://www.cnbc.com/2018/04/19/amazon-to-be-the-no-1-apparel-retailer-in-the-us-morgan-stanley.html [Last accessed 12/6/2018].

5 Author research; Google finance.

6 Author research; Amazon 10-K; 18 markets outside US as of June 2018, as per confirmation from Angie Quenell at Amazon.

7 Securities and Exchange Commission (nd) Amazon 10-K for the fiscal year ended 31/12/17. Available from: https://www.sec.gov/Archives/edgar/data/1018724/000101872418000005/amzn-20171231x10k.htm [Last accessed 12/6/2018].

8 Sender, Hanna, Stevens, Laura and Serkez, Yaryna (2018) Amazon: the making of a giant, *Wall Street Journal*, 14 March. Available from: https://www.wsj.com/graphics/amazon-the-making-of-a-giant/ [Last accessed 12/6/2018].

9 Siegel, Rachel (2018) The Amazon stat long kept under wraps is revealed: Prime has over 100 million subscribers, *Washington Post*, 18 April. Available from: https://www.washingtonpost.com/news/business/wp/2018/04/18/the-amazon-stat-long-kept-under-wraps-is-revealed-prime-has-over-100-million-subscribers [Last accessed 12/6/2018].

10 Kowitt, Beth (2018) How Amazon is using Whole Foods in a bid for total retail domination, *Fortune*, 21 May. Available from: http://fortune.com/longform/amazon-groceries-fortune-500/ [Last accessed 12/6/2018].

Why Amazon is not your average retailer: introduction to retail strategy

02

Flywheel *A heavy revolving wheel in a machine which is used to increase the machine's momentum and thereby provide greater stability or a reserve of available power.*

Amazon is full of contradictions. The retailer whose strategy was to be 'unprofitable for a long time' is now the second most valuable company in the world. Amazon is a retailer that doesn't own most of the stuff it sells. Amazon is both a feared competitor and, increasingly, retail partner. Depending on who you ask, the phrase 'The Amazon Effect' can either mean putting a company out of business or drastically enhancing the customer experience.

Amazon sells everything from nappies to treadmills, but it also produces hit television shows and provides cloud computing services to the US Government. Amazon is a hardware manufacturer, payment processor, advertising platform, ocean freight business, publisher, delivery network, fashion designer, private label business, home security provider and an airline. It doesn't stop there. Amazon wants to be a supermarket, a bank, a healthcare provider and, by the time you're reading this, it will probably be on the cusp of disrupting at least one more industry.

Amazon is aware that, to the outside world, such diversification seems scattered and illogical. Is Amazon simply a jack of all trades, but master of none? 'As we do new things, we accept that we may be misunderstood for

Figure 2.1 Market capitalization: select US retailers (7 June 2018)

SOURCE Author research/NBK Retail; Google Finance

long periods of time,'[1] the retailer stated on its website in 2018. To understand Amazon, you first need to understand their strategic framework: the flywheel.

Losing money to make money

Created by management theorist Jim Collins, the flywheel effect describes a virtuous cycle that makes companies ever more successful. On his website, Collins states: '[T]here is no single defining action, no grand program, no one killer innovation, no solitary lucky break, no miracle moment. Rather, the process resembles relentlessly pushing a giant, heavy flywheel, turn upon turn, building momentum until a point of breakthrough, and beyond.'[2]

So how does this apply to Amazon? In his book, *The Everything Store*, published in 2013, Brad Stone explains the initial thinking:

> Bezos and his lieutenants sketched their own virtuous cycle, which they believed powered their business. It went something like this: lower prices led to more customer visits. More customers increased the volume of sales and attracted more commission-paying third-party sellers to the site. That allowed Amazon to get more out of fixed costs like the fulfilment centres and the servers needed to run the website. This greater efficiency then enabled it to lower prices further. Feed any part of this flywheel, they reasoned, and it should accelerate the loop.[3]

After two decades of investment, the flywheel is now spinning. Amazon continues to diversify its business, looking well beyond the borders of retail, to feed the flywheel. Amazon isn't satisfied with being the Everything Store,

Figure 2.2 The flywheel: the key to Amazon's success

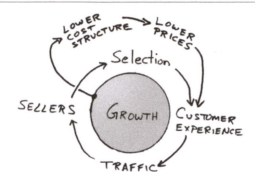

it also wants to be the Everywhere Store. Intentions to disrupt entirely new sectors like banking and healthcare may seem incongruous with the core retail division, but we have to remember two things:

1 Every new service is another spoke on the wheel. Amazon's success cannot be measured by looking at one business unit in isolation.

2 The one thing linking all of Amazon's seemingly irrational moves is the opportunity to improve the customer experience, further embedding itself with shoppers in the process.

In 2018, Bain & Company predicted that a banking service from Amazon could attract more than 70 million customer accounts within five years – which would make Amazon the size of the third-largest American bank, Wells Fargo.[4] Trust and loyalty to the Amazon brand is now well established and can be translated across other sectors, although this will not come without greater scrutiny.

Now let's take a closer look at how Amazon's values have shaped their strategy to become one of the most disruptive and influential retail businesses of the 21st century.

Amazon's core principles

'We're a company of pioneers. It's our job to make bold bets, and we get our energy from inventing on behalf of customers. Success is measured against the possible, not the probable.'
Amazon, 2018[5]

Winning combo: customer obsession and passion for invention

Most retailers would consider themselves innovative, customer-centric and results-oriented. The difference with Amazon is that they really mean it.

They started out in books, but for over a decade now Amazon's bold mission has been to become 'Earth's most customer-centric company' – full stop. They have remained unwaveringly committed to this goal, ensuring that every decision made will ultimately add value to the customer. The whole point of retail, after all, is to serve the shopper.

> 'If you want to get to the truth about what makes us different, it's this. We are genuinely customer-centric, we are genuinely long-term-oriented and we genuinely like to invent. Most companies are not those things.'
> **Jeff Bezos, 2013**[6]

Amazon is clearly not the first retailer in the world to obsess over its customers. In fact, one might argue that inspiration was taken from the late Sam Walton, founder of Walmart, who genuinely embraced the 'customer is king' mantra and once famously said, 'There is only one boss. The customer. And he can fire everybody in the company from the chairman on down, simply by spending his money somewhere else.'[7]

What sets Amazon apart, however, is their relentless dissatisfaction with the status quo. They are continuously looking for better ways of serving their customers and making the shopping experience even more convenient. When retailers talk of innovation, they tend to mean things like pop-up stores and digital displays. With Amazon, it's underwater warehouses and robotic postmen.

In his 2016 letter to shareholders, Jeff Bezos wrote:

> There are many advantages to a customer-centric approach, but here's the big one: customers are always beautifully, wonderfully dissatisfied, even when they report being happy and business is great. Even when they don't yet know it, customers want something better, and your desire to delight customers will drive you to invent on their behalf.

Bezos makes the point that no one ever asked Amazon to create the Prime membership programme 'but it sure turns out they wanted it.'[8] Amazon has the solution before the customer need even exists.

In 2017, the retailer spent over \$20 billion on research and development – more than any other US company.[9] Yet despite Amazon's deep pockets for R&D, the company considers frugality to be a key leadership principle as it helps to breed resourcefulness, self-sufficiency and invention.

Frugality is a common trait among the world's most successful retailers. In the early days, Amazon famously used doors as desks. Walmart got its very name because it only had seven letters, which was shorter than the alternative suggestions and therefore cheaper to install and light the exterior neon sign. Meanwhile, senior executives at Spain's largest retailer Mercadona are thought to keep a one-euro-cent coin in their pockets to remind them that they are working to cut costs for the shopper.[10]

Similarly, Amazon will only spend money when there's a clear benefit to the customer. 'Jeff would never dream of changing a pixel, a button, a place on the checkout or anything on that website unless you articulated to Jeff what it was going to do to the customer', said Brian McBride, ASOS Chairman and former Amazon UK boss, speaking at a retail technology conference in 2018. 'Unless there was something in it for the customer, why do it?'[11]

Amazon's leadership principles

1 Customer obsession.

2 Ownership.

3 Invent and simplify.

4 Leaders are right, a lot.

5 Learn and be curious.

6 Hire and develop the best.

7 Insist on the highest standards.

8 Think big.

9 Bias for action.

10 Frugality.

11 Earn trust.

12 Dive deep.

13 Have backbone; disagree and commit.

14 Deliver results.

Innovating at scale

So how does Amazon create a culture that thrives on agility? How do they innovate at scale?

One example is the 'working backwards' approach. Amazon has always been quite a vocal critic of PowerPoint slides (easy for the presenter, difficult for the audience). Instead, meetings are structured around six-page narratives which are silently read at the start of each meeting. The memos, according to Bezos, force a deeper clarity, particularly when it comes to new product development. They're designed to read as a mock press release announcing the finished product while conveying the benefits to the customer in layman's terms – or as Ian McAllister, currently Director of Alexa International, calls it, 'Oprah-speak', not 'Geek-speak'.

'Working backwards makes you accountable for how it will work for the customer.'
Paul Misener, Amazon Vice President for Global Innovation Policy and Communications, 2017[12]

These are 'centred around the customer problem, how current solutions (internal or external) fail, and how the new product will blow away existing solutions.' If the benefits don't sound appealing, then the product manager continues to tweak the internal document. 'Iterating on a press release is a lot less expensive than iterating on the product itself (and quicker!)', McAllister wrote in a 2012 blog.[13]

The result? Rapid innovation. A great example of this is Prime Now, Amazon's one- to two-hour delivery service, which went from product idea to launch in just 111 days.[14] This is how Amazon differentiates: their unique approach to product development enables them to marry a start-up mentality with the scale and resources of a large company.

The best place in the world to fail

Amazon values curiosity and risk taking, but not everything they touch turns to gold. Their biggest flop was arguably the Fire phone, which was no match for iPhones and Androids and eventually led to a $170 million write-off. Other short-lived experiments included: travel website Amazon Destinations, Groupon-like deals site Amazon Local and Amazon Wallet, an app that allowed shoppers to store gift cards and loyalty cards on their phone.

'Many of life's failures are people who did not realize how close they were to success when they gave up.'
Thomas Edison[15]

Innovation and failure, according to Bezos, are 'inseparable twins'. It is Amazon's acceptance of failure as a learning experience that sets them apart from other businesses. '[E]very single important thing that we have done has taken a lot of risk taking, perseverance, guts, and some of them have worked out, most of them have not', says Bezos. Let's be clear, the ones that have worked out – for example, Prime, Amazon Web Services (AWS) and Amazon Echo – have been colossal successes for the company.

The 20-year bet and importance of consistency

'We're going to be unprofitable for a long time. And that's our strategy.'
Jeff Bezos, 1997[16]

Wall Street is inherently short-termist, leaving most public companies focused on maximizing profitability and stock performance from quarter to quarter. Amazon does the exact opposite.

Since day one, Amazon has prioritized growth over profitability, measuring their own success by customer and revenue growth, the degree to which customers purchase from them on a repeat basis, and brand equity. The plan has always been to establish market leadership, which in turn would strengthen Amazon's economic model. The flywheel concept isn't designed for overnight success, it's about building long-lasting relationships with customers.

Not to be overlooked here is the importance of consistency in Amazon's strategy: its first-ever shareholder letter from 1997 reads as if it was written yesterday. Bezos didn't predict the future, he created it. Two decades ago, he laid out his vision to focus relentlessly on customers in a bid to create long-term value for both shoppers and shareholders. Don't forget that in 1997 Amazon was an online bookseller, nothing like the retail goliath it has become today, but nonetheless their strategy was crystallized.

For Amazon's plan to work, Bezos had to be in it for the long haul. He is now the richest person on the planet, though much of his net worth is tied

Figure 2.3   Playing the long games: Amazon sales vs profits

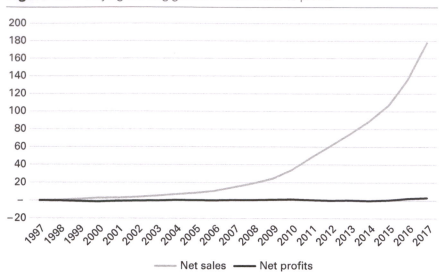

—— Net sales —— Net profits

SOURCE   Author research; Amazon 10-Ks

up in Amazon stock. Having him at the helm for more than two decades has helped to keep Amazon from wavering from the original vision. A thick skin and extraordinary focus were needed to shrug off the critics and quell shareholder fears. At the time of writing in 2018, Amazon has reported annual profits just 13 of its 21 years in existence, and even today profit margins remain lacklustre and erratic, far from the upwards linear movement that the financial markets expect to see. Most retail CEOs would have been fired by now, but Bezos trained his shareholders to be patient.

'Amazon, as best I can tell, is a charitable organization being run by elements of the investment community for the benefit of consumers.'
Matthew Yglesias, Executive Editor of Vox, 2013[17]

In the early years, however, a whole lot of people were betting against Amazon. By 2000, the year the dot-com bubble burst and Amazon's sixth in operation, the retailer had yet to report a profit and was haemorrhaging millions of dollars in losses. Wall Street analysts were convinced Bezos was building a house of cards,[18] with Lehman Bros analyst Ravi Suria predicting Amazon would run out of cash in a matter of months unless it could 'pull another financing rabbit out of its rather magical hat.'[19] Suria wasn't alone here. The same year, finance magazine *Barron's* put out a list of 51 internet companies that were expected to go bust by the end of 2000. The Burn Rate 51 included now-forgotten names like CDNow and Infonautics – and Amazon.

Headlines such as 'Can Amazon Survive?'[20] and 'Amazon: Ponzi Scheme or Wal-Mart of the Web?'[21] illustrated doubts over Amazon's future. Amazon was expected to be yet another victim of the dot-com bubble.

Despite the broader scepticism and genuine befuddlement over its unconventional business model, Amazon managed to persuade enough shareholders by telling a compelling story. He requested their patience and surprisingly they agreed. 'I think it comes down to a consistent message and consistent strategy, one that doesn't deviate when the stock goes down or goes up', said Bill Miller, the Chief Investment Officer at Miller Value Partners.[22] Today, investors are often confused when Amazon reports the occasional profit – they've come to expect Amazon to recycle any cash back into the business.

Former Amazon executive Brittain Ladd believes that companies either play a finite or infinite game. With a finite game, the company believes it can beat their competitors. It is characterized by an agreed set of rules and clearly defined mechanisms for scoring the game.

Speaking to the authors, Ladd commented:

> Amazon, however, plays an infinite game where the goal is to outlast competitors. Amazon understands that competitors will come and go. Amazon understands that it can't be the best at all things. Amazon has made a strategic decision to place its focus on outlasting its competitors by creating an ecosystem that flawlessly meets and serves the needs of consumers across an ever-expanding array of products, services and technology.

Cheap capital and sustainable moats

Amazon clearly play by their own set of rules. Without Bezos' vision, they wouldn't have earned the confidence of the investment community. Without the confidence of their shareholders, they wouldn't have been able to invest in the necessary infrastructure for the core e-commerce business or to innovate well beyond the borders of retail, adding those critical spokes to the flywheel. There would be no AWS, no Prime, no Alexa. Amazon wouldn't be Amazon.

Speaking at a logistics conference in 2018, Sir Ian Cheshire, Chairman of Debenhams, noted that the average retailer reinvests 1–2 per cent of its revenues into systems. Amazon reinvests 6 per cent. 'That's a factor of 5:1 which is going back into a better toolkit, testing and infrastructure', he said.[23]

NYU professor Scott Galloway takes this one step further with this assertion that Amazon is 'playing unfair and winning'. He explains: 'They have access to cheaper capital than any company in modern history. Amazon can now borrow money for less than the cost of what China can borrow money [for]. As a result, they're able to throw up more stuff against the wall than any other firm.'[24]

As a competitor, how can you possibly keep up with a company that has zero obligation to report a profit? A company whose primary expectation from their investors is to keep ploughing money into new areas of growth?

'You really develop very sustainable moats around a business when you run it at low margins', says Mark Mahaney, RBC Capital Managing Director who has covered internet stocks since 1998. 'Very few companies want to come into Amazon's core businesses and try to compete with them at 1 per cent margins or 2 per cent margins.'[25]

And that's just the retail business. Many of Amazon's 'non-core' businesses are in fact loss leaders. Prime subscription fees may now be a healthy top-line contributor, but most analysts agree that Amazon is likely still losing money on postage in a bid to encourage more frequent shopping.[26] Meanwhile, its devices such as Kindles and Echos[27] are typically sold at cost price or at a loss. Like Google, Amazon aims to lock in as many shoppers as possible and then make money on the content purchased through the device[28] (as well as gain valuable data about buying habits). Given that Echo owners spend 66 per cent more than the average Amazon shopper, the retailer is very clearly incentivized to subsidize sales[29] of its devices.

Uneven playing field: tax

We can't talk about Amazon's competitive advantages without mentioning tax. Over the past 15 years (2002–17), Walmart paid $103 billion in corporate income tax. That is 44 times the amount Amazon paid during the same period.[30]

Amazon is now the third-largest retailer in the world, in revenue terms, and, in 2018, became the second company in the US (following Apple) to hit $1trillion in market value.[31]

But companies don't pay tax on revenues – they pay tax on profits. Amazon's unconventional profit-sacrificing strategy has allowed them to minimize, sometimes even eliminate, their tax burden. In 2017, they reported $5.6 billion in profits but paid zero in federal taxes, the result of various tax credits and tax breaks for executive stock options.[32]

As an online retailer, Amazon has historically – and controversially – benefited from a 1992 Supreme Court ruling – Quill Corp. vs North Dakota – that prevented states from collecting sales tax from e-commerce companies unless those retailers have a physical presence in that state (in the form of an office or warehouse, for example). This is one of the reasons why Bezos was initially attracted to Washington as Amazon's headquarters: the state had a small population and its capital Seattle was becoming a technology hub. It's worth pointing out here that Bezos' first choice is said to have been a Native American reservation near San Francisco, which would have presented generous tax breaks had the state not intervened.

Amazon spent its early days building warehouses in small states like Nevada and Kansas, allowing them to deliver to nearby populous states like California and Texas, but without collecting sales taxes.[33] For years, the ability to sell stuff tax-free gave Amazon and other online retailers a gargantuan edge over bricks and mortar rivals. However, as Amazon continued to expand and its focus shifted to ever faster delivery, it had little choice but to open more fulfilment centres in closer proximity to its customers. 'When that strategy no longer became tenable, and as Amazon wanted to add more warehouses in more states to support its growing Prime two-day delivery program, the company often negotiated to get the taxes delayed, deferred, or reduced as a condition of collecting them',[34] Jeremy Bowman of the *Motley Fool* wrote in 2018.

Many states subsequently signed on to an agreement that allowed retailers to voluntarily collect sales tax. By 2017, Amazon was collecting sales tax from all 45 states that have a state-wide sales tax,[35] which meant that by the following year, when the Supreme Court finally overturned the 1992 ruling, the impact on Amazon was fairly minimal. It did, however, mean that Amazon's third-party merchants had to begin charging sales tax on their products (Amazon had previously only collected tax on the items it owned).[36]

> 'Quill creates rather than resolves market distortions. In effect, it is a judicially created tax shelter for businesses that limit their physical presence in a State but sell their goods and services to the State's consumers, something that has become easier and more prevalent as technology has advanced.'
> **Supreme Court of the United States, 2018**[37]

Meanwhile, in its search for a second headquarters in 2018, Amazon solicited bids from cities and regions across North America, promising $5 billion in investment and 50,000 new jobs over the next decade. The *Hunger Games*-style competition resulted in over 200 bids, with extraordinary offers ranging from New Jersey's $7 billion in tax incentives to Chicago's promise that employees would have to pay part of their salary back to Amazon as 'income tax'.

In Europe, Amazon's tax structure has been equally controversial. After over a decade of channelling sales through entities in Luxembourg, in 2015 Amazon began accounting for sales and paying taxes in Britain, Germany, Spain and Italy. The EU has since ordered Amazon to pay back €250 million in taxes, the result of an unfair tax break the company was given by Luxembourg in 2003, and has proposed a new 3 per cent digital tax on revenues – rather than profits – of large tech companies.

Meanwhile, in the UK, a 2017 revaluation of business rates disproportionately benefited Amazon and other online retailers. The rates, deemed by many as archaic, were calculated to take into account the rise in property prices since 2008; as most of Amazon's warehouses are located out of town, they actually saw their value (and therefore business levy) decline while many high street retailers saw their bill go up – some by up to 400 per cent. Another massive competitive advantage for Amazon.

Amazon's tax fight is far from over. President Trump, who himself said during the 2016 presidential debates that not paying his own taxes makes him 'smart', now has a bee in his bonnet over Amazon's tax planning. Ironically, the Trump Administration's 2017 Tax Act – which saw the rate slashed from 35 per cent to 21 per cent – is directly benefiting Amazon. In 2018, the retailer reported a provisional tax benefit of nearly $800 million.[38] Still, the threat of greater scrutiny looms, but more on this later.

Tweet

I have stated my concerns with Amazon long before the Election. Unlike others, they pay little or no taxes to state & local governments, use our Postal System as their Delivery Boy (causing tremendous loss to the U.S.), and are putting many thousands of retailers out of business! @realDonaldTrump 4:57 AM, 29 Mar 2018.

Three pillars: Marketplace, Prime, AWS

Tax loopholes and unique access to cheap capital have given Amazon a sustained competitive advantage over its bricks and mortar rivals. As we've touched on previously, this allowed Amazon to more rapidly invest in new areas for growth, resulting in what they describe as the three pillars of the business: Marketplace, Prime and AWS.

These businesses have played an instrumental role in growing Amazon's revenue and accelerating the flywheel. With the exception of AWS (which can perhaps be excused given this is Amazon's main profit engine), these businesses have directly added value to customers. What is more, they are largely unique to Amazon.

Marketplace

As one of the first retailers to open its site to third-party sellers, Amazon has been able to achieve its dream of offering 'Earth's biggest selection'. Customers benefit by having millions of products across dozens of categories at their fingertips, while Amazon reduces both inventory cost and risk. Its Marketplace has enabled Amazon to become the first port of call for even the most obscure products – from silicone wine glasses to cat scratch turntables – which when combined with Prime delivery becomes a very compelling proposition.

Marketplace has also proved to be a fruitful revenue stream, as Amazon takes a cut of about 15 per cent of the price of the merchandise.[39] From 2015 to 2017, revenues generated from third-party seller services nearly doubled to $32 billion, making it Amazon's largest source of revenue after retail product sales and ahead of AWS.[40]

Figure 2.4   Growing importance of services: Amazon net sales by business segment

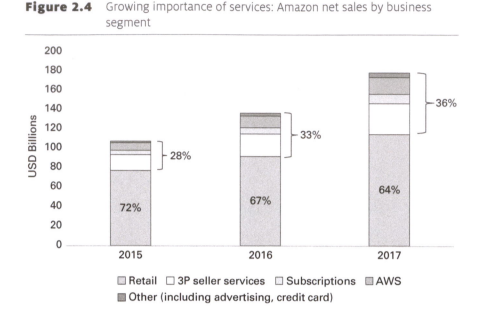

A growing number of Marketplace sellers are not only opting to sell through Amazon but are also looking to the retailer to store their products and, when an order comes in, to process payments and pick, pack and deliver the item to shoppers. The programme, called Fulfilment by Amazon (FBA), means that these products become eligible for fast Prime shipping and also have a greater chance of winning the Buy Box (so that the product appears in the first 'Add to Basket' button on the product detail page). For Amazon, FBA allows them to make better use of excess capacity while simultaneously increasing shipping volumes, and therefore leverage, with the likes of UPS and FedEx. But perhaps the best part of FBA is that it would take decades for another retailer to replicate.

Prime

Amazon's membership scheme has proven to be the glue of their ecosystem. With over 100 million members around the globe, Prime has become so much more than a loyalty programme – it's become a way of life. Amazon has cleverly taken Prime from a scheme that initially centred on delivery perks to an all-encompassing content-streaming, book-lending, photo-storing beast of a membership programme. The result? Higher spend, shopper frequency and retention. We'll discuss this in greater detail in the next chapter.

Amazon Web Services

Amazon's cloud storage service may not directly benefit shoppers, but it has certainly proven to be Amazon's white knight. Operating margins are consistently in the high single digits and in 2017 the division was responsible for more than 100 per cent of Amazon's operating profit. Remember Brad Stone's point about feeding *any* part of the flywheel to accelerate it? A uniquely profitable division within Amazon means greater opportunity to reinvest in the core retail division.

Figure 2.5 Amazon operating margin by segment

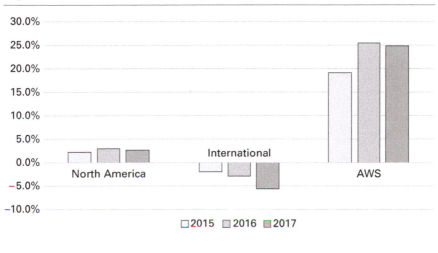

'Many characterized AWS as a bold – and unusual – bet when we started. "What does this have to do with selling books?" We could have stuck to the knitting. I'm glad we didn't.'
Jeff Bezos, 2016[41]

AWS is now the clear market leader in the public cloud business, powering hundreds of thousands of businesses in nearly 200 countries around the world,[42] allowing Amazon, in analyst Ben Thompson's words, to 'take a cut of all economic activity'.[43] Unsurprisingly, major competitors like Walmart and Kroger are steering clear of AWS (much to the advantage of Google and Microsoft), but Amazon still provides cloud computing services to a number of retail brands which, as of 2018, included Brooks Brothers, Eataly and Ocado.

AWS might be the outlier of an already eclectic and wide-ranging mix of business units at Amazon, but it still bears all the traditional Amazonian hallmarks: customer-obsessed, inventive and experimental, and long-term-oriented.

It's no secret that Amazon is on the hunt for its fourth (and fifth and sixth …) pillar. Amazon Studios and Alexa have been touted as the next possible pillars, with Alexa in particular having been a phenomenal, perhaps somewhat unexpected, success. We believe that Alexa is actually more powerful as a hardware extension of the flywheel that drives consumption of the three existing pillars. That's not to say that it won't be a key area of growth for Amazon in the future; Bezos has promised to 'double down' on voice technology.

Tech company first, retailer second

As we established earlier in the chapter, Amazon's technology roots and passion for invention are what sets them distantly apart from rivals. In fact, many of Amazon's past innovations can be easily forgotten because they have simply become today's normal. Cast your mind back to the late '90s: online shopping used to quite a laborious process. Amazon cut the friction out by launching 1-click shopping, personalized product recommendations and user-generated ratings and reviews.

Delivery, meanwhile, wasn't always fast and free. Prime significantly raised customer expectations, leaving competitors with little choice but to invest in their own fulfilment capabilities. Amazon tackled one of the biggest barriers to online shopping – missed deliveries – with the 2011 launch of Amazon Lockers. Today, virtually every major Western retailer offers click & collect.

E-readers sounded like science fiction before Amazon introduced the Kindle. Although the broader category has seen a slowdown in sales (we can blame screen fatigue), the convenience of storing hundreds of books on a single device was a gamechanger at launch.

'We may be a retailer, but we are a tech company at heart. When Jeff started Amazon, he didn't start it to open [a] book shop.'
Amazon CTO Werner Vogels, 2016[44]

Amazon is the ultimate disruptor. These are just a handful of initiatives that have revolutionized shopping and consumption habits. Most of Amazon's innovations catch competitors on the back foot, leaving them in the undesirable position of reacting to rather than leading change. But there is certainly one beneficiary – the customer. Ceaseless innovation from Amazon raises customer expectations, which in turn leads competitors to raise their game and ultimately creates a better experience for the shopper. In today's retail world, there is certainly no room for complacency.

> 'Digital transformation is like an arrival of the railways in the Victorian era, but it's going to happen much faster.'
> **Doug Gurr, Amazon UK Country Manager UK, 2018**[45]

The big question is, of the experiments currently brewing, which will be the ones to stick and transform the industry once again? Amazon has already been a phenomenal catalyst for change in areas like delivery, checkout and voice technology, and is almost singlehandedly shaping the future of retailing in the Western world. Here are our predictions:

- **Amazon's move into bricks and mortar will be the final nail in the coffin for pure-play e-commerce.** As technology breaks down the barriers between physical and digital, those retailers without a bricks and mortar presence – already under pressure to offset shipping and customer acquisition costs – will be severely disadvantaged. More digitally native e-commerce brands will make the leap into the physical realm primarily via flagships, pop-ups, concessions and as acquisition targets by legacy retailers.

- **There will be a greater divergence between functional and fun shopping.** In the future, consumers will spend significantly less time buying the essentials. Our homes, powered by Amazon, will do all the mundane reordering so shoppers will never have to go into a supermarket to buy bleach or toilet paper again. Instead, these products will be automatically replenished – the ultimate test of brand loyalty. Amazon's quest to take the chore out of food shopping and facilitate a frictionless experience creates an opportunity for competitors to focus on WACD: What Amazon Can't Do.

- **Winning in retail today means excelling where Amazon cannot, and therefore focusing less on product and more on experience, services, community and expertise.** The store of the future will go from transactional to experiential as competitors look to distance themselves from the utilitarian aspect of buying online. Amazon is great for purchasing, not so compelling for shopping. We believe the design, layout and broader purpose of the physical store will evolve to better reflect shifting consumer priorities. It won't just be a place to buy, but also a place to eat, work, play, discover, learn and even borrow.

- **Amazon will democratize online grocery, as technology dismantles the barriers traditionally associated with grocery e-commerce in the US.** More anti-Amazon alliances will form with the likes of Google and Ocado particularly benefiting from Amazon's grocery ambitions. Once Amazon convinces shoppers that they're a credible alternative to the supermarkets, then they've cleared that final hurdle to becoming the Everything Store. Capturing that high-frequency purchase makes it easier to cross-sell and bait shoppers into their broader ecosystem, making Amazon the default shopping option. And that's when things get ugly, not just for the supermarkets but for all of retail: Amazon shoppers tend to be loyal, lifelong customers.

- **As Prime transitions to a bricks and mortar setting, retailers will have to drastically rethink their own loyalty schemes.** The notion of swiping a plastic card at the till in exchange for points is dated. The next evolution of loyalty will see retailers ditch the 'more you shop, more you earn' concept. Points-based schemes will become a thing of the past as the loyalty battleground shifts from saving customers money to saving them time, energy and effort. Hyper-personalization through real-time mobile rewards will become the norm. There is an urgency to go beyond the transaction, developing a deep, emotional bond with shoppers.

- **One-hour delivery will become the norm in urban areas, as legacy retailers reconfigure their best assets – their stores – to act as mini warehouses.** Retailers must also utilize their physical locations to appease today's 'on my terms' shopper with instore collection and to address the Achilles heel of online retail – product returns. Expect to see more collaboration, even with Amazon itself, in this area as retailers join forces to better serve the customer. The store of the future won't just become a hub for experience but also for fulfilment.

- **Amazon will continue to relentlessly innovate on behalf of the customer, wowing shoppers and disrupting more sectors in the process.** In the future, the notion of skipping the checkout will feel natural (and not like we're shoplifting); in-home or in-car delivery will be an acceptable alternative to traditional unattended delivery; and the barriers to buying clothes online – sizing and returns – will be largely eliminated. Meanwhile, the combination of more sophisticated AI and penetration of Alexa into the home and on our phones could lead to the era of the truly personalized shopping assistant.

- **By 2021, Amazon will have transitioned into a predominantly service-based company.** Retail, as a percentage of overall sales, continues to decline (from 72 per cent in 2015 to 64 per cent in 2017). We believe the tipping point, when the majority of Amazon's sales come from services rather than first-party goods, will be in 2021. Although there is still plenty of opportunity to grow its core retail offering internationally, Amazon is building out a portfolio of wide-ranging services for suppliers and other businesses (advertising, Marketplace, AWS); for consumers (core Prime membership, music/video streaming, home security installation, grocery subscriptions, the list goes on); and even for other retailers. What is more, as third-party sales continue to grow as a percentage of total paid units, Amazon's stated sales become less reflective of the gross merchandise volume moving through Amazon (because this only accounts for their take of the third-party vendor's sale, not the full order value). Amazon is moving from retail merchant to indispensable infrastructure.

- **In the future, more retailers will run on Amazon's rails.** Retailers themselves are increasingly content to overlook the huge competitive threat posed by Amazon to take advantage of their physical and digital infrastructure. Some may consider it playing with fire – certainly retailers like Toys R Us, Borders and Circuit City would. They were among Amazon's very first 'frenemies' in the early noughties when they outsourced their e-commerce businesses to the giant – all three have since gone bankrupt. But we believe more retailers will cozy up to Amazon if it helps them to achieve greater reach (Marketplace), drive traffic to stores (Amazon pop-ups, click & collect, instore returns) or improve the customer experience (same-day delivery, voice-activated shopping). The unique dual role of competitor and service provider is becoming more apparent by the day. 'Co-opetition' is a key theme for the future.

In summary, Amazon is not your average retailer because it's not actually a retailer. It's a tech company whose sole purpose is perpetual innovation on behalf of their customers. And it happen to sell a lot of stuff in the process.

Notes

1 Amazon's website (2018). Available from: https://www.amazon.jobs/en/ principles [Last accessed 19/6/2018].

2 https://www.jimcollins.com/concepts/the-flywheel.html

3 Stone, B (2013) *The Everything Store: Jeff Bezos and the age of Amazon*, Bantam Press, London.

4 Thompson, Scott (2018) We'll all be banking with Amazon in 10 years: agree? *Tech HQ*, 22 May. Available from: http://techhq.com/2018/05/well-all-be-banking-with-amazon-in-10-years-agree-or-disagree/ [Last accessed 19/6/2018].

5 Amazon's website (2018). Available from: https://www.amazon.jobs/en/ principles [Last accessed 19/6/2018].

6 Stone, B (2013) *The Everything Store: Jeff Bezos and the age of Amazon*, Bantam Press, London.

7 Tonner, Andrew (2016) 7 Sam Walton quotes you should read right now, *The Motley Fool*, 8 September. Available from: https://www.fool.com/ investing/2016/09/08/7-sam-walton-quotes-you-should-read-right-now.aspx [Last accessed 19/6/2018].

8 Amazon 2016 letter to shareholders (2017), *Amazon.com*. Available from: http://phx.corporate-ir.net/phoenix.zhtml?c=97664&p=irol-reportsannual [Last accessed 19/6/2018].

9 Molla, Rani (2018) Amazon spent nearly $23 billion on R&D last year – more than any other US company, *Recode*, 9 April. Available from: https://www.recode.net/2018/4/9/17204004/amazon-research-development-rd [Last accessed 19/6/2018].

10 Delgado, Cristina (2013) Butcher's boy who has discreetly risen to become Spain's second-richest man, *El Pais*, 11 November. Available from: https:// elpais.com/elpais/2013/11/11/inenglish/1384183939_312177.html [Last accessed 19/6/2018].

11 Sillitoe, Ben (2018) 10 tips from a UK retail stalwart: ASOS chairman Brian McBride, Retail Connections, 9 May. Available from: http://www.retailconnections.co.uk/articles/10-tips-uk-retail-boss-brian-mcbride/ [Last accessed 19/6/2018].

12 Misener, Paul (13 September 2017) Retail Innovation at Amazon presentation, Retail Week. Tech event, 2017 Agenda. Available from: http://rw.retail-week. com/Video/TECH/AGENDA/PDF/MAINSTAGE_AGENDA.pdf [Last accessed 2/4/2018].

13 McAllister, Ian (2012) What is Amazon's approach to product development and product management? *Quora*, 18 May. Available from: https://www.quora.com/What-is-Amazons-approach-to-product-development-and-product-management [Last accessed 19/6/2018].

14 Gonzalez, Angel (2016) For Amazon exec Stephenie Landry, the future is Now, *Seattle Times*, 21 May. Available from: https://www.seattletimes.com/business/amazon/for-amazon-exec-stephenie-landry-the-future-is-now/ [Last accessed 19/6/2018].

15 https://www.goodreads.com/quotes/6071-many-of-life-s-failures-are-people-who-did-not-realize

16 MacLean, Rob (2000) What business is Amazon.com really in? *Inc.*, 21 February. Available from: https://www.inc.com/magazine/20000201/16854.html [Last accessed 19/6/2018].

17 Yglesias, Matthew (2013) Amazon profits fall 45 percent, still the most amazing company in the world, *Slate*, 29 January. Available from: http://www.slate.com/blogs/moneybox/2013/01/29/amazon_q4_profits_fall_45_percent.html [Last accessed 19/6/2018].

18 Khan, Lina (2017) Amazon's antitrust paradox, *Yale Law Journal*. Available from: https://www.yalelawjournal.org/note/amazons-antitrust-paradox [Last accessed 19/6/2018].

19 Pender, Kathleen (2000) Scathing report of Amazon is a must-read for stock owners, *SF Gate*, 30 June. Available from: https://www.sfgate.com/business/networth/article/Scathing-Report-of-Amazon-Is-a-Must-Read-for-2750932.php [Last accessed 19/6/2018].

20 Anonymous (2000) Can Amazon survive? *Knowledge at Wharton*, 30 August. Available from: http://knowledge.wharton.upenn.edu/article/can-amazon-survive/ [Last accessed 19/6/2018].

21 Anonymous (2000) Amazon: Ponzi scheme or Wal-Mart of the web? *Slate*, 8 February. Available from: http://www.slate.com/articles/business/moneybox/2000/02/amazon_ponzi_scheme_or_walmart_of_the_web.html [Last accessed 19/6/2018].

22 Corkery, Michael and Nick Wingfield (2018) Amazon asked for patience. Remarkably, Wall Street complied, *New York Times*, 4 February. Available from: https://www.nytimes.com/2018/02/04/technology/amazon-asked-for-patience-remarkably-wall-street-complied.html [Last accessed 19/6/2018].

23 Baldwin, Caroline (2018) Sir Ian Cheshire on how to compete with Amazon, *Essential Retail*, 30 January. Available from: https://www.essentialretail.com/news/sir-ian-cheshire-amazon/ [Last accessed 28/6/2018].

24 Lee, Nathaniel, Shana Lebowitz and Steve Kovach (2017) Scott Galloway: Amazon is using an unfair advantage to dominate its competitors, *Business Insider*, 11 October. Available from: http://uk.businessinsider.com/scott-galloway-why-amazon-successful-2017-10 [Last accessed 28/6/2018].

25 Fox, Justin (2013) How Amazon trained its investors to behave, *Harvard Business Review*, 30 January. Available from: https://hbr.org/2013/01/how-amazon-trained-its-investo [Last accessed 28/6/2018].

26 Hern, Alex (2013) How can Amazon pay tax on profits it doesn't make? *Guardian*, 16 May. Available from: https://www.theguardian.com/commentisfree/2013/may/16/amazon-tax-avoidance-profits [Last accessed 28/6/2018].

27 Nellis, Stephen and Paresh Dave (2018) Amazon, Google cut speaker prices in market share contest: analysts. Reuters, 3 January. Available from: https://www.reuters.com/article/us-amazon-alphabet-speakers/amazon-google-cut-speaker-prices-in-market-share-contest-analysts-idUSKBN1ES0VV [Last accessed 28/6/2018].

28 Santos, Alexis (2012) Bezos: Amazon breaks even on Kindle devices, not trying to make money on hardware, *Engadget*, 12 October. Available from: https://www.engadget.com/2012/10/12/amazon-kindle-fire-hd-paperwhite-hardware-no-profit/ [Last accessed 28/6/2018].

29 Williams, Robert (2018) Study: Amazon Echo owners are big spenders, *Mobile Marketer*, 4 January. Available from: https://www.mobilemarketer.com/news/study-amazon-echo-owners-are-big-spenders/514050/ [Last accessed 28/6/2018].

30 Authors' analysis of company 10-ks and annual reports.

31 La Monica, Paul R (2018) Apple is leading the race to $1 trillion, *CNN*, 27 February. Available from: http://money.cnn.com/2018/02/27/investing/apple-google-amazon-microsoft-trillion-dollar-market-value/index.html [Last accessed 28/6/2018].

32 Shephard, Alex (2018) Is Amazon too big to tax? *The New Republic*, 1 March. Available from: https://newrepublic.com/article/147249/amazon-big-tax [Last accessed 28/6/2018].

33 Soper, Spencer, Matthew Townsend and Lynnley Browning (2017) Trump's bruising tweet highlights Amazon's lingering tax fight, *Bloomberg*, 17 August. Available from: https://www.bloomberg.com/news/articles/2017-08-17/trump-s-bruising-tweet-highlights-amazon-s-lingering-tax-fight [Last accessed 28/6/2018].

34 Bowman, Jeremy (2018) Analysis: Trump is right. Amazon is a master of tax avoidance. *USA Today*, 9 April. Available from: https://www.usatoday.com/story/money/business/2018/04/09/trump-is-right-amazon-is-a-master-of-tax-avoidance/33653439/ [Last accessed 28/6/2018].

35 Isidore, Chris (2017) Amazon to start collecting state sales taxes everywhere, *CNN*, 29 March. Available from: http://money.cnn.com/2017/03/29/technology/amazon-sales-tax/index.html [Last accessed 28/6/2018].

36 Finley, Klint (2018) Why the Supreme Court sales tax ruling may benefit Amazon, *Wired*, 21 June. Available from: https://www.wired.com/story/why-the-supreme-court-sales-tax-ruling-may-benefit-amazon/ [Last accessed 27/82018].

37 https://www.supremecourt.gov/opinions/17pdf/17-494_j4el.pdf?mod=article_inline

38 Amazon 10-K for the fiscal year ended December 31, 2017. Available from: https://www.sec.gov/Archives/edgar/data/1018724/000101872418000005/amzn-20171231x10k.htm [Last accessed 28/6/2018].

39 Ovide, Shira (2018) How Amazon's bottomless appetite became corporate America's nightmare, *Bloomberg*, 14 March. Available from: https://www.bloomberg.com/graphics/2018-amazon-industry-displacement/ [Last accessed 28/6/2018]

40 Amazon 10-K for the fiscal year ended December 31, 2017. Available from: https://www.sec.gov/Archives/edgar/data/1018724/000101872418000005/amzn-20171231x10k.htm [Last accessed 28/6/2018].

41 Amazon 2015 letter to shareholders (2016), Amazon.com, Available from: http://phx.corporate-ir.net/phoenix.zhtml?c=97664&p=irol-reportsannual [Last accessed 28/6/18]

42 Amazon's website (nd). https://aws.amazon.com/about-aws/ [Last accessed 28/6/18].

43 Thompson, Ben (2017) Amazon's new customer, *Stratechery*, 19 June. Available from: https://stratechery.com/2017/amazons-new-customer/ [Last accessed 28/6/2018].

44 Miller, Ron (2016) At Amazon the Flywheel Effect drives innovation, *TechCrunch*, 10 September. Available from: https://techcrunch.com/2016/09/10/at-amazon-the-flywheel-effect-drives-innovation/ [Last accessed 28/6/2018].

45 Fedorenko, Sasha (2018) Doug Gurr of Amazon UK on four ways digital transformation is changing retail, *Internet Retailing*, 14 June. Available from: https://internetretailing.net/strategy-and-innovation/doug-gurr-of-amazon-uk-on-four-ways-digital-transformation-is-changing-retail-17895 [Last accessed 28/6/2018].

The Prime ecosystem: redefining loyalty for today's modern shopper

03

'"All-you-can-eat" express shipping.'[1] This is how Jeff Bezos described Amazon Prime when it launched back in 2005. The idea was simple – shoppers pay an annual fee in exchange for unlimited two-day shipping. No longer would customers have to worry about consolidating orders or minimum purchase requirements. Bezos wanted fast shipping to become an everyday experience rather than an 'occasional indulgence'.[2]

The company had already been offering Super Saver Shipping, which catered to those time-rich customers who didn't mind waiting a bit longer for their orders to arrive (this still exists today, but is just called free shipping). This set the stage for new delivery services such as Prime, an idea first proposed by Amazon engineer Charlie Ward. In his book, *The Everything Store*, Brad Stone writes:

> Why not create a service for the opposite type of customer, Ward suggested, a speedy shipping club for consumers whose needs were time sensitive and who weren't price conscious? He suggested that it could work like a music club, with a monthly charge.[3]

Amazon is no stranger to risk taking, and this was quite a gamble. Not only would the promise of unlimited two-day shipping disproportionately raise customer expectations and add significant cost pressure, particularly in the short term, but were customers willing to pay for the privilege of shopping with Amazon? Sure, warehouse clubs like Costco were charging a membership fee – but this was recouped in the form of lower prices instore. Could Amazon convince shoppers that fast shipping alone was worth the initial $79 fee?

> 'It was never about the seventy-nine dollars. It was really about changing people's mentality so they wouldn't shop anywhere else.'
> **Vijay Ravindran, ex-Amazon Director, 2013**[4]

It appears so. By 2018, Amazon was shipping more than 5 billion items worldwide and had over 100 million paid Prime members globally, making it one of the world's largest online subscription schemes.[5]

Shipping, shopping, streaming and more

The Prime model is classic Amazon – customer-obsessed with a long-term view of success. Today, Prime is about so much more than just shipping perks. Amazon has spent the past decade relentlessly building out the Prime flywheel to the extent that it is now described as 'the gateway to the best of Amazon', according to Prime Director Lisa Leung.[6] The retailer has significantly expanded an already impressive range of Prime-eligible products (from 20 million in 2014 to 100 million by 2018[7]) while also tacking on a plethora of new services in a bid to provide customers with ever greater value. Today, there are more reasons than ever before to join Prime.

> 'They come for shipping. They stay for digital.'
> **Aaron Perrine, Amazon General Manager, 2018**[8]

As part of a broader strategy to spread their tentacles across new sectors, Amazon has greatly bolstered the entertainment aspect of Prime. Let's not forget that Amazon's chief raison d'être, according to Doug Gurr, Amazon's country manager for the UK,[9] is 'improving the shopping and entertainment experience for the consumer'. Amazon addressed the latter back in 2011 by adding unlimited, commercial-free, instant streaming of thousands of TV shows and films to its Prime offer. It has since taken greater control of production through its Amazon Studios subsidiary, offering Prime members exclusive content such as the TV shows *Bosch*, *Transparent* and *The Marvellous Mrs Maisel*. Today, Prime Video is a viable competitor to Netflix. The service has helped to lock in loyalty by making the Prime bundle even more attractive while simultaneously feeding the flywheel. 'When we win a Golden Globe, it helps us sell more shoes', Bezos said.[10]

Table 3.1   Amazon membership benefits

Category	Amazon Prime Benefit
Ship	'Free' delivery on over 100 million items in two days or less
	'Free' same-day or one-day delivery on over 1 million items in 8,000 US cities and towns
	Release day delivery by 7pm on new videos, games, books, music, movies and more
	Prime Now one- to two-hour delivery
Stream	Prime Video: stream or download thousands of TV shows and movies
	Twitch Prime: perks for gamers such as free in-game loot every month
	Prime Music: stream over 2 million songs without any ads
	Prime Originals: Amazon-exclusive TV shows and movies such as *The Marvellous Mrs Maisel*
Shop	Whole Foods benefits: exclusive savings, 5% cash back with Visa card and two-hour delivery
	Alexa: voice shopping and reordering
	Just for Prime: early access to deals and exclusive access to own-label products
	Amazon Family: save 20% off diapers and baby food with five or more subscriptions
Read	Choose from over 1,000 top Kindle books, magazines, comics, kids' books and more
	First reads: each month, download one of six editors' picks for free ahead of publication
More	Earn 5% cashback with select credit cards; earn 2% rewards with Amazon Prime Reload
	Prime photos: unlimited photo storage

SOURCE Author research; Amazon, as of June 2018

And this isn't just a US phenomenon. In Japan, for example, membership increased 16 per cent just three months after the launch of Prime Video. In India, where Amazon is heavily investing in Prime Video, Amazon added more new Prime members in its first year than any other market in the company's history. In 2018, Amazon added its first entertainment benefit, Prime Reading, to its scheme in China.[11] The strength of the bundle proposition today makes it easier to drive member adoption and retention in international markets.

Convenience has always been the premise, but these days Amazon is taking this to the next level by granting access to an entire *lifestyle of convenience*. Want one-hour delivery? Want to use a Dash Button to reorder laundry detergent? Want to shop via Alexa? Want in-home or in-car deliveries? Guess what – you need to be a Prime member.

> 'Our goal with Amazon Prime, make no mistake, is to make sure that if you are not a Prime member, you are being irresponsible.'
> **Jeff Bezos, 2016[12]**

Prime is also increasingly about access to *products* as much as it is *services*. As part of Amazon's efforts to tap into the food and fashion sectors, the retailer has been quietly building out a wide-ranging portfolio of private label products, many of which are reserved for members. This creates a heightened sense of exclusivity, and one that is impossible to replicate in a physical setting. Can you imagine Walmart banning certain customers from taking Great Value products off its shelves? Amazon cleverly gets away with this in a digital environment and is clearly motivated to grow its private label portfolio as a means of providing greater value to customers while differentiating from its peers in a margin-accretive manner.

It's important to point out that Prime membership also acts as the gateway to those services that come with additional fees such as AmazonFresh, Prime Pantry or Prime Now. Amazon's online grocery shoppers must first and foremost be a Prime member before then paying a $15 monthly add-on fee for food delivery, a reflection of the higher costs associated with delivery of perishable foods and one that is generally accepted by US consumers. But this means that every single customer that buys fresh food through Amazon is a member of their loyalty scheme – and therefore Amazon knows quite a lot about them. Imagine if Tesco had stores exclusively dedicated to Clubcard members – the opportunities for personalization would be endless. It's no surprise that Amazon is in a hurry to absorb Whole Foods' loyalty scheme into Prime.

Prime offers exceptional value to its members but without promising rock-bottom prices. In fact, in the early days, Amazon employees wanted to call the programme Super Saver Platinum, which Bezos rejected on the basis that it was not designed to be a money-saving scheme.[13] (It is thought that the name Prime was eventually chosen due to the prime position of fast-track pallets in fulfilment centres.[14]) Today, however, there are a growing number of financial incentives to become a Prime member. In addition to the main shipping benefit, members have access to exclusive deals, can get cashback on Amazon and Whole Foods purchases by using a Prime-branded Visa card and, as Amazon moves further into bricks and mortar, members will find lower prices in stores.

What is more, Amazon has created an entire shopping event – Prime Day – exclusively for its members. The Black Friday-esque event, guised as a celebration of Amazon's 20th birthday for its 2015 launch, is designed to artificially stimulate demand in an otherwise sluggish period while simultaneously rewarding members of the Prime club with more than 24 hours' worth of deals. At the time of launch, it was also a clever way to soften the blow of a recent price hike – for the first time in history, Amazon raised the price of Prime from $79 to $99 (it has since been raised again to $119, most certainly not the last fee hike). In any case, Prime Day is as much about brazen customer acquisition as it is about reminding existing members of the value of Prime.

In summary, the aim is to make Prime so attractive that, in Bezos' own words, shoppers would be 'irresponsible' not to join. By clustering their services under one umbrella, with each intended to make the customer's life either easier or more enjoyable, Amazon can tap into consumer needs that far supersede price. They don't just want share of wallet, they want share of life.

But is Prime actually a loyalty programme?

It's a hotly debated question in the retail industry – can we really call Prime a loyalty programme? In their essence, these schemes are designed to drive repeat business by rewarding a retailer's most important customers. In this sense, Amazon Prime is the very epitome of a loyalty scheme. After all, not many other retailers have 100 million customers paying for the privilege of shopping with them.

However, the term 'loyalty scheme' is often associated with the plastic cards we carry around in our wallets, habitually swiping them at the till in exchange for (often unquantifiable) points. Let's be very clear here – these types of loyalty schemes are on the way out.

The term 'loyalty card' is a misnomer. They don't drive loyalty. If they did, we would only have one loyalty card in our wallets. Instead the average shopper in markets like the US, Canada or UK holds around three or four cards.[15] By focusing on discounts and vouchers, these cards often end up encouraging the very opposite behaviour as shoppers cherry-pick the best deals. This is also a reflection of changing shopping habits and proliferation of choice, particularly in markets like the UK where consumers have ditched the weekly shop. Instead, shoppers are buying more frequently, in smaller quantities and across a range of different retailers. The idea of being loyal to one and only one supermarket is a thing of the past.

So when it comes to driving loyalty today, retailers must ditch the 'more you shop, more you earn' concept in favour of convenience, service and experience. With Prime, Amazon is spearheading this next evolution of loyalty – the battleground is quickly shifting from saving customers money to saving them time, energy and effort. Retailers will drive loyalty through greater personalization and by delighting shoppers with instore perks. Waitrose, for example, has been wildly successful in offering its loyalty card-holders free coffee and newspapers, welcoming shoppers into their stores as you would welcome a guest into your home.

Loyalty cards will evolve to become more digitally led – after all, if checkout-free stores are about to take off, there will be nowhere to swipe your plastic card! Loyalty schemes will morph to become part of a wider bundle that not only rewards shoppers for their custom but also sends them personalized, real-time offers instore and reduces friction by allowing them to find and pay for products – all in one app.

Price-oriented retailers, of course, are the exception here and will continue to drive loyalty by offering their shoppers exceptional value for money. We would argue that there is merit to ditching costly loyalty schemes altogether, in this case, to invest in everyday low prices. After all, Aldi and Lidl don't operate loyalty schemes and they have some of the most devoted customers out there. At the end of the day, the key to driving loyalty is understanding what your customers value.

For Amazon, this is ease and convenience. It's instant gratification. And increasingly it's about entertaining them in the process. If Amazon achieves this, then the benefits to their wider business are bountiful.

What does Amazon get out of Prime?

Extreme loyalty. Lifelong, monogamous shoppers. Customers that wear Prime blinders and don't bother checking other retail sites. They make

Amazon their first port of call, their default shopping option, even if it's not always the cheapest. Addicted to the convenience offered by Prime, shoppers become less price-sensitive – all to the advantage of Amazon's algorithms. This is behavioural modification at its best.

So what does that look like in numbers?

- **Spend**: the average Prime member spends $2,486 – nearly five times more than non-members,[16] according to Morgan Stanley. As with most subscriptions, members typically feel the need to get their money's worth, which can lead to irrational decision making: in this case, shoppers justify the annual Prime fee by spending more with Amazon. The sunk cost fallacy works to Amazon's advantage.

- **Frequency**: according to Consumer Intelligence Research Partners, Prime customers shop with Amazon nearly twice as often (25 times per year) as non-Prime members, making Bezos' initial vision – using Prime as a tool to remove barriers to more frequent shopping – a reality.[17]

- **Retention**: it is estimated that retention rates are higher than 90 per cent.[18]

Through Prime, Amazon also gets access to a treasure trove of customer data, giving them an unrivalled understanding of the online purchasing behaviour of their most important shoppers. This allows for greater personalization, from helpful product recommendations to perhaps less-than-welcome dynamic pricing (according to Profitero, Amazon changes its prices more than 2.5 million times a day).

Prime also enables upsell opportunities, as discussed in relation to AmazonFresh, Prime Pantry and Prime Now, but more importantly, Prime baits shoppers into Amazon's wider ecosystem. While other retailers' loyalty schemes focus on top-tier customers, Amazon cleverly draws as many shoppers it can into its ecosystem, thereby maximizing customer value over their lifetime. There's a good reason the retailer practically gives Prime memberships away to college students and then offers Prime members 20 per cent off nappies and baby food – they can capture tomorrow's consumers at critical life stages, locking them in as loyal members of the club.

Another bonus for Amazon? Prime is nearly impossible to replicate. It is wide-reaching, probably too generous and certainly unique in scope, giving Amazon a compelling point of differentiation. Not many other retailers have the scale, infrastructure or cross-sector dominance to produce a copy-cat version.

Despite being one of the most powerful retailers in the world, Walmart tried and failed to match Amazon's ecosystem. Walmart's Prime-like 'ShippingPass' offered unlimited two-day shipping but for a lower fee of $49. Here's why this didn't work. First, although it was cheaper than Prime, Walmart's scheme did not offer additional benefits beyond delivery. This is testament to the strength and uniqueness of the bundle proposition that Amazon has created through Prime. With over half of US households already holding a Prime membership, it would have been difficult – particularly for the more price-conscious Walmart shopper – to justify an additional membership without all the bells and whistles of Prime. Sure, prices might have been lower through Walmart but the assortment didn't match Amazon's and, what's more, customer expectations around speed and cost of delivery were quickly changing. The retailer couldn't get away with charging for a service that was becoming the norm. Walmart scrapped the short-lived programme in 2017, instead offering free two-day shipping on more than 2 million items – no membership required.

Going global

Amazon has exported its Prime model to almost all international countries of operation. Shoppers in Amazon's three largest global markets – Germany, Japan and the UK – were naturally the first to get a taste for Prime when it first went global in 2007. However, in recent years, Amazon has been backfilling existing markets with Prime, which is arguably a far more compelling proposition today than when it was first exported over a decade ago. From 2016–2018, Amazon added Prime to six markets including a couple of new ones altogether – Singapore and Australia. Prime is now available in every Amazon market except for its Souq operations in the Middle East (Egypt, UAE, Saudi Arabia, Kuwait) and Brazil.

Table 3.2 Amazon Prime international presence

Year Launched	Market
2005	US
2007	Germany
2007	UK
2007	Japan
2008	France
2011	Italy
2011	Spain
2013	Canada
2016	India

(continued)

Table 3.2   (Continued)

Year Launched	Market
2016	China
2017	Mexico
2017	Netherlands
2017	Singapore
2018	Australia

SOURCE   Author research; Amazon
Excludes markets where Amazon does not have a live site, ie Belgium as of June 2018

This hasn't gone unnoticed among Brazilian competitors. Local retailer B2W has capitalized on Amazon's slow start by launching its own shopping club that charges an annual fee for fast shipping and they've aptly named it... Prime. Meanwhile, MercadoLibre, Latin America's answer to eBay, has begun storing and shipping third-party goods in a similar vein to Amazon's Fulfilled by Amazon programme. Amazon has been present in Brazil since 2012 but primarily through e-readers, books and streaming movies; five years later, they finally opened their site to third-party vendors. We believe that Amazon will eventually bring its full retail business to Latin America's largest retail market, and with it will come Prime.

Equally, we can expect Amazon to introduce Prime to the Middle East once it fully integrates its Souq division, which it acquired in 2017, and builds on its 2018 entry into Turkey. Amazon has barely scratched the surface when it comes to international expansion of Prime – this will be a key focus over the next decade as growth opportunities dry up at home.

But can Prime work in a physical setting?

It's been fascinating for industry analysts like us to watch how Prime would unfold in a physical setting. Sure, it's easy to tier shoppers online where you can enable or disable access to certain products and services. In a physical setting, it's slightly more delicate. However, Prime forms the very DNA of Amazon's retail business. As Amazon moved further into the physical world of retail, omitting Prime was never going to be an option. We caught the first glimpse of how Amazon would translate Prime in a bricks and mortar setting through Amazon Books – its first full-size, traditional store concept. We'll discuss the details of this unique concept later in the book but for now it's important to understand that, at its 2015 launch, there were no tangible benefits for Prime members. However, less than a year later, Amazon very boldly moved towards a tiered pricing model – prices for Prime customers are now equivalent to those offered on Amazon's website, and everyone else must pay the list price.

Now you can argue that this isn't entirely different to what American supermarkets have done for decades by scanning a loyalty card at the checkout. However, the supermarkets give shoppers a discount on *select* items, while Amazon's scheme is designed for every *single* item to have two prices. If you're not a Prime member, there is no reason to shop there – aside from perhaps testing out Amazon devices like the Echo or Kindle. It's one step short of charging admission to enter the store.

It should come as no surprise to learn that these stores don't contribute much to the top line. In fact, we would argue that they should be considered a marketing expense as their sole intention is to raise awareness of the benefits, and ultimately drive adoption, of Prime. But how would this work in a supermarket setting? Amazon couldn't get away with such a visibly tiered pricing policy, as shoppers would simply vote with their feet. The challenge would be striking the right balance of rewarding Prime shoppers in a discreet enough way so as not to lose customers, while still conveying the benefits of Prime to those non-members. This would first and foremost come through services, which are easier to justify as an exclusive perk for members. For example, AmazonFresh Pickup, the drive-through supermarket trial launched in 2017, is only available to Prime members. This makes sense because you must already be a Prime member to order groceries through AmazonFresh. Making this work in Whole Foods stores would be a much bigger challenge. When the Whole Foods acquisition was announced in mid-2017, the authors put forth a series of predictions of how Prime would unfold instore. We expected Amazon to introduce a blanket discount at the checkout; offer personalized, real-time offers instore; add Whole Foods to the Prime Now service; offer tiered pricing in non-food merchandise (similar to Amazon Books); Prime-only checkout lanes; and VIP online order collection and returns points.

Have our predictions come true? At the time of writing, in mid-2018, Amazon has done the following:

- offered Prime-exclusive promotions (for example, Thanksgiving turkeys discounted for Prime members, breaking Whole Foods' all-time record);
- launched free two-hour delivery on Whole Foods orders over $35 for Prime members in select cities;
- expanded the benefits of the Amazon Prime Rewards Visa Card, giving Prime members 5 per cent back when shopping at Whole Foods;

- added Whole Foods private label products like 365 Everyday Value on Amazon;
- began the technical work to integrate Prime at the point of sale. It is thought that once that is complete, Prime members will receive an additional 10 per cent discount at checkout.

So we weren't too far off, and it's still early days. Integrating Prime at the point of sale will be the priority and then we will likely see additional perks roll out instore. We believe Amazon will feel emboldened with Prime instore given that approximately 75 per cent of Whole Foods shoppers are already Prime members.[19] However, less than 20 per cent of Prime members are Whole Foods shoppers so there is an opportunity to drive customer traffic while also using Amazon's fulfilment capabilities to enhance the appeal of Whole Foods' e-commerce offer.

Prime 2.0

The future is certainly a greater physical presence, but Prime's core digital proposition will also evolve to become even more attractive, increasingly flexible and ultimately more expensive.

More bells and whistles

Amazon will continue to enrich the Prime offer, adding new benefits that either add to the stickiness of Prime or tie in with Amazon's broader strategic focus. For example, Amazon launched its first fashion benefit – Prime Wardrobe – in 2017 as part of its efforts to build trust and credibility in the category. The service brings the fitting room to the shopper by allowing Prime members to receive up to 15 items of clothing, shoes or accessories to try in the comfort of their own homes. Shoppers are provided with prepaid labels and resealable boxes for free returns, and they are only charged when they decide what they'd like to keep. This tackles some of the biggest barriers to buying clothes online today – sizing and returns (with the former being further addressed through Amazon's acquisition of Body Labs, a 3D body-scanning start-up).

Inspired by the niche services offered by brands like Stitch Fix and Trunk Club, Prime Wardrobe is the first of its kind among mainstream clothing retailers. Within months of its launch, UK-based online fashion retailer ASOS introduced its own try-before-you-buy service along with same-day delivery, most likely preparing itself for when Amazon brings Prime Wardrobe across the Atlantic. This is the Amazon Effect in action, kicking competitors into gear and improving the experience for the customer.

Looking to new demographics for growth

According to a 2016 Piper Jaffray survey, a whopping 82 per cent of US households that earn more than $112,000 per year hold a Prime membership.[20] Amazon has cornered the affluent market and now must look outside its core customer demographic for future growth. The same survey shows that Amazon's reach is lowest among those who earn less than $41,000.

The main barriers for this lower-income customer group have historically been the annual Prime fee, limited internet access and lack of a credit card. More than a quarter of American households have no or limited access to checking and savings accounts.[21]

In recent years, Amazon has ramped up efforts to target lower-income shoppers. For example, it launched a pay-monthly Prime membership scheme in 2016. For shoppers, this option actually works out more expensive on an annual basis ($156 versus $119) but provides an alternative way to access Amazon if customers are unwilling or unable to pay the annual fee in one lump sum.

Meanwhile, Amazon has homed in on the unbanked/underbanked consumer by launching a discounted Prime membership for those receiving government assistance, as well as Amazon Cash, a scheme that allows shoppers to deposit cash into their Amazon account by scanning a barcode at participating stores. This has since been rolled out in the UK as well, where it is branded Top Up.

This is a blatant attempt to win share from a demographic that was traditionally served by bricks and mortar retailers, most notably Walmart. It's estimated that around 20 per cent of Walmart's shoppers pay for groceries with food stamps and, for years, Walmart has allowed customers to 'pay with cash' online (payments are made at Walmart's stores).[22]

So what's Amazon's next move? At the time of writing in mid-2018, Amazon was in talks with JP Morgan and other banks about setting up an Amazon-branded checking account for its customers. This would be a natural extension of the services Amazon already provides and is also being offered by global e-commerce retailers like Alibaba and Rakuten.

But more fee hikes are inevitable

Amazon is therefore very motivated to grow its Prime membership base for the dual purpose of feeding the flywheel (or, in simple terms, growing sales) and offsetting rising shipping costs. As discussed in Chapter 2, alternative revenue streams such as AWS, advertising and increasingly subscriptions (around 90 per cent of which is Prime revenues) are vital for Amazon to continue to invest in the core retail division.

We believe that Prime subscriptions could generate $20 billion in revenues by 2020.[23] Prime revenue growth will be achieved through international customer acquisition, but also good old-fashioned fee hikes.

In 2005, the original Prime fee was $79 – but let's not forget that at the time of launch Prime was purely about shipping. After nearly a decade of maintaining that original price, Amazon raised the fee for the first time to $99 in 2014. This was a reflection of rising shipping costs and investments in the Prime offer with new services such as video streaming. Prime got more expensive again in 2018, jumping 20 per cent to $119, and it's fair to say this won't be the last increase.

Amazon spends billions of dollars on shipping, something we'll explore in greater detail later in the book. In theory, as shoppers spend more, volumes increase and shipping costs go down, resulting in better deals with suppliers and consequently lower prices for customers. However, as Amazon moves further into fast-moving consumer goods categories, this becomes harder to achieve given the low-value/high-frequency nature of the category. It's estimated that Prime makes up about 60 per cent of shipping costs[24] and that, in order to break even on Prime, Amazon would have to increase the fee to $200. That won't happen. Yes, we can expect to see additional fee hikes every few years but let's not forget the all-important flywheel effect that is at the very heart of the Prime scheme. As intangible as it may be, Prime encourages shoppers to spend more and Amazon must strike the right balance so as not to jeopardize that.

For many, Amazon is now so deeply embedded in their everyday lives that they will accept future price increases. It's imperative that Amazon continues to invest in digital content and the core shipping offer, while also exploring new loyalty avenues, in order to maintain its incredibly high consumer value proposition. But it's fair to say that Prime will remain the engine of Amazon's retail machine.

Notes

1 Amazon press release, 2005. Amazon.com announces record free cash flow fueled by lower prices and free shipping; introduces new express shipping program – Amazon Prime, *Amazon.com*, 2 February. Available from: http://phx.corporate-ir.net/phoenix.zhtml?c=176060&p=irol-newsArticle&ID=669786 [Last accessed 28/6/2018].

2 ibid.

3 Stone, Brad (2013) *The Everything Store: Jeff Bezos and the age of Amazon*, Bantam Press, London.

4 ibid.

5 Siegel, Rachel (2018) The Amazon stat long kept under wraps is revealed: Prime has over 100 million subscribers, *Washington Post*, 18 April. Available from: https://www.washingtonpost.com/news/business/wp/2018/04/18/the-amazon-stat-long-kept-under-wraps-is-revealed-prime-has-over-100-million-subscribers [Last accessed 12/6/2018].

6 Amazon UK Analyst Briefing, London, July 2018.

7 Disis, Jill and Seth Fiegerman (2018) Amazon is raising the price of Prime to $119, *CNN*, 26 April. Available from: http://money.cnn.com/2018/04/26/technology/business/amazon-prime-cost-increase/index.html [Last accessed 28/6/2018].

8 Stevens, Laura (2018) Amazon targets Medicaid recipients as it widens war for low-income shoppers, *Wall Street Journal*, 7 March. Available from: https://www.wsj.com/articles/amazon-widens-war-with-walmart-for-low-income-shoppers-1520431203 [Last accessed 28/6/2018].

9 Amazon UK Analyst Briefing, London, 2017.

10 McAlone, Nathan (2016) Amazon CEO Jeff Bezos said something about Prime Video that should scare Netflix, *Business Insider*, 2 June. Available from: http://uk.businessinsider.com/amazon-ceo-jeff-bezos-said-something-about-prime-video-that-should-scare-netflix-2016-6 [Last accessed 2.7.2018]

11 Amazon press release (2018) Amazon.com announces first quarter sales up 43% to $51.0 billion, *Amazon*, 26 April. Available from: http://phx.corporate-ir.net/phoenix.zhtml?c=97664&p=irol-newsArticle&ID=2345075 [Last accessed 28/6/2018].

12 Kim, Eugene (2016) Bezos to shareholders: It's 'irresponsible' not to be part of Amazon Prime, *Business Insider*, 17 May. Available from:http://uk.businessinsider.com/amazon-ceo-jeff-bezos-says-its-irresponsible-not-to-be-part-of-prime-2016-5 [Last accessed 28/6/2018].

13 Stone, Brad (2013) *The Everything Store: Jeff Bezos and the age of Amazon*, Bantam Press, London.

14 ibid.

15 Vizard, Sarah (2016) Loyalty cards aren't convincing British consumers to shop, *Marketing Week*, 7 December. Available from: https://www.marketing-week.com/2016/12/07/loyalty-cards-nielsen/ [Last accessed 28/6/18].

16 Columbus, Louis (2018) 10 charts that will change your perspective of Amazon Prime's growth, *Forbes*, 4 March. Available from: https://www.forbes.com/sites/louiscolumbus/2018/03/04/10-charts-that-will-change-your-perspective-of-amazon-primes-growth/#5d364e813fee [Last accessed 28/6/2018].

17 Braverman, Beth (2017) Amazon Prime members spend a whole lot more on the site than non-members, *Business Insider*, 7 July. Available from: http://www.businessinsider.com/is-amazon-prime-worth-it-2017-7?IR=T [Last accessed 28/6/2018].

18 Soper, Spencer (2018) Bezos says Amazon has topped 100 million Prime members, *Bloomberg*, 18 April. Available from: https://origin-www.bloomberg.com/news/articles/2018-04-18/amazon-s-bezos-says-company-has-topped-100-million-prime-members [Last accessed 28/6/2018].

19 Hirsch, Lauren (2018) Amazon plans more Prime perks at Whole Foods, and it will change the industry, *CNBC*, 1 May. Available from: https://www.cnbc.com/2018/05/01/prime-perks-are-coming-to-whole-foods-and-it-will-change-the-industry.html [Last accessed 28/6/2018].

20 Molla, Rani (2017) For the wealthiest Americans, Amazon Prime has become the norm, *Recode*, 8 June. Available from: https://www.recode.net/2017/6/8/15759354/amazon-prime-low-income-discount-piper-jaffray-demographics [Last accessed 28/6/2018].

21 Hirsch, Lauren (2018) Amazon wants to make it easier to shop its website without a credit card, *CNBC*, 5 March. Available from: https://www.cnbc.com/2018/03/05/amazons-talks-with-jp-morgan-may-build-on-services-to-the-unbanked.html [Last accessed 28/6/2018].

22 Anonymous (2017) Amazon to discount Prime for US families on welfare, *BBC*, 6 June. Available from: https://www.bbc.com/news/technology-40170655 [Last accessed 28/6/2018]

23 Authors' own estimates.

24 Saba, Jennifer (2018) Priming the pump, *Reuters*, 19 April. Available from: https://www.breakingviews.com/considered-view/amazons-10-bln-subsidy-is-prime-for-growth/ [Last accessed 28/6/2018].

Retail apocalypse: reality or myth?

04

'For so long, people have predicted the demise of movie theatres, but people still like to go to the movies.'
Jeff Bezos, 2018[1]

You don't have to look very hard today to find an article or piece of research that positions e-commerce as the death knell for the bricks and mortar store. The word 'apocalypse' has officially entered the retail lexicon and is arguably too well documented in the media these days – it even has its own Wikipedia page.

Doom and gloom make good headlines, and we'll spend most of this chapter defying the apocalypse narrative, but first let's make one thing very clear: we have too many stores. Today, we have an oversupply of retail space; we have retail space that is no longer fit for purpose.

So, naturally stores are shuttering – and it's happening quickly. According to Cushman & Wakefield, there were nearly 9,000 major chain store closures in the US in 2017, with another 12,000 expected for 2018.[2] In the same year, there were more than 20 retail bankruptcies – from clothing chains like The Limited to iconic brands like Toys R Us.[3] Meanwhile, shopping malls are becoming an endangered species: by 2022, up to one quarter of US malls are expected to have closed.[4]

While this is especially pronounced in the overbuilt suburbs of the US, it's by no means an American phenomenon. In the UK, the Centre for Retail Research has predicted that total store numbers will fall by 22 per cent in 2018,[5] while in Canada, shoppers have bid farewell to major retail chains such as Sears and Target in recent years.

Meanwhile, global shopper demand and expectations for online retail are booming. According to McKinsey, China now has more online shoppers than any other nation and accounts for 40 per cent of global e-commerce sales.[6] In the UK, according to the Office for National Statistics, online sales of non-food items have doubled in the past five years and currently account for 25 per cent of the overall market.[7]

> 'Every Industrial Revolution has brought long-term benefits but always goes through short-term pain.'
> **Doug Gurr, Amazon UK Country Manager, 2018[8]**

There is no denying that the growth of e-commerce is partially happening at the expense of legacy brick and mortar chains – but is it all Amazon's fault? Not entirely. In a nutshell, mature modern retail markets are overstored, there has been a titanic shift in shopping habits, mobile has turned retail on its head, people are spending less on stuff and more on experiences, and new, disruptive brick and mortar retailers – think fast fashion and discount grocery – are stealing share from more established players. We are at the intersection of major technological, economic and societal changes that are profoundly reshaping the retail sector.

Now let's take a closer look at these shifts, and more specifically, how they're leading retailers to rightsize their store portfolios.

The on-my-terms shopper is born

> 'In the new distributed commerce world that allows consumers to buy any product, anytime, anywhere, it really doesn't matter whether a customer shops in a company's store or on its website or mobile app. It's all retail. Today's retailers sell to shoppers any way they want to buy.'
> **Matthew Shay, President & CEO of the National Retail Federation, 2017[9]**

Technology isn't just raising customer expectations and creating new ways to shop – it's fundamentally revolutionizing retail. This will naturally be a key theme throughout the book, but here we'd like to specifically explore how technology is resetting customer expectations by enabling a more convenient, frictionless shopping experience.

First, we must acknowledge that the world is much more joined up than it was a decade ago: two-thirds of the global population is now connected via mobile and today there are more mobile devices than there are people on the planet.[10] It's hard to imagine that the iPhone, a device that has become such an integral part of our everyday lives, has only been around since 2007. Google believes that we no longer 'go online'; today we 'live online'. With the average person looking at their phone 150 times per day, it's fair to say that our mobile phones have simply become an extension of us as consumers.[11]

> 'There aren't store customers or online customers – there are just customers who are more empowered than ever to shop on their terms.'
> **Erik Nordstrom, Co-President of Nordstrom, 2017[12]**

In this age of ubiquitous connectivity, the consumer is king. Retailers have been challenged to cater to these 'always on' and connected consumers since the introduction of e-commerce, accessible through increasingly portable computing devices. The ability to shop on a mobile phone while sitting on a train or waiting for the dentist has empowered consumers with a whole new level of convenience and accessibility, while also bridging the divide between physical and digital retail which we will discuss further in the next chapter.

Another technological development that has transformed the way we shop includes payment, enabled via online banking and mobile wallets. PayPal, which saves time and adds extra security on entering payment information, introduced consumers to online payments in the same way that contactless cards are paving the way for other mobile payment schemes instore.

And the advent of mobile has only served to accelerate the growth of e-commerce retailers including Amazon. Additional technology developments, fuelled by the demand for more immersive and portable experiences, have included mobile-optimized websites, apps, and larger devices such as tablets, with bigger touchscreens to interact with them on and wearables. And security is also evolving from the use of myriad forgettable passwords, to single-sign-on access via Google, Facebook, etc, two-factor authentication, and biometric fingerprint and facial recognition.

Likewise, retail has evolved in its use of these technology advances to make the online shopping experience as simple as possible. Amazon's 'click to buy' patent revolutionized online checkout, while brands are working out how to make social shopping pay, with shoppable pins on Pinterest and WeChat's app-within-app payments dominance in China as notable early successes. But in future the quest for ease and convenience, driven by customer expectations set by online, will advance beyond mobile and touchscreen technology. We can already see this happening now, with Connected Home heating and lighting systems, as well as auto- and simplified replenishment via voice.

These technological improvements, which have put billions of products right at shoppers' fingertips, have been matched by similar advances in fulfilment. Lead times are getting shorter as online retailers look to replicate the sense of immediacy that was once reserved for bricks and mortar retailers. Today, customers expect shipping to be fast, reliable and free.

The result of all of this? Online shopping has become utterly effortless. Mobile commerce in particular is booming and is poised for impressive future growth. By 2021, global m-commerce sales are expected to more than double to reach US $3.6 trillion, accounting for an astounding 73 per cent of the global e-commerce market.[13]

This shift is naturally also reflected in the retail rankings. In 2012, the top five global retailers – Walmart, Carrefour, Kroger, Seven & I and Costco – were all predominantly bricks and mortar-based retailers. By 2017, three of the top five were primarily online players – Alibaba, Amazon and JD.com – and by 2022 the authors are predicting that, after decades at the top, Walmart will finally be knocked from its throne as Alibaba becomes the world's largest retailer, with Amazon a close second.

Bricks and mortar retailers must ensure they can appease today's super-charged shopper who enters their store with heightened, and at times conflicting, expectations. On one hand, customers are demanding ultra-convenience, a frictionless shopping experience, transparency and instant gratification. But on the other hand, they also expect the environment in which they shop to be hyper-personalized and, increasingly, experiential.

The future is certainly fewer but more impactful stores: we expect retailers to continue rightsizing – while simultaneously investing in the store experience – as they adjust to this new reality of shifting spending patterns. Those retailers lacking the agility to re-engineer themselves for today's modern consumer will find themselves with no choice but to shutter stores.

Amazon Effect: killing the category killer

Like the phrase 'retail apocalypse', the 'Amazon Effect' is also effective click-bait for many retail articles today. Stores closing? It's the Amazon Effect.

Retailers investing online? The Amazon Effect. Acquisitions, bankruptcies, redundancies… These days, we can find a way to link, however tenuously, most retail developments to the Seattle-based behemoth.

Nonetheless, the notion of being 'Amazoned' is very real for some. In 2018, Shira Ovide of Bloomberg wrote, 'Other companies become verbs because of their products: to Google or to Xerox. Amazon became a verb because of the damage it can inflict on other companies. To be Amazoned means to have your business crushed because the company got into your industry.'[14]

When the actual product can be delivered digitally – think music, video, games, books – and e-commerce penetration nears the 50 per cent mark, there is little hope for the physical space selling those goods. 'Category killers', highly focused retailers that are typically dominant in one product category, were naturally the first casualties of e-commerce. The likes of Blockbuster, Circuit City, CompUSA and, more recently, Toys R Us have been consigned to the pages of the history books. Many of these companies went from being the disruptor to the disrupted, a stark reminder of the danger of complacency.

Borders, for example, used to be America's second-largest bookstore chain. In a 2008 interview, transcribed on hedge fund manager Todd Sullivan's site, CEO George Jones said, 'I do not think that technology and self-service in our stores will even vaguely replace the fact that you can come into our stores and there is someone who greets you and is knowledgeable about books. That is and will always be a huge part of our business.'[15] Borders went bust three years later.

What was once a competitive advantage for the category killer – a deep product assortment and large store network – ultimately led to its own demise. It's no coincidence that Amazon started out selling books as this was a commodity category that early internet shoppers would feel comfortable buying online. It's also important to understand that when Amazon was getting into books, there were three million books in print worldwide, far more than any bookstore could ever stock.[16] Cue the beginning of the end for category killers.

Amazon's very existence impacts every single retail business. They are hands down the most disruptive retailer in the Western world. No other retailer has been so effective at eliminating complacency and irrelevance in the sector, ultimately driving change for the benefit of the customer. But naturally, this means a future with less bricks and mortar retail space: 28 per cent of shoppers globally cite Amazon as the key reason for visiting physical stores less often.[17]

Overspaced, with questionable relevance

According to the International Council of Shopping Centers, the number of American shopping centres grew by 300 per cent – or more than twice as fast as the population – from 1970 to 2015.[18] Today, with 23.5 square feet of retail space *per person*, the US is by far the most over-retailed country in the world. In fact, the US has 40 per cent more shopping space per capita than Canada, five times more than the UK and 10 times more than Germany.[19] A retail apocalypse has long been looming.

The demise of the shopping centre has been exacerbated by the Great Recession and the growth of e-commerce. After all, the online marketplace is simply a modernized, digital version of the shopping mall – but open 24/7 and with infinite assortment.

However, the US retail sector was considered overstored well before the e-commerce boom. According to Bloomberg, this was the 'result of investors pouring money into commercial real estate decades earlier as the suburbs boomed. All those buildings needed to be filled with stores, and that demand got the attention of venture capital. The result was the birth of the big-box era of massive stores in nearly every category – from office suppliers like Staples Inc. to pet retailers such as PetSmart Inc. and Petco Animal Supplies Inc.'[20]

Fast forward to 2019 and there is another important factor at play: consumers are simply buying fewer clothes. *The Atlantic* reported in 2017 that the apparel sector's share of total US consumer spending has dropped by a whopping 20 per cent this century.[21]

We are spending less on clothes

So what's driving this? First, discretionary spend is being diverted towards experiences, leaving shoppers with less money in their pockets to splash out on fashion. In the UK, Barclaycard data showed that spending on entertainment, in pubs and in restaurants all individually saw double-digit growth in 2017, while spending on women's clothing dropped 3 per cent.[22] New clothes are discretionary in the best of times, but the combination of squeezed disposable income and shifting consumer priorities have really dented the apparel sector.

Second, there has been a noticeable absence of any new must-have fashion trends. Skinny jeans have kept us going for the past decade. Third, we have an ageing population – women generally tend to buy fewer new clothes as they get older. This is one of the many problems faced by UK department store retailer Marks & Spencer, whose core customer sits in the 55-plus demographic. In fact, in 2016, CEO Steve Rowe said that 60 per cent of female shoppers are buying fewer clothes than they were compared to the decade before.[23]

There is also a growing awareness of recycling and sustainability among consumers, which is leading the fashion sector to aim for complete circularity. As more shoppers think twice before buying new, services such as H&M's 'Take Care' in Germany are being introduced. The aim is to help shoppers extend the life of their clothes with free repairs and advice on getting stains out. Zara also has its #joinlife recycling programme. Great for consumers and of course for the planet – not so great for fashion sales.

Lastly, workplaces are more casual today, which is resulting in shoppers ditching their blazers and suit jackets in favour of a more blended wardrobe. Charles Tyrwhitt founder Nick Wheeler has openly expressed his frustration with ties going out of fashion: 'It's the only bloody product that has a decent margin.'[24]

Malls, department stores and superstores: a slow death?

The reduced consumer demand for new clothes is particularly worrying for shopping malls given that 70 per cent of their square footage was traditionally dedicated to apparel. Today, it's more like 50 per cent[25] and we expect that figure to continue to decline over time. The ideal modern mall, according to Sandeep Mathrani, CEO of shopping centre operator GGP, in a 2017 Bloomberg interview, would be built around a department store, a supermarket, an Apple store, a Tesla store, and businesses that started out online, such as Warby Parker.[26] We'd argue that an Amazon returns area should also be part of the mix, but more on that later.

According to Cushman and Wakefield, mall visits dropped by 50 per cent between 2010 and 2013 and have been in decline ever since.[27] However, it's important to call out here that higher-end 'A malls', those primarily located in urban or touristy areas, are bucking this trend. In fact, just 20 per cent of malls make up nearly three-quarters of mall sales.[28] For these top-performing shopping centres, reinvention will be the primary requirement for future-proofing their businesses. For everyone else, rationalization is inevitable: between 20 and 25 per cent of US malls are expected to close by 2022.[29]

Of course, it's not just malls that are overspaced and lacking relevance today. Following the demise of the category killer, we believe that out-of-town superstores and department stores are the most at-risk retail formats today. Despite the many differences between these two formats, the original premise of both department stores and superstores is the same: one-stop shopping. In the past, it made sense to dedicate 100,000-plus square feet of retail space to these 'palaces of consumption', aggregating a significant number of brands under one roof. Macy's famously boasts about its 2.5 million-square-foot flagship New York store being the 'World's Largest Store' – it does cover an entire city block – while in Europe some Carrefour and Tesco hypermarkets were so massive that employees used to wear roller skates to get around. Piling it high may have worked in the past; today, however, with Amazon alone stocking millions of Prime-eligible products, the idea that a bricks and mortar retailer can still offer 'everything under one roof' becomes laughable.

But retail moves fast. It was only a couple of decades ago that Walmart was banking on its Supercenter concept as the future of retail. And let's not forget, for its time, it was incredibly innovative. No longer did shoppers have to visit multiple speciality retailers; the convenience of one-stop shopping and low prices was a winning combination. Back in 1997, then CEO of Walmart David Glass predicted: 'I believe Supercenters will be to the next decade what discount stores were to the last.' It's worth pointing out that at the time Walmart, like most retailers, were only just beginning to explore 'futuristic ideas [such] as Internet shopping.'[30]

Glass was certainly right with his predictions (although we're pretty sure Bezos could update that claim with e-commerce being to the following decade what superstores were to the previous one). From 1996–2016, Walmart opened an average of 156 Supercenters each year. The majority of these openings were conversions of existing discount stores as opposed to new builds; however, this was the most significant food retailing conversion process in US history. Walmart was able to bring its winning formula of low prices and wide grocery assortment to previously under-served areas.

Back in 2012, Natalie and esteemed retail analyst and co-author Bryan Roberts predicted that Walmart would reach saturation with its Supercenter format by 2020.[31] This was based on three factors: discount conversion opportunities drying up, slow population growth and the cannibalization of bricks and mortar sales by online retail.

Today, the superstore concept is at serious risk of becoming obsolete in many parts of the world. After two decades of opening hundreds of big-box stores annually, in 2017, Walmart US opened less than 40.[32] We have yet to see a net decline in store numbers, but we stand by our previous claim that the format will reach saturation in the very near future.

The 'death of the hypermarket' is far more pronounced in markets such as the UK where the retail sector is more heavily influenced by online and discount channels which pose the largest threat to superstores. According to the Office for National Statistics, at the time of writing in 2018, e-commerce made up 17 per cent of total retail sales[33] in the UK, nearly double the US figure.[34] Meanwhile, Aldi and Lidl alone account for 12 per cent of the grocery sector,[35] according to Kantar. The explosive growth in these two channels over the past decade has led to titanic shifts in shopping behaviour and expectations, the most significant of which has been the death of the weekly shop.

'This is a once in 50- to 60-year change. The last big change was the supermarket [in the 1950s]. I think what you are seeing now is as fundamental.'
Lord Mark Price, former Waitrose MD, 2014[36]

Today, an astounding 65 per cent of UK shoppers visit a supermarket more than once per day,[37] according to the 2017–18 Waitrose Food & Drink report. No longer do customers need to trek to an out-of-town superstore for low prices or wide assortment. Online retail is well and truly eroding the superstore proposition; meanwhile, proximity retailing no longer comes with a premium price tag. Shoppers today buy little and often; they are shopping 'for tonight' and as a result they are visiting a multitude of brands.

The most tangible evidence of this fundamental shift in shopping habits can be found at the very entrance of a supermarket. In that same report, Waitrose stated that the average store traditionally provided 200 large shopping carts and 150 shallow ones for the 'daily shopper'. By 2017, that had been reversed: there are now 250 shallow trolleys and just 70 large ones.[38] 'The notion that you are going to go and push a trolley around for the week is a thing of the past', said Price.

Department stores, meanwhile, won't be as fortunate. Since 2000, department store sales across the US have plummeted by 40 per cent. Almost all major listed department store retailers saw a decline in store productivity over the past decade. Sears – once iconic but now dying a slow death – witnessed the most dramatic decline: sales per square foot fell by 56 per cent from $218 in 2006 to just $97 in 2016.[39] The obvious answer to this problem? A whole lot of store closures. Sears, Macy's and JCPenney are in the process of collectively shutting more than 500 stores.[40]

'They've been trying to kill us for centuries. We've been through hypermarkets, supermarkets, the specialists and now pure plays.'
El Corte Ingles Chairman Dimas Gimeno, 2018[41]

A fundamental rule in retail is being relevant to your customers. This is essential in the best of times but becomes all the more critical when the backdrop is an overstored retail landscape and a subdued consumer with shifting priorities. Being all things to all people is no longer an option. In fact, we'd argue that Amazon is probably the only retailer in the world today that can get away with being all things to all people thanks to its unrivalled assortment and accessibility – in both the financial and logistical senses. For everyone else, it's essential to have both a crystal-clear vision of your target customer and a truly differentiated proposition in order to stand out from the crowd.

By their very nature, traditional department stores are simply less relevant today:

- *Online encroachment.* Although Amazon does not break out category figures, it is considered to be one of the largest apparel retailers in the US. We don't believe that online retailers can ever fully replace the physical store experience in categories like fashion and food, but that doesn't mean they won't try. Faster delivery, more generous returns policies and sizing improvements are helping to instil greater confidence in shoppers looking to buy clothes online.

  As we touched on earlier in the chapter, online retail is encroaching on the core premise of the department store: one-stop shopping. According to Cowen and Company, US department stores currently generate approximately 15–25 per cent of their sales online; however, many analysts believe that 35–40 per cent is the maximum penetration level for apparel sales online.[42] So while there is an opportunity to grow department store sales online, this will indeed lead to a glut of empty space in stores. The good news is retailers can get creative about filling this excess space, as we'll discuss later in the book.

It's also important to remind ourselves that, at one time, shoppers turned to department stores for the knowledge and assistance that could be provided by store employees. It was also an opportunity to discover and get inspired by new products. Of course, that is less relevant today as mobile phones have become the shopper's trusted advisor of choice and many people often browse online before coming into the stores. That said, we believe that department stores could do more to capitalize on personal shopping and the fitting room experience more broadly.

- *Product sameness and mid-market positioning.* The department store's pitfalls go far beyond *breadth* of assortment; the range itself is undifferentiated and less compelling these days. In fact, consultants at AlixPartners estimate that there is a 40 per cent overlap in product mix among traditional department stores. But these stores weren't always so homogeneous.[43] At one time, the Sears Wish Book represented the largest selection of toys you could find in one place and, up until the '80s, JCPenney was still selling home appliances and auto products. The subsequent rise of the big-box discounters like Walmart and Target forced the major department store chains to rationalize their general merchandise offerings and shift their focus to fashion. Today, apparel, footwear and accessories make up around 80 per cent of most department stores' sales compared to just 50 per cent a few decades ago.[44]

An increased focus on fashion may have once helped to differentiate from a growing superstore threat but today, despite their best efforts to invest in exclusive ranges and collaborate with other brands, department stores are left looking quite vulnerable. The so-called fast fashion chain Zara can take a coat from design stage to the sales floor in 25 days.[45] Off-price retailers meanwhile offer prices up to 70 per cent lower than traditional department stores.[46] The rise of these bricks and mortar disruptors means that department stores are no longer the cheapest, nor are they the most fashionable or the most convenient. And we all know that in retail the middle ground is a very dangerous place to position yourself.

The initial knee-jerk reaction to these new competitive threats was a period of seemingly perpetual discounting; however, this race to the bottom simply eroded margins, devalued brand perception and trained shoppers to only buy on promotion. Now department stores are opting for a more sustainable 'if you can't beat 'em, join 'em' approach by ramping up their own off-price presence. In fact, at the time of writing in 2018 a growing number of traditional department store chains have more outlet and off-price stores than full-price shops.[47] Despite the risk of cannibalizing existing stores, this format is far more relevant for today's modern shopper.

Department stores are no stranger to reinvention, and we will discuss in more detail how they can co-exist with Amazon and other online retailers later in the book; however, for now there is no denying that there will be fewer of them in the future.

Millennials, minimalism and mindful spending

In a *Journal of Retailing* essay in 1955, economist and retail analyst Victor Lebow wrote:

> Our enormously productive economy demands that we make consumption
> our way of life, that we convert the buying and use of goods into rituals, that
> we seek our spiritual satisfactions, our ego satisfactions, in consumption. The
> measure of social status, of social acceptance, of prestige, is now to be found in
> our consumptive patterns. The very meaning and significance of our lives today
> is expressed in consumptive terms... We need things consumed, burned up,
> worn out, replaced and discarded at an ever-increasing pace.

For the past century, American culture has been defined by consumerism. But that's all changing. Millennials, defined as those born between 1980 and 1996, now outnumber Baby Boomers, those born between 1946 and 1964, making them the largest living generation in the US[48] according to Pew Research. There are of course subsequent demographics like Generation Z to take into account and many more to follow. However, millennials are of particular interest, having reached peak spending age, but with values and spending habits that are vastly different to previous generations.

As Morgan Stanley observed in 2016:

> Educational spending may come to define the Millennials the way owning
> a house and two-car garage was emblematic of the Boomers. On average,
> Millennials under 25 use twice as much of their total spending on education as

their parents did. Higher costs have meant more student debt, which has put a damper on spending.[49]

In fact, from 2005 to 2012, the average amount of student debt for Americans under 30 has almost doubled from $13,340 to $24,897, according to Morgan Stanley. Educated but saddled with debt, Millennials are increasingly opting for minimal yet meaningful, socially conscious lifestyles. This is resulting in a generational shift in buying habits and will have huge implications for the retail sector for decades to come.

Battle for share of wallet will intensify not only as digitally native Millennials reign as the dominant consumer group, but also as we continue to see a cross-generational shift away from buying material things and towards experiences such as travel, entertainment and dining out. In a speech at the Shoptalk conference in 2017, Sarah Quinlan, SVP at Mastercard, noted how the #1 Christmas gift in the US in 2016 was a plane ticket – and #2 was a hotel voucher.[50] Meanwhile, Ikea believes that we've reached 'peak stuff'[51] and Boots CEO (ex-Dixons Carphone boss) Seb James thinks that 'shoppers are now only grazing on ownership.' Later in the book, we'll discuss how retailers can adapt their stores to cater to the rise in both the sharing and experience economies.

While there is no denying that asset-light Millennials place a high value on experiences – with social media in particular fuelling the FOMO (Fear of Missing Out) factor – the shift towards experiential spending is not just a Millennial thing. Mastercard's Sarah Quinlan summed it up nicely in a 2017 corporate interview:

> Before, if you acquired more and more goods, you could measure your social status. Now... we really like our family and friends again and want to spend time with them. Thus, we've seen a rise in spending on travel, on hotels, on airlines, on trains, on concert tickets and the like. And that's what people prize – it's going out for a meal with family and friends versus buying goods.[52]

In 2015, for the first time on record, Americans spent more money in restaurants and bars than in supermarkets,[53] according to the US Census Bureau. Spending in the discretionary categories of 'food away from home' and 'entertainment' continued to rise in 2016, up 5 per cent and 3 per cent respectively, after increasing by 8 per cent and 4 per cent the previous year.

It's no surprise then that retailers are frantically reinventing their bricks and mortar locations to position themselves as less transactional and more experiential, a topic we'll explore in greater detail later in the book. 'It's not enough simply to have the stuff,' says Debenhams Chairman Sir Ian Cheshire, 'you've got to wrap it in a set of experiences.'[54]

It's also important to point out that consumers are having to dig deeper when it comes to necessities such as healthcare and insurance as well as pensions. According to Deloitte, healthcare as a percentage of total personal consumer expenditure rose from 15.3 per cent in 2005 to 21.6 per cent in 2016.[55]

The bottom line is that with less money being spent on material goods, retailers will naturally have to adapt their store portfolios to reflect the seemingly permanent changes in expenditure patterns.

In summary? An apocalypse for some, but transformation for most.

Notes

1   Kumar, Kavita (2018) Amazon's Bezos calls Best Buy turnaround 'remarkable' as unveils new TV partnership, *Star Tribune*, 19 April. Available from: http://www.startribune.com/best-buy-and-amazon-partner-up-in-exclusive-deal-to-sell-new-tvs/480059943/ [Last accessed 2/11/2018].

2   Wylie, Melissa (2018) No relief for retail in 2018, *Bizjournals*, 2 January. Available from: https://www.bizjournals.com/bizwomen/news/latest-news/2018/01/no-relief-for-retail-in-2018.html [Last accessed 29/3/2018].

3   Thomas, Lauren (2017) Bankruptcies will continue to rock retail in 2018, *CNBC*, 13 December. Available from: https://www.cnbc.com/2017/12/13/bankruptcies-will-continue-to-rock-retail-in-2018-watch-these-trends.html [Last accessed 29/3/2018].

4   Isidore, Chris (2017) Malls are doomed: 25% will be gone in 5 years, *CNN*, 2 June. Available from: http://money.cnn.com/2017/06/02/news/economy/doomed-malls/index.html [Last accessed 29/3/2018].

5   Armstrong, Ashley (2018) What will 2018 have in store for the retail sector?, *Telegraph*, 2 January. Available from: https://www.telegraph.co.uk/business/2018/01/02/will-2018-have-store-retail-sector/ [Last accessed 29/3/2018].

6   Marinova, Polina (2017) This is only the beginning for China's explosive e-commerce growth, *Fortune*, 5 December. Available from: http://fortune.com/2017/12/04/china-ecommerce-growth/ [Last accessed 29/3/2018].

7   Bowsher, Ed (2018) Online retail sales continue to soar, *Financial Times*, 11 January. Available from: https://www.ft.com/content/a8f5c780-f46d-11e7-a4c9-bbdefa4f210b [Last accessed 28/6/2018].

8   BRC (2018) 'Every Industrial Revolution has brought long-term benefits but always goes through short-term pain', Doug Gurr, UK Country Manager, @

AmazonUK #BRCAnnualLecture [Twitter] 12 June. Available from: https://twitter.com/the_brc/status/1006597059615608832 [Last accessed 29/6/2018].

9 Reynolds, Treacy (2017) Holiday Retail Sales Increased 4 percent in 2016, *National Retail Federation*, 13/1. Available from: https://nrf.com/blog/holiday-retail-sales-increased-4-percent-2016 [Last accessed 29/6/18]

10 Boren, Zachary Davies (2014) There are officially more mobile devices than people in the world, *Independent*, 7 October. Available from: https://www.independent.co.uk/life-style/gadgets-and-tech/news/there-are-officially-more-mobile-devices-than-people-in-the-world-9780518.html [Last accessed 29/3/2018].

11 Anonymous (2017) Push Growth Seminar 15 May 2017 [Blog] *The Internet Retailer* 17 May. Available from: http://www.theinternetretailer.co.uk/582-push-growth-seminar-15th-may-2017-google-headquarters-st-giles-high-street-london/ [Last accessed 29/3/18].

12 Andrews, Travis M (2017) Nordstrom's wild new concept: a clothing store with no clothes, *Washington Post*, 12 September. Available from: https://www.washingtonpost.com/news/morning-mix/wp/2017/09/12/nordstroms-wild-new-concept-a-clothing-store-with-no-clothes/?noredirect=on&utm_term=.bed99d644159 [Last accessed 29/6/18].

13 Emarketer (2018) Worldwide retail and ecommerce sales. Available from: https://www.emarketer.com/Report/Worldwide-Retail-Ecommerce-Sales-eMarketers-Updated-Forecast-New-Mcommerce-Estimates-20162021/2002182 [Last accessed 29/2/2018].

14 Ovide, Shira (2018) How Amazon's bottomless appetite became corporate America's nightmare, *Bloomberg*, 17 March. Available from: https://www.bloomberg.com/graphics/2018-amazon-industry-displacement/ [Last accessed 29/3/2018].

15 Sullivan, Ted (2008) Borders: Interview with CEO George Jones, *Seeking Alpha*, 7 October. Available from: https://seekingalpha.com/article/98837-borders-interview-with-ceo-george-jones [Last accessed 28/6/2018].

16 Stone, Brad (2013) *The Everything Store: Jeff Bezos and the age of Amazon*, Bantam Press, London.

17 PWC (2017) 10 retailer investments for an uncertain future. Available from: https://www.pwc.com/gx/en/industries/assets/total-retail-2017.pdf [Last accessed 29/3/2018].

18 Fung Global Retail & Technology (2016) Deep dive: the mall is not dead: part 1. Available from: https://www.fungglobalretailtech.com/wp-content/uploads/2016/11/Mall-Is-Not-Dead-Part-1-November-15-2016.pdf [Last accessed 29/3/2018].

19 Cowen and Company (2017) Retail's disruption yields opportunities – store wars! Available from: https://distressions.com/wp-content/uploads/2017/04/Retail_s_Disruption_Yields_Opportunities_-_Ahead_of_the_Curve_Series__Video_-_Cowen_and_Company.pdf [Last accessed 29/3/2018].

20 Townsend, Matt et al (2017) America's 'retail apocalypse' is really just beginning, *Bloomberg*, 8 November. Available from: https://www.bloomberg.com/graphics/2017-retail-debt/ [Last accessed 29/3/2018].

21 Thompson, Derek (2017) What in the world is causing the retail meltdown of 2017? *The Atlantic*, 10 April. Available from: https://www.theatlantic.com/business/archive/2017/04/retail-meltdown-of-2017/522384/ [Last accessed 29/3/2018].

22 Next PLC 2017 annual report (2018) Available from: http://www.nextplc.co.uk/~/media/Files/N/Next-PLC-V2/documents/reports-and-presentations/2018/Final%20website%20PDF.pdf [Last accessed 28/6/2018].

23 Felsted, Andrea and Shelly Banjo (2016) Apparel Armageddon across the Atlantic, *Bloomberg*, 31 May. Available from: https://www.bloomberg.com/gadfly/articles/2016-05-31/women-curtailing-clothes-shopping-hit-uk-us-retailers-iov824k1 [Last accessed 28/6/2018].

24 Goldfingle, Gemma (2018) Charles Tyrwhitt founder Nick Wheeler laments the fact that no-one buys ties anymore: 'It's the only bloody product that has a decent margin', #TDC18 [Twitter] 30 January. Available from: https://twitter.com/gemmagoldfingle/status/958279318068760578 [Last accessed 29/3/2018].

25 Anonymous (2017) This whole 'malls are dying' thing is getting old, mall CEOs say, *Investors.com*, 12 April. Available from: https://www.investors.com/news/this-whole-malls-are-dying-thing-is-getting-old-mall-ceos-say/ [Last accessed 29/3/2018].

26 Ibid.

27 Thompson, Derek (2017) What in the world is causing the retail meltdown of 2017? *The Atlantic*, 10 April. Available from: https://www.theatlantic.com/business/archive/2017/04/retail-meltdown-of-2017/522384/ [Last accessed 29/3/2018].

28 Fung Global Retail & Technology (2016) 'Deep Dive: The Mall Is Not Dead: Part 1' [Online] https://www.fungglobalretailtech.com/wp-content/uploads/2016/11/Mall-Is-Not-Dead-Part-1-November-15-2016.pdf [Last accessed 29.3.18]

29 Isidore, Chris (2017) Malls are doomed: 25% will be gone in 5 years, *CNN*, 2 June. Available from: http://money.cnn.com/2017/06/02/news/economy/doomed-malls/index.html [Last accessed 29/3/2018].

30 Walmart 1997 Annual Report. Available from: http://stock.walmart.com/
    investors/financial-information/annual-reports-and-proxies/default.aspx [Last
    accessed 28/6/2018].

31 Berg, Natalie and Bryan Roberts (2012) *Walmart: Key insights and practical
    lessons from the world's largest retailer*, Kogan Page, London.

32 Walmart 10-Ks, author research.

33 Office for National Statistics (2018) Retail sales, Great Britain: February 2018.
    Available from: https://www.ons.gov.uk/businessindustryandtrade/retailindus-
    try/bulletins/retailsales/february2018#whats-the-story-in-online-sales [Last
    accessed 29/3/2018].

34 U.S. Census Bureau News (2018) Quarterly retail e-commerce sales 4th quar-
    ter 2017. Available from: https://www.census.gov/retail/mrts/www/data/pdf/
    ec_current.pdf [Last accessed 29/3/2018].

35 McKevitt, Fraser (2017) Lidl becomes the UK's seventh largest supermarket,
    Kantar. Available from: https://uk.kantar.com/consumer/shoppers/2017/
    september-kantar-worldpanel-uk-grocery-share/

36 Ruddick, Graham (2014) Supermarkets are 20 years out of date, says Waitrose
    boss, *Telegraph*, 22 October. Available from: http://www.telegraph.co.uk/
    finance/newsbysector/epic/tsco/11178281/Supermarkets-are-20-years-out-of-
    date-says-Waitrose-boss.html [Last accessed 29/3/2018].

37 John Lewis Partnership (2017) The Waitrose Food & Drink Report 2017–
    2018. Available at: http://www.johnlewispartnership.co.uk/content/dam/cws/
    pdfs/Resources/the-waitrose-food-and-drink-report-2017.pdf [Last accessed
    29/3/2018].

38 Ibid.

39 Fung Global Retail & Technology (2017) Deep dive: the mall is not dead:
    part 2. Available at: https://www.fungglobalretailtech.com/wp-content/
    uploads/2017/09/The-Mall-Is-Not-Dead-Part-2%E2%80%94-The-Mall-
    Is-in-Need-of-Transformation-September-6-2017.pdf [Last accessed
    29/3/2018].

40 Garfield, Leanna (2017) 17 photos show the meteoric rise and fall of Macy's,
    JCPenney, and Sears, *Business Insider*, 3 September. Available from: http://
    uk.businessinsider.com/department-store-sears-macys-jcpenney-closures-
    history-2017-8 [Last accessed 29/3/2018].

41 Hardy, Emily (2018) Alvarez says (unsurprisingly) that 'department stores are
    great & have a great future'. 'They've been trying to kill us for centuries. We've
    been through hypermarkets, supermarkets, the specialists & now pure plays.
    It's just about finding what makes you different.' [Twitter] 19/4. Available
    from: https://twitter.com/Emily_L_Hardy/status/986958259801198592 [Last
    accessed 28/6/18].

42 Cowen and Company (2017) Retail's disruption yields opportunities – store wars! Available from: https://distressions.com/wp-content/uploads/2017/04/Retail_s_Disruption_Yields_Opportunities_-_Ahead_of_the_Curve_Series__Video_-_Cowen_and_Company.pdf [Last accessed 29/3/2018].

43 Wahba, Phil (2017) Can America's department stores survive? *Fortune*, 21 February. Available from: http://fortune.com/2017/02/21/department-stores-future-macys-sears/ [Last accessed 29/3/2018].

44 Ibid.

45 Bain, Marc (2017) A new generation of even faster fashion is leaving H&M and Zara in the dust, *Quartz*, 6 April. Available from: https://qz.com/951055/a-new-generation-of-even-faster-fashion-is-leaving-hm-and-zara-in-the-dust/ [Last accessed 29/3/2018].

46 Klepacki, Laura (2017) Why off-price retail is rising as department stores are sinking, *Retail Dive*, 1 February. Available from: https://www.retaildive.com/news/why-off-price-retail-is-rising-as-department-stores-are-sinking/434454/ [Last accessed 29/3/2018].

47 McKinsey (2016) 'The State of Fashion 2017' [Online] https://www.mckinsey.com/~/media/mckinsey/industries/retail/our%20insights/the%20state%20of%20fashion/the-state-of-fashion-mck-bof-2017-report.ashx [Last accessed 29/3/18].

48 Andrews, Travis M (2016) It's official: Millennials have surpassed baby boomers to become America's largest living generation. *The Washington Post*, 26/4. Available from: https://www.washingtonpost.com/news/morning-mix/wp/2016/04/26/its-official-millennials-have-surpassed-baby-boomers-to-become-americas-largest-living-generation/?utm_term=.84adab7ac6d2 [Last accessed 29/3/18].

49 Morgan Stanley (2016) Generations change how spending is trending, 26 August. Available from: https://www.morganstanley.com/ideas/millennial-boomer-spending [Last accessed 11/9/2019].

50 Sarah Quinlan from Mastercard, speech at Shoptalk Copenhagen Oct 2017 based on Christmas 2016.

51 Farrell, Sean (2016) We've hit peak home furnishings, says Ikea boss, *Guardian*, 18 January. Available from: https://www.theguardian.com/business/2016/jan/18/weve-hit-peak-home-furnishings-says-ikea-boss-consumerism [Last accessed 29/3/2018].

52 Mastercard News (2017) Sarah Quinlan on how consumers choose experiences and services over goods (Online video). Available from: https://www.youtube.com/watch?v=hCiZqtSDumY [Last accessed 28/6/2018].

53 Thompson, Derek (2017) What in the world is causing the retail meltdown of 2017? *The Atlantic*, 10 April. Available from: https://www.theatlantic.com/

business/archive/2017/04/retail-meltdown-of-2017/522384/ [Last accessed 29/3/2018].

54 Cahill, Helen (2017) Debenhams boss shuns selling stuff, *City A.M.*, 4 April. Available from: http://www.cityam.com/262339/debenhams-boss-shuns-selling-stuff [Last accessed 29/3/2018].

55 Barua, Akrur and Daniel Bachman (2017) The consumer rush to 'experience': Truth or fallacy? *Deloitte*, 17 August. Available from: https://dupress.deloitte.com/dup-us-en/economy/behind-the-numbers/are-consumers-spending-more-on-experience.html#endnote-sup-5 [Last accessed 29/3/2018].

End of pure-play 05 e-commerce: Amazon's transition to bricks and mortar retailing

'Being a pure e-commerce player is less unique than it was. There is more competition. Increasingly, consumers won't think about online and offline – they will just think about retail.'
Sir Terry Leahy, former CEO of Tesco[1]

Now that we have established that many more stores will need to close in order to adapt to the change in shopping habits, you might rightly ask why we are now talking about the death of e-commerce and not death of the store.

The simple answer is because, despite the explosive growth of online retail, a whopping 90 per cent of all global retail sales take place in bricks and mortar stores.[2] Physical retail must evolve, but it certainly isn't dying. The underperformers will be weeded out. The undifferentiated will be exposed. The overcapacity issue will be addressed. But make no mistake – the bricks and mortar store will continue to play a crucial role in retail for decades to come.

'Physical stores aren't going anywhere. E-commerce is going to be a part of everything, but not the whole thing.'
Jeff Bezos, 2018[3]

In fact, we would argue that as technology continues to break down the barriers between online and offline, those retailers *without* a physical presence are the ones looking vulnerable today. Gone are the days when pure-play online retailers could boast lower overhead costs – and consequently lower prices – due to foregoing physical space requirements. The structural economic advantages once held by online-only retailers have disappeared.

Back in 2015, Natalie authored a report predicting that pure-play e-commerce would largely cease to exist by 2020.[4] This was met with a degree of scepticism at the time, the most notable of which was perhaps when the very well-regarded Alex Baldock, then CEO of Shop Direct, publicly rebutted our claim in his speech at a *Retail Week* conference.[5] But would you expect the boss of a pure-play e-commerce retailer to do anything other than to make a case for pure-play e-commerce?

Today the notion of moving 'online to offline' has become a justified trend and even has its own acronym: O2O. Since our report was published, we've seen dozens of prominent, digitally native brands make the leap into the physical realm. The most notable of these are e-commerce giants Amazon and Alibaba which, through the launch of new retail concepts ranging from tech-infused bookstores to checkout-free supermarkets, are sending a clear signal to the retail community that their vision of the future very much includes physical stores. And this goes beyond the odd flagship store – online retailer JD.com is looking to open 1,000 stores *a day* in China.

Jack Ma, founder of Alibaba, has since taken our initial prediction one step further with his belief that 'pure e-commerce will be reduced to a traditional business and replaced by the concept of New Retail – the integration of online, offline, logistics and data across a single value chain.'[6]

In this chapter, we will explore the factors driving the online to offline trend, how Amazon specifically is shifting gears to take on bricks and mortar retailing, and how the accelerated convergence of physical and digital worlds will require retailers to adapt their own business models.

Next-generation retail: the quest for omnichannel

Before we dive into the O2O trend, it's important to understand the broader convergence of physical and digital retail. Consumers today are genuinely channel- and device-agnostic. 'The consumer does not care about online and offline,' says Terry von Bibra, Alibaba's General Manager of Europe. 'No consumer in the world gets up in the morning and says, "I'm going to buy some shoes online", or goes into an electronics store and says, "I'm going to buy a refrigerator offline". The only people that care about that are the people that sell shoes or refrigerators.'[7]

> 'The era of channel [either online or store] is over. What we're really embarking on now is a world where, for consumers, channels are completely merged and we need to think that way.'
> **Paula Nickolds, Managing Director of John Lewis, 2017**[8]

What the consumer does want is a frictionless experience. Seamless shopping is now a firmly embedded expectation, regardless of the number of channels or devices used to research, browse, purchase or collect an item. Meeting this demand is no easy feat. In fact, we have calculated that there are more than 2,500 ways to shop today. The path to purchase is no longer linear – new customer touchpoints are popping up outside of traditional retail channels which, when combined with the proliferation of delivery services, means shoppers have more choice than ever before.

It's no surprise then that terms like *omnichannel, connected, seamless* and *frictionless retail* and – dare we use the horrific portmanteau – *phygital* have dominated industry discussions over the past decade. Despite having an element of buzzword bingo to it, their intent is valid – bricks and mortar retailers must not only invest in digital capabilities, but also ensure a genuinely cohesive online and offline experience. In other words, retailers need to start thinking like their shoppers.

> 'There's still no substitute for touching, feeling, seeing the product. We'll see more merging in the future.'
> **Doug Gurr, Amazon UK Country Manager, 2018**[9]

So what does omnichannel retailing look like in practice? A mom needs to buy her son a new pair of shoes. She researches online – desktop, mobile or tablet – then goes to the store to have her son's feet measured. The shoe she'd like is out of stock, so the store associate offers to check availability at another branch or to have it delivered to the customer's home. In this instance, the customer has left satisfied despite not walking out with the product she intended to buy. The retailer was able to offer excellent customer service – enabled by technology.

This might sound fairly simplistic by today's standards, but an overwhelming number of retailers lack a single view of inventory and many are simply not structured in a way that allows for this level of service. Despite an industry-wide focus on creating a unified customer experience, many retail businesses are still operating in silos, with online and bricks and mortar divisions working towards different sets of objectives.

But we have come a long way since the very early days of the smartphone when it wasn't unheard of for anxious retailers to deploy wireless signal jammers to prevent shoppers using their devices to search for a better price. Little did they then know how the advent of 'showrooming', as it became known, would have as profound an impact on shopping as we know it as the growth of e-commerce itself.

Equally, in the early days of e-commerce, retail store managers complained that customers who had bought an unwanted product from the retailer online increasingly wanted to return it to the store. This is easiest from the perspective of the customer, who does not want to repack and potentially pay for postage. Why should they make an extra trip to the post office when the retailer has a branch a few metres away on their main, local shopping street?

But many retailers weren't prepared for the impact on their reverse logistics, which led in some early cases to store managers refusing to accept online returns. And, yet, retailers soon realized the value of the convenience in offering this service, turning it to their advantage by enabling online fulfilment instore, with click & collect. Nowadays, if a shopper doesn't like the shoes she chose and had delivered, she can often return them via post free of charge or return them to the store, while the store is often credited with sale (and return) by virtue of where the order is placed or paid for.

For those retailers who have seen their business model come under threat from the dual whammy of the Amazon Effect and 'showrooming', digital store integration or transformation has become an important strategic imperative. Not only does this mean, perhaps counterintuitively, embracing showrooming by offering free, secure customer Wi-Fi (especially where mobile data signals fail to reach), but using that connection to capture more detailed information about customer footfall, traffic flows, dwell times and purchase behaviour, and using it to improve the customer experience and offer in a store.

As technology rapidly breaks down the barriers between online and offline, retailers are being pushed to offer a more connected retail experience that results in greater customer satisfaction. Let's now look at the specific technologies and innovations that are making this happen.

Key drivers of convergence of physical and digital retail

The pivotal role of mobile

As discussed in the previous chapter, mobile has genuinely transformed the way we shop, not only by creating endless new shopping opportunities but also by acting as a much-needed bridge between online and offline retail.

Knowledge is power

Armed with their own personal shopping companion, consumers can make far more informed decisions both in and out of the store. So how has this impacted the bricks and mortar shopping experience? Put simply, it's given the customer a heightened sense of empowerment. The assistance of our mobile phones has greatly improved the instore experience – and raised expectations in the process – when it comes to access, speed and convenience. Today, the majority of sales are digitally influenced.[10] Gone are the days when price comparisons meant visiting multiple physical locations. And today, when shoppers want to learn more about a product, it's often quicker to consult our phones than to seek out a store associate.

It's worth pointing out here that the number one destination for online product search isn't Google. It isn't even a search engine. It's Amazon.[11] The combination of Amazon's unrivalled assortment and treasure trove of customer reviews makes it both a trustworthy and convenient source for consumers looking to gain product information. In fact, over half of online shoppers in the US trust Amazon the most for useful product information.[12] That statistic alone is enough to send shivers down the spine of the entire retail sector, and for bricks and mortar retailers specifically, it highlights the dual challenge of price transparency and availability. If the product is out of stock or the price isn't right, then Amazon is in a prime position to gobble up that sale in the form of a mobile transaction.

> 'Many people think our main competition is Bing or Yahoo. But, really, our biggest search competitor is Amazon.'
> **Ex-Google Chairman Eric Schmidt, 2014**[13]

The use of mobile devices instore is now even helping shoppers to make more informed decisions when buying groceries. In the future, for example, Walmart wants its shoppers to be able to point their phones at a piece of fruit to determine how fresh it is.

Frictionless, personalized experience – mobile and beyond

Mobile devices have also opened countless opportunities for retailers to create a more convenient and tailored experience for their customers. But prior to even entering the store, retailers should have a compelling online offer to win at the online 'search, browse and discovery' phase that is clearly linked to physical presence. Once that is achieved, retailers need to then give the customer a reason to visit the physical store. Many already try to drive online customers into stores by offering wish lists, and recipe or shopping lists, as well as discounts, special events and local promotions that can be accessed instore.

But once there, retailers must address two of the biggest shopping bugbears (particularly in a grocery setting), which are finding products and then waiting in a queue to pay for them. Mobile is playing a huge role in both areas. First, in terms of improving navigation, retailers are embracing instore mapping systems using a range of technologies including Wi-Fi, Bluetooth, audio, video and magnetic positioning, augmented reality (AR) and 3D virtualization, allowing customers to use their mobile devices to find the products they are looking for more quickly. In the future, expect more retailers to bundle instore navigation services with personalized, real-time offers in a bid to replicate the deeply tailored experience that traditionally could only be experienced online. Beacon technology and augmented reality, accessed via mobile devices, are creating new opportunities for retailers to target instore shoppers with such offers. With technology, retailers are always treading that fine line between convenient and creepy but research suggests that the majority of shoppers are receptive to receiving real-time offers that are relevant to them.[14] As previously touched on, we believe that plastic, points-based loyalty cards will become a thing of the past as retailers look to digitize loyalty schemes – and mobile will naturally play a key role here.

Secondly, reducing friction at the checkout has become a hot topic, with Amazon most famously attempting to bypass the payment process, let alone checkouts, altogether in its Amazon Go convenience store. We'll discuss this in greater detail later in the book but here it's important to point out that digital integration and the more pragmatic move towards more cashless transactions is being applied instore to speed up the authorization and therefore queuing process. Grocers, for example, are no strangers to self-checkout, relying on the customer to scan, bag and check out their own goods to deliver a faster throughput rate than a manned checkout. Or even queue-busting systems can enable a sales associate to check out customers waiting in a queue. Accepting 'tap and go' contactless or mobile wallet payments is another step to helping customers bypass the friction of queuing at the checkout altogether.

In addition, digital displays, replacing traditional paper tags and posters, can become convenient connection points for customers to access information – on the digital shelf tag itself, by connecting to the customer's mobile device, or via an app. While mobile plays an essential role in digitizing the instore experience, it's important to highlight additional technologies that are helping to break down the barriers between online and offline retail. Digital displays, for example, also have the benefit of enabling the retailer to change prices and promotions dynamically, and so exploit another way to keep pace with online. Fashion retailers can use so-called smart or 'magic' mirrors to help shoppers see complementary and alternative product recommendations, share their outfit plans with friends on social networks, or even simply call an assistant to request more sizes, for example. Meanwhile, endless aisles and mobile kiosks allow retailers to offer infinite assortment beyond traditional, physical constraints.

Those retailers furthest ahead in terms of integrating digital technologies into their stores understand how these efforts can combine the best that online has to offer, in terms of means of access and availability, with those attributes that cannot be replicated online, and only the physical store can offer: the ability to feel and touch the product. In this instance, some have started equipping their store staff with the same access to product, pricing and availability information as their customers, so they can 'save the sale' by having products shipped from another store for collection or ordered from the store online, for home delivery and collection. For example, shoe retailer Dune's single view of stock allows them to move thousands of pairs of shoes each week and, during end of season clearance sales, they can ensure the correct merchandise is sent to the appropriate store. Crucially, it also gives the retailer the agility to fulfil from any channel, even if they are down to their last pair of shoes.

Meanwhile, retailers are blurring the boundaries even further by employing AR and virtual reality (VR) experiences. For example, fashion chain Zara, under increased competition from pure-play online rivals like ASOS and Boohoo, began testing an AR experience in 2018. Instore shoppers hold their mobile phones to a store window or sensor where they can then see models superimposed over the image on their screens. Not only does this enable instore shoppers to click through to buy the item, but online shoppers can also use the app by hovering their phone over a package delivered from Zara. Mobile devices are truly enabling a far more blended shopping experience, and this is only set to accelerate in the future.

Click, collect and return

The boundaries between online and offline are also blurring when it comes to fulfilment. For many shoppers today, visiting a physical location is the preferred method of receiving and returning online orders. Retailers are equally incentivized to drive this behaviour, as leveraging their stores as pick-up points is far more cost-effective than delivering to individual homes and typically results in additional spend once instore. At Target, one-third of shoppers that collect online orders instore buy something else, while at Macy's shoppers typically spend an additional 25 per cent instore once their order has been picked up.[15]

In less than five years, click & collect has gone from a quirky business model traditionally associated with UK retailer Argos (unknowingly ahead of its time) to a retailing prerequisite. Today, it's difficult to think of any retailer in a mature retail market that doesn't allow its customers to pick up their online orders instore. The phenomenal growth of click & collect is proof that shoppers want to marry the benefits of online shopping – assortment and convenience – with the ease of collecting instore. After all, 90 per cent of Americans live within 10 miles of a Walmart store[16] and, in France, shoppers can find a Carrefour store within an eight-minute drive.[17] Let's not underestimate the physical infrastructure advantage held by the large multinationals.

Retailers are also reconfiguring their stores to cope with a higher volume of returns. Historically, the return rate for retail has been just under 10 per cent of sales. Today, thanks to the growth of e-commerce and heightened customer expectations, it's more like 30 per cent and in categories like apparel it can be as high as 40 per cent.[18] Shoppers today naturally expect to be able to return unwanted online orders to wherever is most convenient for them – regardless of channel used for purchase.

Once again, this highlights the evolving, critical role of the physical store. A whopping 85 per cent of Home Depot's online returns take place instore.[19] BORIS (the affectionate acronym for Buy Online Return In Store) is yet another opportunity for multi-channel retailers to leverage their physical stores to piggyback off the growth of online retail – not only from the point of view of pleasing today's very demanding customer but, as with click & collect, retailers are likely to benefit from incremental purchases. According to UPS, two-thirds of shoppers who return online orders to a physical store then make a new purchase during that visit.[20]

With 60 per cent of shoppers preferring to return online orders to a bricks and mortar store, the BORIS trend highlights yet another disadvantage for pure-play online retailers.[21] It's no coincidence that Amazon's foray into physical retail – and one of the first changes to Whole Foods stores following the acquisition – was the implementation of Amazon Lockers, providing shoppers with an alternative to the post office for collecting and returning online orders.

Equally, many pure-play e-commerce retailers are collaborating with bricks and mortar retailers to provide shoppers with greater choice and convenience. For example, in the UK, Walmart-owned Asda allows shoppers to collect and return orders from online retailers such as ASOS, Wiggle and AO.com. Meanwhile, some retailers are even teaming up with their competitors. Amazon partnered with department store retailer Kohl's in late 2017 for an instore returns programme while, perhaps a less well-known example, Swiss giant Migros and e-tailer brack.ch have formed a similar click & collect arrangement in the name of better serving the customer, creating a more unified physical and digital retail experience.

Pervasive computing: shopping without stores or screens

Finally, we can't talk about a blended online and offline shopping experience without mentioning the Internet of Things. When we think about the shopping experience blending into the background of consumers' homes, we can already see the impact that AR and VR, as well as voice and simplified replenishment solutions, are having. They are supercharging consumers' already high expectations, set by online, for speed, convenience, value and personalization. And they take advantage of the blended reality that informs most customer decisions today.

VR, for example, can enable a retailer to bring the store into the home using immersive digital displays viewed using a special headset – customers can even buy simply by nodding their head in Alibaba's Buy+ VR mall. This still might sound a bit like science fiction, but Walmart's 2018 launch of 3D virtual shopping will help to take this technology to the masses. Equally, consumers can bring their home into the store – retailers like Ikea, Macy's and Lowe's are all now using VR instore to enable endless aisle capabilities.

'Virtual reality is developing fast and in five to ten years it will be an integrated part of people's lives.'
Jesper Brodin, Ikea Range & Supply Manager, 2018[22]

Amazon meanwhile continues to open the industry's eyes up to the possibility of transplanting retail real estate directly into consumers' homes – from Dash Buttons that enable customers to reorder the product they denote at a touch, to Echo devices that allow shoppers to ask Alexa to add it to their list, all the way through to what the authors consider the holy grail of frictionless commerce – auto-replenishment of goods, where the shopper can completely opt out of the purchasing decision. All share the same aim: for the means of engagement between the shopper and retailer to fade into the background, using more pervasive computing interfaces than keyboard, mouse and even touchscreen.

So, online and offline retail are no longer mutually exclusive. The most successful retailers will be those that, while recognizing the urgency for digital investment, are able to simultaneously reconfigure their stores with the ultimate view that these are assets and not liabilities. Bricks and mortar stores will play a major role in shaping the future of retail as a more convenient, connected and customer-dictated industry.

So what happens if you don't have any stores?

Clicks chasing bricks – the end of online shopping

'I think it's just a race; will the online folks like us figure out brick and mortar retail faster than the brick and mortar retailers figure out online?'
Chieh Huang, founder and CEO of Boxed, 2018[23]

O2O: *incentives for getting physical*

Now that we've established the factors driving the convergence of digital and physical worlds, let's look at what this means for pure-play e-commerce retailers.

In a nutshell, it means that online-only is no longer enough.

Yes, online retail will always win on assortment. But as we have previously established, physical space constraints aside, bricks and mortar retailers are increasingly leveraging technology to offer a more fused customer experience and in doing so they are encroaching on attributes that were traditionally solely associated with online retail – convenience, personalization, transparency of information.

Meanwhile, in the face of rising shipping and customer acquisition costs, online-only retailers are recognizing that there are a growing number of benefits – financial, logistical and marketing – to having bricks and mortar space. As e-commerce becomes a more prominent part of retailers' businesses, it's exposing the often-underreported costs of trading online. According to global consulting firm AlixPartners, these include:

- shipping and handling charges: free and/or fast shipping and packaging costs;
- costs associated with increased returns and restocking, reverse logistics, and lost margin on SKUs returned to a channel that was not intended to sell it;
- corporate headcount growth to support e-commerce divisions (including merchandising, planning, marketing, content creation, web development and IT, to name a few);
- balancing additional online marketing expenses with traditional expenses;
- incremental distribution and warehousing costs associated with piece picking;
- deleveraged store base and diluted store labour;
- incremental labour and technology expenses associated with omnichannel capabilities (ship from store, buy online, pick up in store, order from store, etc).
- complications associated with inventory management – deciding to share or not to share online and stores' inventory and the costs associated with either decision.[24]

How do these costs stack up against those incurred by a bricks and mortar retailer? Take clothing, for example. According to AlixPartners, a typical $100 clothing purchase made by a shopper in a bricks and mortar outlet comes with a cost of goods sold of about $40. The associated operating costs such as rent, overhead and labour would be $28, leaving the retailer with a profit margin of 32 per cent.[25]

The same $100 clothing transaction made online and intended for home delivery also comes with a cost of goods sold of about $40. However, the costs associated with processing that order are slightly higher than if it had been sold in a physical store. In this instance, the individual order must be picked, packed and shipped from a distribution centre to the shopper's home, which is naturally more expensive than shipping a truckload of inventory from DC to store. In this instance, operating costs would be $30, which leaves the retailer with a profit margin of 30 per cent, or slightly less profitable than if the item had been sold instore.[26]

Shipping costs

Now retailing, of course, is not as black and white as this case study may imply – there are a number of variables that would impact cost such as product category, store format and efficiencies in the supply chain. However, it's worth highlighting how physical space is becoming an attractive option for digitally native brands looking to mitigate costs. And looking ahead, there's no sign of online volumes – and therefore costs – slowing down. By 2019, UPS expects e-commerce shipments to account for over half of its total volume, up from 36 per cent a decade ago.[27]

With Amazon taking roughly 40 cents of every dollar Americans spend online,[28] it's no surprise the retailer is especially motivated to optimize its supply chain and reduce shipping costs. In just three years (from 2014–2017), the cost of sorting and delivering products to customers nearly doubled to $22 billion.[29]

And Amazon continuously stirs the pot, raising customer expectations for free and ever faster delivery as it looks to bolster the value of its broader Prime ecosystem. As a historically online-only retailer, Amazon's ability to compete with bricks and mortar peers on immediacy has been vital. But now the genie has been let out of the bottle. Today, near-instant gratification is a firmly embedded customer expectation, as other retailers have had no choice but to invest in next-day and increasingly same-day delivery capabilities.

The problem? It's not sustainable. And we're beginning to see the first cracks. Amazon is raising transportation fees for suppliers of beverages, nappies and other heavy products that are expensive to ship, while also limiting the number of single, low-priced items (soap and toothbrushes, for example) that shoppers can purchase. As previously discussed, we have even seen Amazon increase Prime fees across its array of subscription options – annual, monthly and student – while also raising fees and minimum spend requirements for its Prime Now one-to-two-hour delivery service. And there will most certainly be more price hikes to come – shoppers should expect to pay more for 'free' shipping in the future.

Amazon is very transparent with investors here, stating that the cost of shipping will continue to increase as more shoppers around the globe become active Prime users and Amazon reduces shipping rates, uses more expensive shipping methods and offers additional services. In the meantime, they are relentlessly exploring ways to take greater control of the last mile to make shipping more cost-effective – drones, robotics, rewarding shoppers for choosing slow delivery, Amazon Flex, Delivery Service Partners, the list goes on. Having a physical presence – whether through lockers, instore concessions, mall pop-up sites or stores themselves – is another piece of this very big fulfilment puzzle. This enables Amazon to provide shoppers with a potentially more convenient and certainly more cost-effective way to receive their online orders, which we'll discuss in greater detail later in the book.

Cost of customer acquisition

But shipping expenses aren't the only challenge – the cost of attracting new shoppers is higher without stores. In fact, the customer acquisition costs for buy-online, ship-from-warehouse models include overhead IT and marketing costs that can make distribution costs four times higher than instore methods.[30]

A shopper may stumble upon a bricks and mortar store and decide to pop in for a browse, but the concept of 'walk-in traffic' doesn't translate online,[31] particularly for small and medium-sized retailers. Real estate in the digital realm is becoming increasingly crowded and expensive. There are close to a million online retailers all vying for the customer's attention via one portal – Google.[32] Despite millions being spent on digital marketing, paid search listings make up just 10 per cent of clicks from Google results,[33] according to a report by Gartner L2. It states, 'The remaining 90 per cent of clickshare goes to organic listings – suggesting natural search optimization is essential to maintaining online traffic and e-commerce market share for all retailers.'

Meanwhile, only 6 per cent of consumers visit the second page of Google search results.[34] And even if a retailer is listed on the first page, this doesn't guarantee clicks; the first five results on that first page receive 68 per cent of clicks.[35]

A bricks and mortar store, however, can act as a billboard for the brand, allowing shoppers to engage with the retailer in a way that can't be achieved via a screen. Ironically, this helps to drive online sales. A 2017 study from British Land found that, when a retailer opens a new store, traffic to its website from the surrounding area rises by more than 50 per cent within six weeks of opening. Interestingly, retailers with fewer than 30 stores receive the most impact, with web traffic boosts of up to 84 per cent.[36]

It should be getting clearer by now – online retailers can't do it on their own anymore. They're recognizing the value of a physical presence as a means of offsetting rising shipping and customer acquisition costs.

O2O: who and how

'There is a problem in being online-only, which is, it's not a great service experience to not be able to try on clothes before you buy them, if that's what you want to do.'
Andy Dunn, CEO, Bonobos, 2016[37]

Some call it the industry's 'stupidest acronym'; to others it's a 'trillion dollar opportunity'. Either way, the O2O trend is certainly gaining momentum now following the highly publicized moves into the physical realm by e-commerce giants like Amazon and Alibaba.

However, one of the most famous, and certainly one of the earliest, examples of a retailer successfully going from online to offline is an American eyewear retailer called Warby Parker. The New York City-based retailer started out online in 2010. Three years later, it opened its first store and at the time of writing there were close to 70. The irony is that by opening physical locations, which are largely profitable, Warby Parker is able to grow online sales. Co-founder Dave Gilboa said, 'We also see a halo effect where stores themselves become a great generator of awareness for our brand and drive a lot of traffic to our website, as well and accelerate our e-commerce sales.'

Since Warby Parker made that initial leap into bricks and mortar, dozens of pure-play e-commerce retailers around the globe have followed suit: Amazon, Alibaba, JD.com, Bonobos, Indochino, Birchbox, Zalando, Farfetch, Missguided, Boden, Gilt, Depop, Everlane, Brandless, Swoon Editions, Blue Nile, Rent the Runway, the list goes on.

Whether pop-ups, showrooms, concessions or permanent locations, all these retail brands were beginning to recognize the value of having some form of a physical presence – and some were even catching the eye of legacy retailers looking to accelerate their digital presence.

Speaking at the 2018 eTail West conference, Matthew Kaness, CEO of Modcloth, the online fashion chain gobbled up by Walmart, summed it up:

> 2010–2014 was a real moment of expansion where, in the e-commerce world, there was this sense that it was going to overtake retail. A lot of people were famous for saying they were never going to open stores and that stores were dead… people got used to traffic going up every year and customer acquisition getting more efficient.[38]

However, in 2015, organic reach became more difficult due to Facebook and Google's decisions to change their algorithms. Kaness continued:

> It became harder to acquire new customers, it became harder to raise venture capital in the category… that was the impetus for a lot of what you're seeing on the sell side. Shareholders, boards, founders and investors are realizing that to build a brand that sustains and scales, in most cases it needs to be multi-channel.[39]

In 2015, Modcloth began testing pop-up stores in cities across the US and in the following year it opened its first permanent store in Austin, Texas. In 2017 it was acquired by Walmart and by 2018 it had announced plans to open 13 inventory-free stores across the US (a trend we'll touch on later in the book).

But Modcloth wasn't Walmart's first target. The world's largest retailer has taken a bold acquisition-based approach to digital transformation. The most notable of these deals was the 2016 purchase of Amazon competitor Jet.com, which saw founder and ex-Amazonian Marc Lore join Walmart to lead the company's global e-commerce business. Since joining Walmart, he has spearheaded the buying spree that has included Modcloth as well as men's clothing specialist Bonobos, footwear retailer Shoebuy, home furnishings retailer Hayneedle and outdoorwear business Moosejaw.

'For us, a big part of it is being paranoid. We're at our best when we've got a competitor that's really challenging us.'
Walmart chairman Greg Penner, 2017[40]

Under Lore, Walmart.com has been taking a two-pronged approach to digital acquisitions, targeting either 1) speciality retailers with deep merchandising expertise, strong product content and established relationships with vendors; or 2) digitally native vertical brands in a bid to differentiate from the competition. And by the competition, we mean Amazon.

Amazon makes it move

Jeff Bezos was asked in a 2012 interview whether he would ever consider opening stores. 'We would love to but only if we can have a truly differentiated idea. One of the things that we don't do very well at Amazon is do a me-too product offering.'

He continued, '…when I look at physical retail stores, it's very well served. The people who operate physical retail stores are very good at it. The question we would always ask before we would embark on such a thing is, what's the idea? What would we do that would be different? How would it be better?'[41]

Since that interview, Bezos has opened:

- Amazon-branded kiosks in shopping centres across America;
- collection lockers in retail stores, malls, libraries, universities and even apartment buildings;
- from LA to London, pop-up stores that swap price tags for scannable barcodes;
- bookstores that aren't really designed to sell books;
- America's first cashier-less supermarket;
- Alexa concessions and Amazon product returns areas in some of its most feared competitors' stores;
- Treasure Truck (essentially Black Friday on wheels);
- a 4-star store that only stocks products with high online ratings;
- and a couple of drive-through supermarkets.

No, Amazon is not a me-too retailer.

Table 5.1 Evolution of Amazon's bricks and mortar presence

Year launched	Concept	Primary function	Description	Exclusive to Prime
2011	Amazon Lockers	Fulfilment	Parcel delivery lockers found in retail stores, shopping centres, offices, libraries, gyms and more. Allows Amazon to overcome two of the biggest barriers to online shopping: missed deliveries and inconvenient returns.	No
2014	Amazon Pop-Up	Technology	300–500 sq ft sites that allow shoppers to interact with Amazon's devices such as Kindles, Fire tablets and Echo in real life. Started out in malls; now also features in Whole Foods and Kohl's stores (Best Buy in the US and Shoppers Stop in India also feature smaller Alexa concessions).	No
2015	Campus Pick-Up Point	Fulfilment	Amazon's first fully-staffed pickup and drop-off collection point. Caters to college students across US campuses. In 2017, this was enhanced with the launch of Instant Pickup, allowing shoppers to collect from a nearby locker within two minutes of placing the order (since discontinued).	No
2015	Amazon Books	Retail/ Technology	Bookstores with uniquely digital features: book covers face out and Prime members receive preferential pricing. About 75% of space dedicated to books. Designed to drive Prime membership and, as with the pop-ups, get shoppers interacting with Amazon technology in a physical setting.	No
2016	Treasure Truck	Retail	Amazon handpicks daily deals which are communicated to shoppers by text. Shoppers are then alerted to the location of the truck to collect their goods. Creates an urgency to buy and adds an element of fun to what is typically a functional shopping experience.	No

Year	Name	Type	Description	
2017	AmazonFresh Pickup	Fulfilment	Online grocery collection service very similar to popular French 'Drive' concept. Amazon uses licence plate recognition technology to reduce waiting times, and orders are delivered directly into the trunk of the shopper's car.	Yes
2017	The Hub	Fulfilment	Parcel delivery lockers for apartment buildings. Like the famous yellow Amazon lockers, The Hub is fully self-service, open 24/7, and accepts deliveries from all carriers.	No
2017	Whole Foods Market	Retail	Acquisition of 450+ supermarkets across North America and the UK. Amazon was attracted to Whole Foods for its strong perishable offer (67% of sales); strong own label; urban presence; and strong overlap with Prime customer base. Amazon is officially no longer a pure-play online retailer.	No
2017	Amazon Returns	Fulfilment	Unique agreement with Kohl's department stores where Amazon shoppers can return unwanted online orders to their local Kohl's. Addresses the perennial headache that is online returns, while driving footfall to Kohl's. We expect this to be rolled out internationally.	No
2018	Amazon Go	Retail	First checkout-free store. Shoppers scan their Amazon app to enter. The high-tech convenience store uses a combination of computer vision, sensor fusion and deep learning to create a frictionless customer experience.	No
2019 and beyond	Fashion or furniture stores would be a logical next step			

NOTE Amazon Go officially opened its doors to the public in 2018
SOURCE Amazon; author research as of June 2018

Historically, Amazon's physical space was designed to serve one of two purposes: showcase their devices or act as a collection site for online orders. As you can see from Table 5.1, Amazon's initial move into bricks and mortar retailing was through collection lockers, college campus drop-off/pick-up sites and mall pop-ups.

However, it was Amazon's rather ironic launch of physical bookstores in 2015 that marked a genuine shift in strategy, as this was the first time Amazon mimicked digital merchandising and pricing in a physical setting. 'We've applied 20 years of online bookselling experience to build a store that integrates the benefits of offline and online book shopping', said Jennifer Cast, Vice President of Amazon Books.[42]

The most helpful online review is displayed as well as the overall rating and number of customer reviews. Product recommendations in the form of 'if you like this, then you'll love…' signage has been brought to the physical shelf. Book covers face out as they would do online, and books must have at least 4-star recommendations to make it on to the shelf. This means a much more curated assortment; the stores only stock about five titles per three linear feet of shelving, while most bookstores offer more than triple that figure.[43] Around 25 per cent of the space is dedicated to sales of non-book items such as Bose speakers and French presses, but also a lot of Amazon's own devices – Kindles, Echo speakers, Fire tablets as well as its own-label Basics range of electronic accessories.

Figure 5.1   Amazon's first-ever bricks and mortar retail concept, Amazon Books, launched in 2015

Perhaps what's most intriguing about the Amazon Books concept, however, is its bold approach to pricing. The books do not feature price tags; instead, shoppers must scan the item and – if they are a Prime member – they will be offered the Amazon.com price while non-members pay the list price. The stores are clearly designed to drive Prime membership and, like Amazon Pop-Ups, to encourage shoppers to interact with Amazon devices, both of which feed the broader ecosystem. Selling books is secondary.

Over the next two years, Amazon continued to experiment with bricks and mortar both as a retailer and technology provider. It would go on to launch new grocery formats such as AmazonFresh Pickup and Amazon Go, which we'll discuss in the coming chapters, while also partnering with existing bricks and mortar retailers such as Kohl's, Best Buy and less well-known examples like mattress start-up Tuft & Needle.

Tuft & Needle – another retailer that started life online – has worked with Amazon to enhance the customer experience as it moves further into physical retailing. Its Seattle store features tablets for shoppers to read product reviews on Amazon, Echo devices to answer customer questions and QR codes that allow for one-click purchasing through the Amazon app. Daehee Park, Tuft & Needle's co-founder, said that after much debate about how to go head-to-head with Amazon, they decided to go in the exact opposite direction. 'We've decided, why not just embrace them? It is the future of retail and e-commerce... We focus on what we're good at and plug in Amazon technology for the rest.'[44]

This could be a model for other brands that are already reliant on Amazon for online sales (Tuft & Needle generates around 25 per cent of its sales through Amazon).[45] Similarly, we believe that Amazon will look to forge more retail partnerships as a means of addressing the ticking time bomb that is online returns. In 2017, Amazon teamed up with Kohl's for designated Amazon returns areas in its Chicago and LA department stores. Some would argue that this is too Trojan Horse-like, especially as Amazon builds up its arsenal of fashion brands, but we believe this is one of the least risky co-opetition routes. It's a unique proposition that drives some much-needed traffic to stores without giving away tons of customer data. For added convenience, there are designated Amazon returns parking spaces near the store entrance, and Kohl's will package and transport the returns to Amazon for free. We could see Amazon striking a similar agreement with other global department store retailers like Marks and Spencer or Debenhams, for example, who are well represented on high streets but could benefit from a boost in footfall. Co-opetition will be a key theme for the future – though not all will be willing to go down that path.

In any case, if there was ever any doubt over Amazon's intentions for physical retail, they were squashed in 2017 when Amazon announced the deal of the decade: they were acquiring Whole Foods Market. Overnight, Amazon picked up 21 million square feet of retail space – and said goodbye to pure-play e-commerce.

Notes

1   Thomson, Rebecca (2014) Analysis: Sir Terry Leahy and Nick Robertson on why delivery has become so crucial, *Retail Week*, 6 February. Available from: https://www.retail-week.com/topics/supply-chain/analysis-sir-terry-leahy-and-nick-robertson-on-why-delivery-has-become-so-crucial/5057200.article [Last accessed 29/6/2018].

2   Fitzgerald, Melanie (2018) Will digital brands spell the death of the physical store? *ChannelSight*. Available from: https://www.channelsight.com/blog/digital-brands-spell-the-death-of-the-physical-store/ [Last accessed 29/6/2018].

3   Kumar, Kavita (2018) Amazon's Bezos calls Best Buy turnaround 'remarkable' as unveils new TV partnership, *Star Tribune*, 19 April. Available from: http://www.startribune.com/best-buy-and-amazon-partner-up-in-exclusive-deal-to-sell-new-tvs/480059943/ [Last accessed 29/6/2018].

4   McGregor, Kirsty (2015) Pure-play etail will cease to exist by 2020, predicts Planet Retail, *Drapers*, 22 July. Available from: https://www.drapersonline.com/news/pure-play-etail-will-cease-to-exist-by-2020-predicts-planet-retail-/5077310.article [Last accessed 29/6/2018].

5   MDJ2 (2015) Ten things we learned at Retail Week Live 2017. Available from: http://mdj2.co.uk/wp-content/uploads/2016/11/Ten-things-we-learned-at-Retail-Week-Live-2017-1.pdf [Last accessed 29/6/2018]

6   Jiang, Moliang (2017) New retail in China: a growth engine for the retail industry, *China Briefing*, 15 August. Available from: http://www.china-briefing.com/news/2017/08/15/new-retail-in-china-new-growth-engine-for-the-retail-industry.html [Last accessed 29/6/2018].

7   Wynne-Jones, Stephen (2017) Shoptalk Europe: an eye-opening journey through the future of retail, *European Supermarket News*, 12 October. Available from: https://www.esmmagazine.com/shoptalk-europe-eye-opening-journey-future-retail/50514 [Last accessed 29/6/2018].

8   Simpson, Emma (2017) New John Lewis boss says department store needs reinventing, *BBC*, 30 March. Available from: https://www.bbc.co.uk/news/business-39441039 [Last accessed 29/6/2018].

9   Amazon UK Analyst Briefing, London, July 2018.

10 Simpson, Jeff, Lokesh Ohri and Kasey M Lobaugh (2016) The new digital divide, *Deloitte*, 12 September. Available from: https://dupress.deloitte.com/dup-us-en/industry/retail-distribution/digital-divide-changing-consumer-behavior.html [Last accessed 29/6/2018].

11 Del Ray, Jason (2016) *55 percent of online shoppers start their product searches on Amazon*, *Recode*, 27 September. Available from: https://www.recode.net/2016/9/27/13078526/amazon-online-shopping-product-search-engine [Last accessed 29/6/2018].

12 Garcia, Krista (2018) Consumers' trust in online reviews gives Amazon an edge, *eMarketer*, 7 March. Available from: https://retail.emarketer.com/article/consumers-trust-online-reviews-gives-amazon-edge/5a9f05e9ebd4000744ae415f [Last accessed 29/6/2018].

13 Kowitt, Beth (2018) How Amazon is using Whole Foods in a bid for total retail domination, *Fortune*, 21 May. Available from: http://fortune.com/long-form/amazon-groceries-fortune-500/ [Last accessed 19/6/2018].

14 Accenture/Salesforce joint report (2016) Retailing, reimagined: embracing personalization to drive customer engagement and loyalty. Available from: https://www.accenture.com/t20161102T060800Z__w__/us-en/_acnmedia/PDF-28/Accenture-Salesforce-Retail-Exploring-Loyalty-ebook.pdf [Last accessed 29/6/2018].

15 Reagan, Courtney (2017) Think running retail stores is more expensive than selling online? Think again, *CNBC*, 19 April. Available from: https://www.cnbc.com/2017/04/19/think-running-retail-stores-is-more-expensive-than-selling-online-think-again.html [Last accessed 29/6/2018].

16 Meyersohn, Nathaniel (2018) Walmart figured out its Amazon strategy. So why's the stock down 13%? *CNN*, 17 May. Available from: http://money.cnn.com/2018/05/16/news/companies/walmart-stock-jet-amazon-whole-foods/index.html [Last accessed 29/6/2018].

17 Transcript of Alexandre Bompard's speech (2018) Carrefour, 23 January. Available from: http://www.carrefour.com/sites/default/files/carrefour_2022_-_transcript_of_the_speech_of_alexandre_bompard.pdf [Last accessed 29/6/18].

18 Bohannon, Patrick (2017) Online Returns: A Challenge for Multi-Channel Retailers. Oracle, 27/1. Available from: https://blogs.oracle.com/retail/online-returns:-a-challenge-for-multi-channel-retailers [Last accessed 29/6/2018].

19 Cochrane, Matthew (2018) Why 2017 was a year to remember for The Home Depot, Inc, *The Motley Fool*, 28 January. Available from: https://www.fool.com/investing/2018/01/28/why-2017-was-a-year-to-remember-for-the-home-depot.aspx [Last accessed 29/6/2018].

20 Ellis, James (2017) Online retailers are desperate to stem a surging tide of returns, *Bloomberg*, 3 November. Available from: https://www.bloomberg.com/news/articles/2017-11-03/online-retailers-are-desperate-to-stem-a-surging-tide-of-returns [Last accessed 29/6/2018].

21 ibid.

22 Ikea website. Available from: https://www.ikea.com/ms/en_US/this-is-ikea/ikea-highlights/Virtual-reality/index.html [Last accessed 29/6/2018].

23 Stern, Matthew (2018) Boxed CEO 'definitely' sees physical stores in its future, *Forbes*, 24 January. Available from: https://www.forbes.com/sites/retailwire/2018/01/24/boxed-ceo-definitely-sees-physical-stores-in-its-future/#619ff68c7cf3 [Last accessed 29/6/2018].

24 Permission received from Tim Yost.

25 Reagan, Courtney (2017) Think running retail stores is more expensive than selling online? Think again, *CNBC*, 19 April. Available from: https://www.cnbc.com/2017/04/19/think-running-retail-stores-is-more-expensive-than-selling-online-think-again.html [Last accessed 29/6/2018].

26 ibid.

27 Carey, Nick and Nandita Bose (2015) Shippers, online retailers seek way around rising delivery costs, *Reuters*, 15 December. Available from: https://www.reuters.com/article/us-usa-ecommerce-freeshipping/shippers-online-retailers-seek-way-around-rising-delivery-costs-idUSKBN1432ZL [Last accessed 29/6/2018].

28 Sender, Hannah, Laura Stevens and Yaryna Serkez (2018) Amazon: the making of a giant, *Wall Street Journal*, 14 March. Available from: https://www.wsj.com/graphics/amazon-the-making-of-a-giant/ [Last accessed 29/6/2018].

29 Amazon 10-K for the fiscal year ended December 31, 2017. Available from: https://www.sec.gov/Archives/edgar/data/1018724/000101872418000005/amzn-20171231x10k.htm [Last accessed 28/6/2018].

30 McGee, Tom (2017) Shopping for data: the truth behind online costs, *Forbes*, 10 August. Available from: https://www.forbes.com/sites/tommcgee/2017/08/10/shopping-for-data-the-truth-behind-online-costs/#53fdecdfc9d7 [Last accessed 29/6/2018].

31 Death of Pureplay Retail report (2016) *Gartner L2*, 12 January. Available from: https://www.l2inc.com/research/death-of-pureplay-retail [Last accessed 29/6/2018].

32 Walsh, Mark (2016) The future of e-commerce: bricks and mortar, *Guardian*, 30 January. Available from: https://www.theguardian.com/business/2016/jan/30/future-of-e-commerce-bricks-and-mortar [Last accessed 29/6/2018].

33 Death of Pureplay Retail report (2016) *Gartner L2*, 12 January. Available from: https://www.l2inc.com/research/death-of-pureplay-retail [Last accessed 29/6/2018].

34 Shelton, Kelly (2017) The value of search results rankings, *Forbes*, 30 October. Available from: https://www.forbes.com/sites/forbesagencycouncil/2017/10/30/the-value-of-search-results-rankings/#fab4b6b44d3a [Last accessed 29/6/2018].

35 ibid.

36 ICSC (2017) The socio-economic impact of European retail real estate. Available from: https://www.businessimmo.com/system/datas/112816/original/europeanimpactstudy-2017_.pdf [Last accessed 29/6/2018].

37 Khan, Humayun (2016) Why the top ecommerce brands are moving into physical retail (and what you can learn from them), *Shopify*, 10 May. Available from: https://www.shopify.com/retail/why-the-top-ecommerce-brands-are-moving-into-physical-retail-and-what-you-can-learn-from-them [Last accessed 29/6/2018].

38 Worldwide Business Research (2018) Putting the customer in the center of your business [Online Video]. Available from: https://slideslive.com/38906045/putting-the-customer-in-the-center-of-your-business [Last accessed 29/6/2018].

39 ibid.

40 O'Keefe, Brian (2017) What's driving Walmart's digital focus? Paranoia, top exec says, *Fortune*, 7 December. Available from: http://fortune.com/2017/12/07/walmart-penner-amazon-alibaba/ [Last accessed 29/6/2018].

41 Bhasin, Kim (2012) Bezos: Amazon would love to have physical stores, but only under one condition, *Business Insider*, 27 November. Available from: http://www.businessinsider.com/amazon-jeff-bezos-stores-2012-11?IR=T [Last accessed 29/6/2018].

42 Denham, Jess (2015) Amazon to sell books the old-fashioned way with first physical book shop, *Independent,* 3 November. Available from: https://www.independent.co.uk/arts-entertainment/books/news/amazon-to-sell-books-the-old-fashioned-way-with-first-physical-book-shop-a6719261.html [Last accessed 29/6/2018].

43 Kurtz, Dustin (2015) My 2.5-star trip to Amazon's bizarre new bookstore, *The New Republic*, 4 November. Available from: https://newrepublic.com/article/123352/my-25-star-trip-to-amazons-bizarre-new-bookstore [Last accessed 29/6/2018].

44 Del Ray, Jason (2017) One of the most popular mattress makers on Amazon is building an Amazon-powered store, *Recode*, 31 July. Available from: https://www.recode.net/2017/7/31/16069424/tuft-needle-seattle-store-amazon-mattresses-echo-alexa-prime-delivery [Last accessed 29/6/2018].

45 ibid.

Amazon's grocery ambitions: create a platform to sell you everything else

06

> 'In order to be a two-hundred-billion-dollar company, we've got to learn how to sell clothes and food.'
> **Jeff Bezos, 2007[1]**

Digital transformation is sweeping across the retail sector, but up until now three categories – furniture, fashion and food – have been relatively insulated. Affected? Yes. Disrupted? No.

These are categories where quality is subjective and cannot always be determined via a screen. These are categories where the desire to see and touch the product traditionally outweighed the convenience of buying online. And therefore, the margin for error in purchasing these categories online was historically higher than when buying commoditized products like books or DVDs, where shoppers knew exactly what they were going to get regardless of where they purchased it.

But that's all about to change.

By 2021, 28 per cent of clothing and footwear sales and 18 per cent of furniture and home furnishing sales in the US are expected to take place online (up from 9 per cent and 6 per cent respectively a decade earlier[2]), according to Kantar. Technology such as augmented reality, visual search and 3D body scanning are breaking down the barriers to online purchasing, reducing friction when it comes to discovery and sizing in fashion and giving shoppers more confidence in buying big-ticket items like furniture. Meanwhile, try-before-you-buy subscription boxes and more generous return policies are also helping to instil trust in shoppers looking to buy clothes online.

US online grocery 2.0?

'I believe the vast majority of grocery volume will be done by customer shopping in stores for a long time to come.'
Doug McMillon, CEO of Walmart, 2017[3]

But what about grocery? The supermarket sector is a notoriously complex, low-margin business with high fixed costs, a fragmented supplier base and product perishability. It only gets more complicated when you add home delivery into the mix. According to Goldman Sachs, it costs supermarkets an astonishing $23 per order to store, pick, pack and deliver groceries, eroding what are already razor-thin margins.[4]

Varying handling and temperature requirements, rejected substitutions and absent customers also add to the complexity. Not even the shopper journey is straightforward – multiple customers may contribute to the basket, adding items right up until the order is picked. Delivering books is a breeze in comparison.

High population density is ideal for any e-commerce operation, but for online grocery it's absolutely essential. You only need to look at the world's most advanced grocery e-commerce markets – South Korea and the UK – for proof. In South Korea, where 83 per cent of the population live in cities, the online grocery penetration reached an astounding 20 per cent in 2017. As a benchmark, the US penetration rate stood at 2 per cent during the same period.[5] A large, densely populated and highly connected country is the perfect breeding ground for online grocery, both in terms of driving supply chain efficiencies and consumer adoption (South Korea has the fastest internet in the world).

In countries with large rural populations like the US, such dense coverage becomes harder to achieve. South Korea has 522 people per square kilometre; the US has just 88.[6] In such a vast, sparsely populated country, most American supermarkets have found it difficult to achieve the economies of scale required to sustain an online grocery model. This resulted in retailers historically either shunning grocery home delivery altogether or limiting it to cash-rich/time-poor city dwellers – ie Peapod and FreshDirect.

According to Credit Suisse, there are 13 independent factors that correlate to online grocery adoption and profitability:

- broadband penetration;
- tablet/smartphone penetration;
- online share of retail spend;
- Amazon penetration;
- start-up/independent culture;
- urban driving infrastructure;
- metropolitan areas with >1 million inhabitants (conducive to in-store picking model);
- metropolitan areas with >5 million inhabitants (conducive to centralized distribution);
- GDP/capita;
- car ownership;
- prevalence of double-income households;
- density of supermarket space;
- inclement seasonal weather.

In addition to limited access, online grocery adoption in the US has also been slow because of the high fees associated with delivery, which have naturally deterred some shoppers from using the service. As of 2018, Walmart was still charging a whopping $10 per order.[7] Meanwhile, the typical 'endless aisle' advantage of buying online is less relevant in grocery and many Americans are still reluctant to let someone else – human or robot – select their produce. The desire to see, touch and even smell fresh food is a key driver to the physical store. Habits are firmly entrenched and there are barriers aplenty.

It's no surprise then that grocery remains one of the most underrepresented categories in online retail. The trend is evident even among die-hard Amazon fans. According to a 2018 NPR/Marist Poll, only 18 per cent of Amazon Prime members in the US have purchased fresh groceries online and a mere 8 per cent have used its Prime Pantry service. The top-cited reason for those who haven't? They simply prefer the instore experience.[8]

So we believe that if Amazon wants to crack grocery, they need stores. Demand for online grocery may be booming among certain consumer demographics (Gen Z, Millennials, busy families, urbanites) but, for many shoppers, it's still more convenient – or in some cases enjoyable – to hop into their car and drive to the grocery store. Don't get us wrong, grocery e-commerce is coming – and it's coming fast – but there will always be a place for the supermarket.

Our view is unsurprisingly shared by the country's largest grocery retailer. Speaking at its 2017 investment community meeting, Walmart CEO Doug McMillon said that to grow a national online grocery business, 'you have to be able to keep perishable products fresh, available and at the right price. To do that, you need a perishable supply chain that supports stores that are near customers.'[9]

In addition to physical stores, McMillon believes that a successful grocery e-commerce business requires 'a lot of general merchandise and apparel to help with the margin mix' as well as 'a lot of scale because volume helps reduce markdowns and throwaways,'[10] Amazon ticks these boxes as well, and is accelerating its incursion into the clothing sector. Remember how earlier we discussed that you cannot look at Amazon's individual categories or business units in isolation and that every service is another spoke on the flywheel? Selling higher-margin clothes, from private label ranges in particular, will help Amazon to offset some of the higher costs of delivering groceries.

Why else does Amazon need grocery stores? Because they'll create a halo effect for the online business through click & collect and same-day delivery, again reinforcing the need for a seamless shopping experience across channels. In many ways, the Whole Foods Market acquisition was an admission that the grocery category will always require an element of physical retail, albeit one of a more versatile nature.

At the same time, as we've already seen with other sectors, technology will dismantle the barriers traditionally associated with buying food online, while continued urbanization will simultaneously drive demand and bring costs down. Automation – from warehouse robotics to driverless delivery trucks – will improve supply chain efficiencies and the rise in third-party delivery services (Instacart and Shipt, for example) will allow more supermarkets to offer speedy delivery without the hefty investment in infrastructure or systems.

Meanwhile, the customer value proposition for online grocery is exploding; today, consumers benefit from improved mobile phone interfaces, single sign-ons, greater personalization and site navigation, automated lists, recipe inspiration, delivery passes, voice-activated shopping, simplified replenishment, same-day delivery and alternatives to home delivery such as click & collect or automated lockers.

Online grocery allows customers to shop on their terms and maximize their time, a trend that will be reinforced in the future as the everyday purchasing of household goods is automated through our connected homes. Technology will take the chore out of grocery shopping.

Food: the final frontier and importance of frequency

'Grocery is the Wild West for online. The size of the prize is huge, and it's growing.'
Carrie Bienkowski, Peapod's Chief Marketing Officer, 2018[11]

Old habits die hard, but they do die. And if anyone can modify behaviour, it's Amazon. Food retailing is attractive to Amazon in that it is the biggest non-discretionary sector – and one that is ripe for disruption. As we'll discuss below, it's also vital in that it enables Amazon to finally tap into a high-frequency purchase.

2022: the online grocery tipping point?

As of 2018, a whopping 20 per cent of US retail spending goes towards food but only 2 per cent of those sales take place online.[12] Technology advances, as laid out above, will help to increase adoption with Amazon firmly in the driving seat. In 2017, the retailer reached 18 per cent share in the US online grocery market – double that of its closest competitor Walmart, according to One Click Retail.[13]

Amazon will do what it does best – act as a catalyst for change, propelling other supermarkets to invest in their own online grocery capabilities, ultimately improving the experience for the customer.

'Amazon had previously made no impact in groceries, so grocers were able to sit back and think food is different. People have realized online is not going to be 1, 2, or 3 per cent of their market. It's going to be 10, 20, 30, or maybe even 60 per cent.'
Tim Steiner, Ocado CEO, 2018[14]

As such, e-commerce grocery adoption is expected to skyrocket from just 23 per cent of US consumers buying food and beverages online in 2016 to 70 per cent by 2024, according to a joint study from the Food Marketing Institute (FMI) and Nielsen. The companies have also brought forward their joint prediction that by 2025, US online grocery sales would reach $100 billion, or 20 per cent of total grocery retail sales. They now believe that 20 per cent tipping point will come as early as 2022, as Amazon fast-tracks online grocery to become mainstream.

Frequency – a big step closer to retail dominance

It's clear that Amazon can't be the Everything Store without food. Not only is it a major part of the consumer spending bucket, but it's also a category that is defined by *frequency* (the average US shopper visits a supermarket 1–2 times per week,[15] according to the FMI) and therefore largely driven by *habit* (85 per cent of the items shoppers put in their carts are the same from week to week).[16] No other sector offers such an incredible customer engagement opportunity.

> '[Grocery is] an everyday way into your life. There's nothing else that happens quite that way.'
> **Walter Robb, former co-CEO of Whole Foods Market, 2018[17]**

Data capture aside, there's a very good reason why Amazon limits its online grocery offering to Prime members. With grocery, Amazon gets frequency. If consumers are doing their weekly food shop through Amazon, bearing in mind they must first be Prime members, then there's a strong chance Amazon will then become their first port of call for other categories. As the former co-CEO of Whole Foods Market Walter Robb puts it, 'Food is the platform for selling you everything else.'[18]

This is why Amazon's move into grocery should worry all retailers, not just supermarkets. Grocery is the path for Amazon to become its customers' default shopping option. Already, according to PWC's 2018 Global Consumer Insights Survey, 14 per cent of consumers around the globe exclusively shop on Amazon.[19] If Amazon can crack grocery, they have the potential to take that figure much higher (though again not without greater scrutiny from the government).

It's no coincidence that Amazon spent years investing in its Prime offer, adding perk after perk and beefing up the content, before delving into the grocery category. It's a combination of the effortlessness of buying through Amazon and attractiveness of Prime that will make it difficult for other retailers to compete. And, as if that's not enough, Amazon also wants to provide services – from voice assistants to video streaming – that become so embedded in shoppers' everyday lives and routines that the retailer eventually makes itself indispensable.

Amazon's food fight: life before Whole Foods Market

However, the idea of luring shoppers in with food and then tempting them with higher-margin general merchandise is by no means a new strategy. This is the very premise of the hypermarket and superstore model. Walmart began adding food to the mix in the late '80s and in just over a decade became the largest food retailer in the US. Meanwhile, Britain's Tesco started life as a grocer and then in the '60s added general merchandise to its stores, enabling it to eventually become the largest retailer in the UK. 'The principle of what Amazon is doing is almost exactly the same', says Jack Sinclair, CEO of 99 Cents Only, who previously ran Walmart's US grocery division.[20]

The Whole Foods acquisition was an inflection point for Amazon, but in order to understand the motives for the deal, we must first go back to the beginning.

CASE STUDY   A lesson in the dangers of overexpansion: Webvan and the dot-com bust

One of the most spectacular failures of the dot-com bust was the online grocery service Webvan. The first major online grocery delivery company was co-founded in 1996 by Louis Borders (of the eponymous, now defunct, bookstore chain) and, as with many companies at the time, the mantra was 'Get Big Fast'. In less than three years, the company burned through $800 million in cash, went public, then filed for bankruptcy and closed down its operations.[21] Its meteoric rise and then fall made Webvan the poster child of the dot-com excess bubble.

Some might argue that Webvan was ahead of its time; after all, the snail-like dial-up connections of the late '90s were hardly conducive to speedy online grocery shopping. Like Amazon, Webvan was placing a big bet on technology's ability to change shopping habits, but its problems ran deeper than that. Its fundamental flaw? Overexpansion without sufficient customer demand.

Webvan shunned the conventional store-based picking model in favour of a centralized approach to online grocery delivery. Not unlike Ocado today, Webvan went on to build state-of-the-art, automated fulfilment centres with the aim of delivering groceries to shoppers within 30-minute time slots. The idea was that its unique technology would drive productivity, enabling Webvan to beat out both online and bricks and mortar rivals.

It wasn't the concept that was bad, it was the execution. Webvan was attempting to simultaneously build a brand and customer base from scratch, while redesigning the very infrastructure of a well-established sector. The capital-intensive plan required Webvan to dish out over $30 million on each large high-tech warehouse, but the lack of customer demand meant that the warehouses weren't running anywhere near full capacity.[22] According to some analysts, Webvan was losing more than $130 per order, when taking into account depreciation, marketing and other overheads.[23]

Richard Tarrant, CEO of MyWebGrocer, said of Webvan in 2013:

> In a low-margin business, where the products can be purchased within three miles by anyone in the United States, they decided to build warehouses and a whole distribution system with delivery trucks, labour, and everything else. But the 36,000 conveniently located grocery stores on every Main Street in America already had all that.[24]

Under pressure to appease investors, expansion was fast and furious. Covering the launch of Webvan's first mega warehouse in Oakland, California, a 1999 *Wall Street Journal* article stated:

> If it thrives, and even if it doesn't, Mr Borders plans to open another enormous grocery warehouse in Atlanta a few months later. Down the road are plans for at least 20 more such facilities throughout the US in practically every city big enough to support a major-league sports team.[25]

Webvan hadn't worked out the initial kinks with its business model before embarking on an aggressive, and ultimately disastrous, expansion plan. Within 18 months, the online grocer was trading in 10 major metro areas across the US.[26] For comparison, it took Ocado over a decade to open its second fulfilment centre.[27] Webvan 'committed the cardinal sin of retail, which is to expand into a new territory – in our case several territories – before we had demonstrated success in the first market', said Mike Moritz, a Webvan board member. 'In fact, we were busy demonstrating failure in the Bay Area market while we expanded into other regions.'[28]

In an effort to gain economies of scale, Webvan acquired rival HomeGrocer in 2000. Coincidentally, Amazon owned a 35 per cent stake in HomeGrocer at the time, which provided a first glimpse of Bezos' vision for the grocery category – taking the 'drudgery' out of the experience. In 1999, he commended HomeGrocer for having 'a fanatical eye for the customer experience. Their shoppers pick out better produce than I could for myself… The company really has an unusual attention to detail.'[29]

The HomeGrocer acquisition wasn't enough to save Webvan and within a year it went bankrupt. This had a lasting effect on the marketplace, souring the appetite for online grocery for years, even decades, to come.

AmazonFresh: rising from Webvan's ashes

Amazon's own online grocery delivery service, AmazonFresh, was born in 2007; though, if you don't live in Seattle, you'd be forgiven for thinking it was a newer concept. Amazon quietly tested the service in its hometown for *five years* before eventually rolling it out to other US cities. If there's one thing Amazon learned from Webvan's crash, it was to nail down its business model before embarking on any kind of expansion.

Leading the AmazonFresh initiative were four former Webvan executives – Doug Herrington, Peter Ham, Mick Mountz and Mark Mastandrea. It's worth highlighting here that Mountz is also the founder of Kiva Systems, the robotics company that Amazon acquired in 2012. Kiva was built on technology originally developed at Webvan and has since become a key part of the AmazonFresh strategy. Interestingly, Webvan was also resurrected in that Amazon purchased the domain – the site was once used to sell Amazon's non-perishable food items, though it's no longer in operation today.

'We had a lot of Webvan DNA in the room and we drew on that experience a lot', said Tom Furphy, who helped start AmazonFresh with Herrington and Ham before moving on to become a venture capitalist. 'That was a good formula for building the business responsibly.'[30]

But the team had their work cut out for them. As a general merchandise retailer, Amazon's site was – and still is today – designed for targeted search but, of course, shoppers tend to browse grocery categories. And while most online transactions comprise two to four items, the average grocery order is comprised of 50 items.[31] Navigating complexities around supply chain and differences in user experience are key to cracking online grocery.

As Amazon began to make its mark, however slowly, it had two big factors working in its favour – timing and an existing customer base. By the mid-noughties, fast broadband connections and higher smartphone penetration were helping to stimulate demand for online grocery, and, unlike Webvan, Amazon was able to tap into an existing pool of shoppers. However, it's worth pointing out here that Prime was only a couple of years old when AmazonFresh was launched. This was another reason for the tortoise-paced roll-out of online grocery – Prime had to be both mature and compelling enough so that Amazon would be equipped with a loyal, sizeable customer base before it got serious about grocery.

In 2013, AmazonFresh had finally begun to expand operations beyond Seattle and within a few years the service was offered in Chicago, Dallas, Baltimore, Seattle, parts of California (Los Angeles, Riverside, Sacramento, San Diego, San Francisco, San Jose, and Stockton), New York City, Northern New Jersey, Philadelphia, Northern Virginia, Connecticut, and, outside of the US, in London.[32]

Over the years, Amazon experimented with different branding and fee structures in order to make the economics of fresh grocery delivery work. For a while, the service was branded Prime Fresh and offered as part of a bundled Prime membership option for a $299 annual fee – triple the price of a normal Prime membership. This turned out to be too big a pill to swallow for many shoppers who were still getting accustomed to ordering groceries online so, in 2016, the AmazonFresh pricing model was changed – it was still limited to Prime members but as a more palatable $14.99 monthly add-on.

Despite the more favourable market conditions, selling fresh food online was no easy feat, which is why Amazon was simultaneously experimenting with a more familiar category – non-perishables.

Subscribe & Save: a first taste of simplified replenishment

Amazon had launched Subscribe & Save in 2007 just several months prior to making its first AmazonFresh deliveries. The subscription programme, which is still running today, allows shoppers to receive automatic delivery of grocery products (from one- to six-month intervals) with discounts of up to 15 per cent. At the time of launch, Amazon's online grocery store, which was separate to the Fresh service, featured over 22,000 non-perishable items from leading brands, including Kellogg's, Seventh Generation and Huggies as well as a wide selection of natural and organic products.[33]

Subscribe & Save was the first step to locking in grocery shoppers, giving Amazon an incredible amount of insight into their brand preferences and price elasticity – a major criticism of the programme is that, despite the discount, it's still subject to Amazon's dynamic pricing, which can negate the effect of cost savings offered through a subscription.

The launch of Subscribe & Save gave us insight at a very early stage as to how Amazon would disrupt the grocery sector – they would take the chore out of grocery shopping. After all, this is what Bezos had admired in HomeGrocer when they acquired a minority stake years earlier. Subscribe & Save was Amazon's first iteration of a simplified replenishment programme. Amazon would go on to launch a number of entirely new customer touch-points, physical and digital, that aimed to make the re-ordering of everyday goods as seamless as possible:

- **Dash Buttons:** Wi-Fi-connected one-click reordering buttons placed in shoppers' homes.
- **Dash replenishment service:** device-driven replenishment scheme, ie smart Brita water pitchers that automatically reorder filters or August home locks that reorder batteries when running low.
- **Alexa:** AI-powered virtual assistant that allows for voice-activated shopping via Echo.
- **Dash Wand:** handheld device that allows for barcode scanning and voice-activated reordering.
- **Dash Virtual Buttons:** as the name implies, one-click reordering buttons available on Amazon's app and site.

In a bid to stay on top of these new competitive threats, in 2017 Walmart filed a patent to integrate IoT (Internet of Things) into its actual products. Like Amazon's Dash replenishment scheme, this would allow for automatic re-ordering of items without any input from the customer. The difference, of course, is that Walmart's patent is for product-driven and not device-driven replenishment, which would generate more widespread usage and accelerate the trend.

'Amazon is about to cement habitual buying, quickly and insidiously, for millions upon millions of people and many product categories.'
Brian Sheehan, Professor of Advertising, Syracuse University, 2018[34]

The automatic replenishment trend will play a significant role in shaping the future of retail. Through these alternative touchpoints, Amazon wants to cut out friction and shorten the path to purchase just as it famously did back in 1999 with its 1-Click purchasing patent. Already today, you can shop without a store or screen. You can be in your kitchen asking Alexa to add items to your basket or pressing a Dash button, and in the future it will become even more seamless as shoppers are able to completely opt out of the purchasing decision. We will go from one-click to no-click.

> 'In grocery, the impact of smart homes, smart kitchens, smart appliances is going to be huge. When it comes to IoT in the home, I see the war of the home hubs happening.'
> **Paul Clarke, Ocado CTO, 2016**[35]

As a result, consumers will spend less time buying the essentials in the future, a trend that we will explore in greater detail later in the book, particularly in relation to its impact on the physical space. But for now, it's important to remember that, in exchange for the ultra-convenience provided by these technologies, purchases are funnelled directly through to Amazon's retail platform. No other retailer has been so successful at infiltrating the consumer's home.

After several years in operation, Subscribe & Save was bolstered through the 2010 launch of Amazon Mom (now more aptly named Amazon Family) and the acquisition of Quidsi. Amazon Mom allowed customers at a critical life stage to get discounts on nappies if they signed up for regular monthly deliveries; meanwhile, rival Quidsi was the parent company of Diapers.com, Soap.com and BeautyBar.com. An interesting side note here – Quidsi was co-founded by Marc Lore, who stayed on to work at Amazon for a few years. He then went on to create the online marketplace Jet.com which, as discussed in the last chapter, was acquired by Walmart in 2016. At $3.3 billion, it was the largest ever purchase of a US e-commerce start-up and a clear indication that Walmart saw Amazon as a fundamental threat to its business. This was an acquisition of both competitor and talent; at the time of writing in 2018, Lore remains the CEO of Walmart's domestic e-commerce operations.

Table 6.1 Amazon's grocery milestones

Year	Amazon's Grocery Milestones	Category
1999	Acquires 35% stake in HomeGrocer.com	Online grocery
2000	Webvan acquires HomeGrocer	Online grocery
2001	Webvan files for bankruptcy; site folded into Amazon.com	Online grocery
2007	Launches AmazonFresh	Online grocery
2007	Launches Subscribe and Save	Online grocery
2011	Acquires Quidsi	Online grocery
2012	Acquires Kiva Robotics	Online grocery
2013	AmazonFresh expands outside of Seattle	Online grocery
2014	Launches Dash wand	Connected home
2014	Launches Prime Pantry	Online grocery
2014	Launches Prime Now	Online grocery
2015	Launches Dash buttons	Connected home
2015	Launches Dash replenishment service	Connected home
2015	Launches Echo/Alexa for voice-activated shopping	Connected home
2015	Launches Amazon Restaurants	Online grocery
2016	AmazonFresh goes international; inks supply deals with Morrisons and Dia	Online grocery
2016	Launches first private label grocery products	Online grocery

2017	Launches AmazonFresh Pickup	Bricks & mortar
2017	Acquires Whole Foods Market	Bricks & mortar
2017	AmazonFresh is scaled back in nine states	Online grocery
2017	Launches virtual Dash buttons	Online grocery
2017	Launches meal kits	Online grocery
2018	Launches Amazon Go	Bricks & mortar

SOURCE Author research; Amazon

Here come the Primes: Pantry and Now

Two more significant launches came in 2014: Prime Pantry and Prime Now. Initially catering to the bulky, typically monthly shop, Prime Pantry allowed shoppers to fill a 4-cubic-foot box with up to 45 pounds of non-perishable household goods for a flat $5.99 fee. As shoppers added items to their online shopping basket, they were told what percentage of the box was full. The concept was innovative and relatively low risk – delivering cereal and laundry detergent wasn't foolproof but it was more economically viable than delivering fresh food. It took Amazon half a decade to expand its AmazonFresh grocery service beyond Seattle; Prime Pantry was rolled out across all 48 contiguous states on the first day.

> 'A box of Cheerios and a book aren't that different. You don't have to fundamentally rewrite or build an entirely new infrastructure.'
> **Ian Clarkson, ex-Amazon executive, 2018[36]**

Prime Pantry allowed Amazon to test demand for products that would have been cost-prohibitive to ship for free. The lack of fresh food was not a deal-breaker for US customers – remember many to this day are still hesitant to purchase perishables online. In international markets like the UK, however, we believe that Prime Pantry is less compelling. Consumers expect to do a full grocery shop online, plus the high density of supermarkets and lack of storage space in comparison to US homes means that British shoppers don't 'bulk buy' in the same way as their American counterparts.

But would American Prime members, who have become trained to expect free shipping, be willing to shell out an additional $6 each time a cardboard box of household goods turned up at their doorstep (bearing in mind some of these items were already available through Amazon's main marketplace)? What is more, Prime members had also come to expect two-day shipping but Pantry delivery took up to four business days. Innovative, yes, but it was difficult to see the real value for customers.

In 2018, Amazon tweaked the model so that instead of paying per delivery, Prime members were charged $5 per month in addition to their annual Prime membership fee. Moving to a subscription model is part of Amazon's broader strategy to add more tiers to their Prime membership scheme and will help them to drive both usage and customer retention.

With Prime Pantry catering to the monthly shop, and AmazonFresh to the weekly shop, Amazon decided to go after yet another shopping mission – convenience. The introduction of free two-hour delivery with Prime Now (or within the hour for a flat fee of $7.99) exclusive to Prime members, changed the game when it came to online shopping; don't forget that same-day delivery was still often a chargeable service ($5.99 for Prime users; $8.99 for others) at the time. Prime Now was significant in that it enabled Amazon to more effectively target specific shopping occasions – and therefore share of wallet – while completely disrupting the sector in the process.

Despite their best efforts, no western competitor could offer as vast a range as Prime Now – 20,000 SKUs across both grocery and general merchandise categories – delivered in as short a window as one to two hours. They certainly couldn't do it for free.

Tesco came closest with its Tesco Now service, which launched in the UK in 2017. Shoppers could have groceries delivered by third-party provider Quiqup within one to two hours, but they could only select 20 items from a range of 1,000 and for a minimum £5.99 fee. Amazon offers 20 times the range at no additional cost to the customer.

Amazon created Prime Now to 'bring a sense of magic to our customers … to give people the time that they need to live their life, rather than go around the town to visit the stores that they need for their grocery shop', explained Mariangela Marseglia, Director, Amazon Prime Now, in a speech at the Shoptalk conference in 2017.

In typical Amazon fashion, Prime Now went from product idea to launch in less than four months. It started out covering just one zip code in Manhattan because Amazon wanted to perfect the customer experience before rolling it out and Marseglia believed that if Prime Now could work in Manhattan, it would work in any other city. In December 2014, Amazon's first Prime Now order, which was for a video game aptly called Rush, came in at 8:51. By 9:00, the item was picked and packed and by 10:01 it was delivered to the customer.

Christmas Eve is one of Prime Now's most popular days, given Amazon's unique ability to cater to the 'crisis' shopping mission. A customer in Manchester, England placed an order for jewellery, women's perfume and a PlayStation console at 10pm one Christmas Eve and had it delivered by 11pm. Amazon is not only satisfying customers but perhaps saving some marriages in the process!

The two other shopping missions that Prime Now caters to are gifting and top-up grocery, the latter of which is becoming more popular in markets such as the UK. According to Jason Westman, UK Head of AmazonFresh and

Prime Now, in order to cater to the 'for tonight' shopping mission, Amazon is pushing its cut-off times to later in the day. In some UK postcodes, shoppers can order as late 4pm and still have their order arrive that evening. 'Time is becoming a more important commodity for everyone', he said in 2018.[37]

We'll discuss the mechanics behind Prime Now later in the book, but for now it's important to understand the immediate impact it had at Amazon and on the wider market. Within a year of its Manhattan launch, Prime Now was rolled out to over 30 cities – primarily in North America but also London, Milan and Tokyo. By 2016, Prime Now was running in more than 50 cities in nine countries around the globe. It was even used as a vehicle for new market entry; in 2017, Amazon launched in Singapore with Prime Now.

Of all of Amazon's grocery services thus far, Prime Now has hands down been the most disruptive. The price wars have been replaced by the time wars, with many supermarkets around the globe now scrambling to offer same-day delivery. This has had an impact on even the most advanced online grocery markets like the UK. Despite holding less than a 2 per cent share of the British grocery sector at the time of writing, Amazon has been a phenomenal catalyst for change when it comes to delivery speed. Since the launch of Prime Now:

- Tesco rolled out same-day delivery nationwide, in addition to launching Tesco Now (via Quiqup);
- Sainsburys introduced Chop Chop, a one-hour delivery service, and offers same-day delivery to 40 per cent of the UK as of 2018 (versus just 11 per cent the previous year);[38]
- Marks & Spencer trialled a two-hour delivery service in partnership with Gophr;
- Co-op teamed up with Deliveroo for fast delivery on snacks, confectionary and alcohol;
- Morrisons and Booths have hopped on the Prime Now bandwagon.

The UK grocers, we believe, were broadly reluctant to offer same-day delivery prior to Amazon's incursion, as a) shoppers weren't crying out for it and b) it added unnecessary cost and complexity. But Amazon let the genie out of the bottle and now there's no putting it back.

As with voice-shopping, Amazon ignited a new trend in same-day delivery, altering shopping behaviour and expectations to such an extent that some competitors have begun turning to Amazon's very own infrastructure in a bid to stay relevant. It's not just Morrisons and Booths in the UK that sell via

Prime Now; Amazon has inked similar supply deals with many national and independent grocers around the world including Dia in Spain, Fauchon and Monoprix in France, and Rossmann and Feneberg in Germany, to name just a few. Meanwhile, a long-standing supply agreement with US natural food retailer Sprouts was unsurprisingly terminated in 2018 after the Whole Foods acquisition – Sprouts has teamed up with Instacart instead.

At the moment, these partnerships are essential for Amazon because, despite their many innovations, Amazon is still not seen as a credible food destination. What good is the infrastructure without a compelling range of stuff? These supply deals, and the Whole Foods acquisition which we'll come on to shortly, give Amazon instant brand recognition and credibility in the competitive grocery category and, crucially, allow Amazon to learn more about how to sell food online.

But this brings up an important point. If Amazon's plan is to differentiate in grocery as it does in non-food – through product choice and convenience – then it needs to take on a host role. It needs to be the gateway to other retailers and brands; it's the marketplace, the infrastructure. In non-food, we're seeing more and more retailers succumb to Amazon's platform because of its undeniable reach. After years of resistance, brands such as Nike have given in to Amazon. In theory, Amazon could have done the same in grocery – but then they bought Whole Foods Market. At some point, they'll need to decide whether they want to be the supermarket or marketplace.

Notes

1 Stone, B (2013) *The Everything Store: Jeff Bezos and the age of Amazon*, Bantam Press, London.

2 Anonymous (2017) The challenge of selling toys in an increasingly digital world, *eMarketer*, 19 September. Available from: https://retail.emarketer.com/article/challenge-of-selling-toys-increasingly-digital-world/59c169efebd4000a7823ab1c [Last accessed 19/6/2018].

3 Walmart (2017) Thomson Reuters Streetevents edited transcript: WMT – Wal-Mart Stores Inc 2017 Investment Community Meeting, 10 October. Available from: https://cdn.corporate.walmart.com/ea/31/4aa1027b4be6818f1a65ed5c293a/wmt-usq-transcript-2017-10-10.pdf [Last accessed 19/6/2018].

4 Kowitt, Beth (2018) How Amazon is using Whole Foods in a bid for total retail domination, *Fortune*, 21 May. Available from: http://fortune.com/longform/amazon-groceries-fortune-500/ [Last accessed 19/6/2018].

5   Harris, Briony (2017) Which countries buy the most groceries online? *World Economic Forum*, 6 December. Available from: https://www.weforum.org/agenda/2017/12/south-koreans-buy-the-most-groceries-online-by-far/ [Last accessed 19/6/2018].

6   ibid.

7   Bowman, Jeremy (2018) Walmart thinks you'll pay $10 for grocery delivery, *The Motley Fool*, 18 March. Available from: https://www.fool.com/investing/2018/03/18/walmart-thinks-youll-pay-10-for-grocery-delivery.aspx [Last accessed 19/6/2018].

8   NPR/Marist (2018) The Digital Economy Poll, June 2018 [Have you ever bought fresh groceries online?] The Marist College Institute for Public Opinion, Poughkeepsie, NY: NPR [distributor]. Available from: http://maristpoll.marist.edu/wp-content/misc/usapolls/us180423_NPR/NPR_Marist%20Poll_Tables%20of%20Questions_May%202018.pdf#page=2 [Last accessed 19/6/2018].

9   Walmart (2017) Thomson Reuters Streetevents edited transcript WMT – Wal-Mart Stores Inc 2017 Investment Community Meeting, 10 October. Available from: https://cdn.corporate.walmart.com/ea/31/4aa1027b4be6818f1a65ed5c293a/wmt-usq-transcript-2017-10-10.pdf [Last accessed 19/6/2018].

10 ibid.

11 Kowitt, Beth (2018) How Amazon is using Whole Foods in a bid for total retail domination, *Fortune*, 21 May. Available from: http://fortune.com/longform/amazon-groceries-fortune-500/ [Last accessed 19/6/2018].

12 ibid.

13 Millerberg, Spencer (2018) Amazon Grocery Year in Review, Clavis Insight, 16 January. Available from: https://www.clavisinsight.com/blog/amazon-grocery-year-review [Last accessed 19/6/2018].

14 Chambers, Sam (2018) Britain's robot grocer is coming to the U.S., *Bloomberg*, 15 June. Available from: https://www.bloomberg.com/news/articles/2018-06-15/britain-s-robot-grocer-ocado-is-coming-to-the-u-s [Last accessed 19/6/2018].

15 Wilkinson, Sue (2017) How my weekly grocery shopping habits relate to U.S. grocery shopper trends, *Food Marketing Institute*, 25 July. Available from: https://www.fmi.org/blog/view/fmi-blog/2017/07/25/how-my-weekly-grocery-shopping-habits-relate-to-u.s.-grocery-shopper-trends [Last accessed 19/6/2018].

16 Kowitt, Beth (2018) How Amazon is using Whole Foods in a bid for total retail domination, *Fortune*, 21 May. Available from: http://fortune.com/longform/amazon-groceries-fortune-500/ [Last accessed 19/6/2018].

17 ibid.

18 ibid.

19 O'Brien, Mike (2018) Google, Amazon and the relationship between paid search and ecommerce, *Clickz*, 29 March. Available from: https://www.clickz.com/google-amazon-paid-search-ecommerce/213753/ [Last accessed 29/6/18].

20 Kowitt, Beth (2018) How Amazon is using Whole Foods in a bid for total retail domination, *Fortune*, 21 May. Available from: http://fortune.com/long-form/amazon-groceries-fortune-500/ [Last accessed 19/6/2018].

21 Bensinger, Greg (2015) Rebuilding history's biggest dot-com bust, *Wall Street Journal*, 12 January. Available from: https://www.wsj.com/articles/rebuilding-historys-biggest-dot-come-bust-1421111794 [Last accessed 19/6/2018].

22 Anonymous (2001) What Webvan could have learned from Tesco, *Knowledge at Wharton*, 10 October. Available from: http://knowledge.wharton.upenn.edu/article/what-webvan-could-have-learned-from-tesco/ [Last accessed 19/6/2018].

23 ibid.

24 Bluestein, Adam (2013) Beyond Webvan: MyWebGrocer turns supermarkets virtual, *Bloomberg*, 17 January. Available from: https://www.bloomberg.com/news/articles/2013-01-17/beyond-webvan-mywebgrocer-turns-supermarkets-virtual [Last accessed 19/6/2018].

25 Anonymous (2001) What Webvan could have learned from Tesco, *Knowledge at Wharton*, 10 October. Available from: http://knowledge.wharton.upenn.edu/article/what-webvan-could-have-learned-from-tesco/ [Last accessed 19/6/2018].

26 Barr, Alistair (2013) From the ashes of Webvan, Amazon builds a grocery business, *Reuters*, 16 June. Available from: https://www.reuters.com/article/amazon-webvan-idUSL2N0EO1FS20130616 [Last accessed 19/6/2018].

27 Ocado website. Available from: http://www.ocadogroup.com/who-we-are/our-story-so-far.aspx [Last accessed 19/6/2018].

28 Barr, Alistair (2013) From the ashes of Webvan, Amazon builds a grocery business, *Reuters*, 16 June. Available from: https://www.reuters.com/article/amazon-webvan-idUSL2N0EO1FS20130616 [Last accessed 19/6/2018].

29 Amazon press release (1999) Amazon.com announces minority investment in HomeGrocer.com, *Amazon*, 18 May. Available from: http://phx.corporate-ir.net/phoenix.zhtml?c=176060&p=irol-newsArticle&ID=502934 [Last accessed 19/6/2018].

30 Barr, Alistair (2013) From the ashes of Webvan, Amazon builds a grocery business, *Reuters*, 16 June. Available from: https://www.reuters.com/article/amazon-webvan-idUSL2N0EO1FS20130616 [Last accessed 19/6/2018].

31 Kowitt, Beth (2018) How Amazon is using Whole Foods in a bid for total retail domination. *Fortune*, 21/5. Available from: http://fortune.com/longform/amazon-groceries-fortune-500/ [Last accessed 19/6/2018].

32 Anonymous (2016) AmazonFresh expands to Chicago, Dallas, *Progressive Grocer*, 26 October. Available from: https://progressivegrocer.com/amazonfresh-expands-chicago-dallas [Last accessed 29/6/18].

33 Amazon press release (2007) Amazon.com's grocery store launches new Subscribe & Save feature allowing automatic fulfillment of most popular items, *Amazon*, 15 May. Available from: http://phx.corporate-ir.net/phoenix.zhtml?c=176060&p=irol-newsArticle&ID=1000549 [Last accessed 29/6/18].

34 Sheehan, Brian (2018) The key to a winning Amazon ad strategy? Go big everywhere else, *Ad Week*, 2 February. Available from: https://www.adweek.com/brand-marketing/the-key-to-a-winning-amazon-ad-strategy-go-big-everywhere-else/ [Last accessed 29/6/18].

35 Paul Clarke, CTO of Ocado, speaking at Salesforce event in London, 2016.

36 Kowitt, Beth (2018) How Amazon is using Whole Foods in a bid for total retail domination, *Fortune*, 21 May. Available from: http://fortune.com/long-form/amazon-groceries-fortune-500/ [Last accessed 19/6/2018].

37 Amazon UK Analyst Briefing, London, July 2018.

38 Macadam, Dan (2018) Can supermarkets really deliver in a day? BBC, 4 February. Available from: https://www.bbc.co.uk/news/business-42777284 [Last accessed 29/6/18].

Whole Foods Market: a brave new era

07

'I don't want people goin' away, thinkin' that nothin's gonna change around here. 'Cause things are gonna change. There's just no question about that.'
John Mackey, Whole Foods Market CEO and Co-Founder, 2017[1]

Recognizing that online and offline are no longer mutually exclusive, retailers are now racing to equilibrium. But the big question is who will get there first? Will legacy bricks and mortar chains successfully crack e-commerce before the digitally native brands figure out how to run physical shops? The clock is certainly ticking.

'We are well positioned to win the future of retail, and I wouldn't trade places with anyone.'
Walmart CEO Doug McMillon, 2017[2]

The convergence of online and offline retail was best exemplified by two major announcements on 16 June 2017: Walmart announced plans to make its fourth e-commerce acquisition in less than a year by acquiring online menswear brand Bonobos, but, more significantly, that same day Amazon announced it would purchase a chain of bricks and mortar stores – Whole Foods Market.

That day changed retail forever. After some dabbling with physical retail, the blockbuster deal cemented Amazon's commitment to bricks and mortar. Immediate reaction in the industry was mixed. On the one hand, Amazon's move into the supermarket space would be one of disruption, requiring legacy grocers to significantly up their game and naturally exposing some losers along the way. But, on the other hand, the deal was also the utmost validation that bricks and mortar retail has a future. Perhaps even a bright one.

Investors seemed to agree. Following the announcement, Amazon's market cap appreciated by $15.6 billion – about $2 billion more than it paid for the supermarket chain. Amazon essentially picked up Whole Foods for free, while the rest of the supermarket sector lost $37 billion in market value.[3] This was a watershed moment for the grocery industry.

In this chapter, we'll explore the rationale behind the Whole Foods deal, how Amazon will redefine the supermarket for the 21st-century shopper, and its impact on the wider sector.

Applying its thirst for invention to the supermarket sector

Based on what we've covered in the book so far, the acquisition of a grocery store operator should come as no great surprise. Just prior to the acquisition announcement, Natalie wrote in May 2017: 'Amazon is, of course, trying to crack grocery themselves in both the physical and digital realms but,

Figure 7.1   Online-only is no longer enough: Amazon acquired Whole Foods Market in 2017

Figure 7.2 Amazon opened its first checkout-free store, Amazon Go, to the public in 2018

without actively acquiring another retailer, they are unlikely to have a meaningful impact on the grocery sector for at least another five years.' Weeks later, the Whole Foods deal was announced.

Prior to the acquisition, three things were very clear: 1) Amazon's wider appetite for bricks and mortar was growing; 2) without physical stores, Amazon would always be underrepresented in grocery; and 3) Amazon had the potential to revolutionize the customer experience.

At the time, the retailer had been quietly experimenting with two new grocery formats in its Seattle hometown: Amazon Go and AmazonFresh Pickup. We'll explore Amazon Go in great detail in the coming chapters, but for now it's important to point out that the convenience store concept lacks something quite fundamental – checkouts.

Meanwhile, its AmazonFresh Pickup service allows Prime members to drive up to a designated site, untethered to a supermarket, and have their groceries brought out to their cars. On a global scale, this isn't exactly revolutionary – French grocers have been operating these 'Drive' concepts for years (as we'll examine in more detail in Chapter 13). But in the US, it was still relatively novel – Walmart was the only retailer actively testing such a service around the same time.

As for bricks and mortar concepts, Amazon Go may get all the glory but AmazonFresh Pickup was the most logical extension into store-based retailing for the retail giant. Amazon brought its rapid fulfilment capabilities to bear, putting its own spin on the concept through its established payment process and even using licence plate recognition technology to speed up waiting times. Shoppers can collect their groceries as quickly as 15 minutes after placing an order.

Although Amazon was always going to have to expand into physical stores, it was never going to slap its logo on a chain of run-of-the-mill supermarkets. The combination of Amazon's customer obsession and thirst for invention meant that the supermarket sector was about to get seriously disrupted. You can always count on Amazon to challenge the status quo and drastically enhance the customer experience, whether that's by delivering groceries to your car or getting rid of queues altogether. But this was just the beginning.

Why Whole Foods Market?

We believe Amazon's end game for grocery is as follows:

1 Democratize online grocery so customers can first and foremost shop on their terms, as they've grown accustomed to doing in general merchandise.

2 Use technology to take the chore out of grocery shopping. Amazon is uniquely positioned to make auto-replenishment a reality for functional, routine-driven consumable categories, and will be particularly motivated to develop private label ranges here.

3 The instore experience will use technology to minimize friction during the navigation and payment parts of the shopping journey, while also enabling real-time, hyper-personalized recommendations and rewards. Being a part of the Amazon family will take Whole Foods from 'class dunce' to 'valedictorian', in Whole Foods' CEO John Mackey's words.[4]

4 Entire categories will be removed from the physical store, freeing up space for: 1) more emotive categories like fresh and prepared foods; 2) blended experiences – from cookery classes to co-working space; 3) click & collect and/or return counters; 4) online grocery fulfilment to cater to demand for same-day delivery.

5 Prime, as previously discussed, will underpin Amazon's grocery strategy. After all, the main incentive for Amazon's move into grocery is to reach shoppers weekly, locking them into its wider ecosystem.

With that in mind, particularly the points about freshness and utilizing stores as mini-fulfilment hubs, you can begin to understand why Amazon was attracted to Whole Foods Market. A strong emphasis on perishables, which account for more than two-thirds of the supermarket chain's sales, theatrical merchandising displays and renowned own-label ranges – including within the coveted fresh category – would compensate for Amazon's relative weaknesses. There had been rumours of Amazon acquiring a mass retailer like Target or BJ's Wholesale Club. But, in our view, Amazon needed a foodie business, not only to establish credibility in perishables, but also because the lack of non-food in Whole Foods stores minimized the potential of range duplication.

Naturally, there was a clear overlap in target customer base, with both retailers having a strong hold among affluent, educated and often time-pressed consumers. In fact, Whole Foods might have done this a little too well – one of Amazon's first moves would be to address its 'Whole Paycheck' reputation by investing in lower prices. This would happen across the board, but with a particular emphasis on sweetening the deal for Prime members, as discussed in Chapter 3. In fact, RBC analyst Mark Mahaney believes that Amazon could double Whole Foods' customer base over a five- to ten-year period purely by giving financial incentives to Prime members.[5]

Whole Foods was also a good fit for Amazon because it had a national presence but it wasn't overstored – Amazon wanted several hundred outlets, not several thousand. This is important, not only because Amazon wants to grow grocery e-commerce sales, thereby lessening the need for physical space, but also because Whole Foods is really a giant test lab for Amazon. It helps to have a more focused, leaner store portfolio as Amazon experiments with pricing, merchandising and layout, iterating on the concept until it finally has a scalable format.

Crucially, Whole Foods is also well represented in urban areas. This means it adds not only a supplemental, but a complementary resource to its last-mile infrastructure, providing it with yet another platform from which to deliver groceries within a couple of hours. As we discussed in the last chapter, Prime Now is one of Amazon's unique competitive advantages in grocery so it's no surprise that they spent most of 2018 rolling this service out across Whole Foods stores nationwide. When Amazon bought Whole Foods, they didn't just acquire 460 stores. They acquired 460 mini-warehouses.

But it's worth highlighting here that, compared to its global peers, Amazon is behind the curve in this regard. In China, the promise of 30-minute delivery to customers within a three-kilometre radius is a key feature among other online-to-offline grocery concepts such as Alibaba's

Hema and JD.com's 7fresh. Unlike Amazon, the Asian giants are moving organically into physical retail, building supermarkets from scratch to suit the modern consumer's needs.

The wake-up call

> 'When Amazon bought Whole Foods, what they did was they sent the signal to the entire grocery/retail landscape that Amazon was coming.'
> **Apoorva Mehta, CEO of Instacart, 2017**[6]

At the time of writing, one year since the deal was completed, Whole Foods stores don't look awfully different than they did pre-Amazon. There were some obvious quick wins, as discussed earlier in the book, such as collection lockers and Echo devices taking up physical real estate instore, and the Whole Foods range going live on Amazon's site. Pricing was sharpened and Prime perks slowly became available instore. But, overall, nothing ground-breaking.

Amazon's pace of innovation may be relentless – every week they appear to be disrupting a new sector – but when it comes to implementation, Amazon is notoriously methodical. The entire industry is now watching with bated breath to see if the retail colossus can do one of the most fundamental things in retail – operate stores. Amazon will take its time, quietly experimenting and tinkering with various bricks and mortar concepts as it tackles the steep learning curve that is grocery. It could very well be years before we see any major changes rolled out across the store estate.

Whole Foods may not have changed all that drastically since the acquisition, but everyone else sure did. The effect of the deal has been largely psychological. It's been a wake-up call for incumbent supermarkets, not only to ramp up their own e-commerce capabilities but also to digitally enhance their store base. To do that, most retailers have had to look externally.

The impetus Ocado was waiting for

Two weeks after the Whole Foods deal, Ocado CEO Tim Steiner was all smiles at the retailer's half-year results meeting in London. One of their biggest threats was also their biggest opportunity. When asked his thoughts on the Whole Foods deal, Steiner noted that it would simply spur on demand for online grocery, which would ultimately help them to grow their business.

'Grocery retailing is changing and we are ideally positioned to enable other retailers to achieve their online aspirations.'[7] Steiner's message echoed that of Instacart CEO Apoorva Mehta who, the same year, called the Amazon-Whole Foods deal a 'blessing in disguise'.[8]

For years, Ocado had been promising investors it would secure an international partner for its grocery delivery technology, Ocado Smart Platform. After missing its first self-imposed deadline of a 2015 announcement, investors began to lose patience as the months and then years rolled on. Perhaps Ocado's ambitions to transition from retailer to global technology provider were inflated?

Ocado finally signed its first long-awaited deal with France's Casino Groupe in 2017 – less than six months after Amazon's Whole Foods acquisition. The agreement enables Casino to have exclusive rights to use Ocado's robotics, online technology and delivery software in France. Since then, Ocado has announced a flurry of deals with global retailers including Sobeys (Canada), ICA (Sweden) and, its most notable to date, Kroger in the US. It's fair to say that Whole Foods was the impetus for these established giants to take action against Amazon.

CASE STUDY   Responding to the Amazon Challenge

Brittain Ladd[9]

The announcement that Amazon was acquiring Whole Foods on June 16, 2017 can best be described as a 'Pearl Harbor moment' in terms of the impact on the grocery industry. Grocery executives who had been convinced Amazon would remain focused on pursuing an online grocery strategy were shocked to discover that, sooner rather than later, Amazon would be a head-to-head competitor.

To compete, many executives chose to reach out to the grocery delivery and order fulfilment company, Instacart. Entering into such an agreement solved a short-term problem of needing the ability to offer customers online grocery ordering, fulfilment and last-mile delivery. However, an agreement with Instacart also posed a threat – to utilize Instacart, grocery retailers had to give the provider access to their data, stores and customers. I was among the first to raise the alarm that retailers were in effect teaching Instacart their business and providing Instacart with data identifying their strengths and weaknesses. If Instacart expand their business model to include opening their own retail stores, or if they are acquired by a competitor such as Walmart, Instacart will be able to leverage that data to their advantage.

Kroger, the second largest retailer in the US and the largest grocery retailer, retained my services in 2018 to provide them with a list of strategies to better compete with Amazon.

Applying my knowledge of Amazon and the global grocery industry, I completed an end-to-end assessment of Kroger's operations and determined that the optimal course of action for Kroger to take would be to acquire Ocado. Kroger operated 42 legacy distribution centres to replenish nearly 2,800 stores, but did not have a supply chain capable of meeting the demands of e-commerce. Acquiring Ocado would give Kroger access to best-in-class grocery fulfilment software capable of transforming their business model. It would also provide them with a competitive advantage. Kroger became convinced through their discussions with Ocado that leveraging Ocado's Customer Fulfilment Centre (CFC) technology would transform their supply chain. However, with a price tag of nearly US $2 billion, Kroger chose to take a 5 per cent stake in Ocado worth $247 million instead of acquiring the company.

Kroger made the official announcement of their intent with Ocado on May 15, 2018. According to the press release, Ocado will provide Kroger with various systems to help the company manage warehouse operations, introduce automation, and provide Kroger with an advanced solution for logistics and delivery route planning. The focus of Ocado's efforts will be on helping Kroger more efficiently fulfil online grocery orders and assembling orders for Kroger's ClickList curbside service. A total of 20 CFCs are scheduled to be built over a three-year period beginning in 2018.

Some analysts and grocery executives believe Ocado's model isn't suited to the US market, given the fact much of the US population is dispersed across many towns and suburbs with small populations, whereas the UK is densely populated; ideal conditions for online grocery and last-mile delivery. Outside urban areas, many analysts believe it makes more sense to focus on having customers shop for groceries inside stores instead of building high-tech automated warehouses.

I voiced similar concerns to Kroger's executive team about Ocado's effectiveness in the UK vs the realities Ocado will encounter in the US. However, I recommended a solution to Ocado and Kroger that if adopted, will eliminate the obstacles Ocado will face. The solution will also transform Ocado's business model, allowing the company to expand into a channel they currently do not serve. Instead of Kroger utilizing Ocado's warehouses, referred to as 'sheds', to fulfil online grocery orders, I recommended the following strategy to Kroger and Ocado:

1 Introduce case-picking technology and robotics to build pallets of products destined for Kroger's store shelves. Leverage the technology to replenish all products to Kroger's stores. If implemented, this strategy will allow Kroger to close the majority of their 42 legacy distribution centres. Ocado executives gave their approval and support.

2 Within the same shed, install modules to fulfil online grocery orders and ClickList curbside orders.

Creating a dual-purpose capability for replenishment and order fulfilment out of each CFC built will greatly reduce Kroger's total logistics costs, increase profitability, and increase Kroger's competitive advantage. Another benefit of Kroger entering into an agreement with Ocado is that Kroger will be able to enter many states they do not currently serve, primarily on the East Coast. Kroger can open CFCs in and around such large, densely populated cities as New York, Philadelphia, Pittsburgh, and Miami among others.

Due to their exclusivity agreement with Kroger, other grocery retailers operating in the US will be unable to access Ocado's technology. I believe grocery retailers will have no choice but to copy Kroger or risk being left behind. CommonSense Robotics – which specializes in building automated grocery distribution facilities that operate in a fashion similar to Ocado's CFCs – is more than likely the primary beneficiary of Kroger's agreement with Ocado.

Brittain Ladd is an expert in strategy and supply chain management. Ladd is also a former Amazon executive who holds the distinction of being one of the first individuals to recognize the need for Amazon to expand their business model to include a physical retail presence. In a 2013 research paper titled 'A Beautiful way to Save Woolworths', Ladd made the argument that Amazon should acquire either the retailer Whole Foods or the Texas-based regional grocery retailer HEB. Ladd worked for Amazon from 2015 to 2017, leading the worldwide expansion of AmazonFresh, Pantry and Groceries.

Amazon's grocery onslaught has certainly created strange bedfellows. While buying alliances aren't unheard of in Europe, it was shocking to see two of the world's largest food retailers – Tesco and Carrefour – announce such an agreement in 2018. Similarly, while we all expected further consolidation in the UK grocery sector, not many people would have predicted Asda and Sainsbury's merging to future-proof their businesses against Amazon.

Tech partnerships are now in vogue, with Google and Microsoft in particular leading the anti-Amazon alliances. Retail acquisitions are also ripe, designed to either keep up with or maintain distance from Amazon – think of Target/Shipt, Walmart/Flipkart (India), and Kroger/Home Chef, just to name a few. Everyone is choosing sides before Amazon strikes.

> 'I would agree that for a lot of retailers, whilst they've put up a great fight, ultimately working with the likes of Amazon is probably a good way to tackle the digital space.'
> **Marcus East, former Marks & Spencer executive, 2018[10]**

Some are even opting for Team Amazon. As we've touched on throughout the book, more retailers are turning to Amazon for their scale and expertise, risking the Trojan Horse element of such partnerships in return for a rapid upscaling of their digital offers. Others, meanwhile, are adamant that teaming up with Amazon is not in their playbook. 'We hate Amazon', said Tarsem Dhaliwal, MD of UK supermarket chain Iceland, in 2018. 'They'll bully us and do horrible things to us. They'll use us; we don't want anything to do with them.'[11]

Table 7.1   Co-opetition: more retail brands are leaning on Amazon

Amazon offering	Retail Relationships	Former Retail Relationships
Amazon.com*	Nike, Under Armour, The Children's Place, Chico's FAS, Adidas, Calvin Klein	
Amazon Lockers	Rite Aid, 7-Eleven, Safeway, Gristedes, Repsol, dm, Edeka, Aldi, Morrisons, Co-op	Radioshack, Staples
Prime Now	Morrisons, Booths, Dia, Monoprix, Bio c'Bon, Fauchon, Rossmann, Feneberg	Sprouts Farmers Market
Alexa integration	Peapod, Ocado, Morrisons, Dominos, Gousto, JD Sports, AO.com, B&H Photo, Woot	
Amazon Pop-Up	Kohl's	
Amazon device kiosks**	Best Buy, Shoppers Stop	
Amazon Returns	Kohl's	
Amazon-powered stores	Tuft & Needle, Calvin Klein	

(continued)

Table 7.1   (continued)

Amazon offering	Retail Relationships	Former Retail Relationships
Collaboration on exclusive product/ service	Best Buy (exclusive line of smart TVs); Sears (installation of Amazon tyres at its auto centres)	
AWS	Brooks Brothers, Eataly, Gilt, Made	

NOTE Examples (list is not exhaustive)
SOURCE Author research, as of mid-2018
* Items from these brands were available on Amazon.com
**Unlike Pop-ups, device kiosks are not staffed by Amazon employees

CASE STUDY Knowing when to concede defeat

Tesco closed its Tesco Direct marketplace in 2018. This was the most transparent admission of defeat to Amazon; Tesco Direct was, after all, designed to compete with the behemoth head-on by replicating their marketplace format, extending Tesco's product range beyond the confines of their superstores and Tesco.com offering. But if there is one rule in retail today, it's this: you cannot out-Amazon Amazon.

Aside from racking up loyalty points on big-ticket purchases, there was very little incentive for shoppers to choose Tesco Direct over Amazon. Tesco's site in comparison was confusing and full of friction. Pricing was inconsistent, it lacked product recommendations and reviews, and the range was neither broad nor compelling enough to make it the go-to destination for general merchandise. Let's not forget that many shoppers today begin their product search not with Google but with Amazon.

Tesco Direct was loss-making and contributed very little to the top line, providing a cautionary lesson that can be learned from Amazon: admitting failure and swiftly moving on. Offering 94 types of treadmill online won't help Tesco to retain its title as the UK's largest food retailer. There's no time for costly distractions when Amazon is on your doorstep. Tesco will be far better off merging grocery and non-food onto one platform, as some competitors did several years ago, and then focusing on logical category extensions to mirror what shoppers would find instore.

The Direct business joins a growing graveyard of Tesco brands including Giraffe, Euphorium, Harris + Hoole, Nutricentre, Hudl, Blinkbox and Dobbies. What was once considered business-critical diversification is now seen as a pricey distraction. Tesco Direct won't be the last of management's culls as they continue to tighten their focus on food by offloading non-core assets. There is, after all, only room for one 'Everything Store'.

Goodbye Whole Foods, Hello Prime Fresh?

Days after the announcement of the Whole Foods acquisition in 2017, Natalie published the following prediction:

> Whole Foods Market branding [will] be significantly reduced or disappear altogether once Amazon establishes trust and credibility in its fresh food offering. This isn't going to happen overnight. Right now, Amazon needs Whole Foods for a number of reasons: strength in perishables, brand equity, overlap in customer base, not to mention bricks and mortar presence. But Amazon's current grocery offering – think AmazonFresh, Prime Pantry, Subscribe & Save, Prime Now – is convoluted and ripe for consolidation. In the future, if Amazon is truly going to make its mark in grocery it will need one cohesive message both online and instore. This must be centred around Prime, which has become the gateway to Amazon's most sought-after services.[12]

It has been over a year since that initial prediction and the authors stand by this claim. Some might disagree – after all, Amazon bought Whole Foods for its brand! But we believe that by 2025, Amazon will have cracked grocery. By 2025, its grocery offering will be seamlessly linked across online and offline channels. By 2025, Amazon will have a scalable supermarket concept which it will export globally, transforming the way consumers around the world shop for food.

We also believe, as per our initial prediction, that Amazon's grocery strategy will be underpinned by Prime. Could we see Whole Foods supermarkets rebranded as Prime Fresh in the future? Could AmazonFresh and Prime Pantry become obsolete? We think so. One thing is for sure – Amazon will continuously refine its grocery strategy until it finds the right model for growth.

So what has changed since that 2017 prediction? Within months of the acquisition closing, the retailer scaled back its AmazonFresh services in nine states. The focus rightly shifted to Prime Now which, as discussed previously, Amazon has been aggressively rolling out across Whole Foods stores. We believe the combination of Whole Foods' physical infrastructure and Prime Now's delivery logistics that enable two-hour delivery will allow Amazon to genuinely disrupt the status quo.

Behind the scenes, the AmazonFresh and Prime Now divisions merged following the Whole Foods acquisition. But from a customer's point of view, there's still a lot of confusion. In her 2018 article, 'Amazon is still sorting out its grocery strategy', Bloomberg journalist Shira Ovide illustrated this complexity with the example of buying something as straightforward as butter:

> If a Prime subscriber in Dallas wants a pound of Whole Foods brand butter delivered, he could order it from Whole Foods and an Amazon courier would bring it to his door. In Boulder, Colorado, where Amazon doesn't have its own delivery option, the butter buyer is directed to set up an account with Instacart.[13]

In Philadelphia, meanwhile, shoppers can have the same item delivered from Whole Foods or AmazonFresh, while in New York, shoppers can buy a couple of dozen different butters (but not the Whole Foods brand) from Prime Now.

Clearly, Amazon's management have their work cut out for them. The short-term complexity can be excused as they integrate Whole Foods and figure out how to do bricks and mortar, but in the longer term, Amazon will need to have a far more coherent grocery strategy.

Notes

1 McGregor, Jena (2017) Five telling things the Whole Foods CEO said about the Amazon deal in an employee town hall, *Washington Post*, 20 June. Available from: https://www.washingtonpost.com/news/on-leadership/wp/2017/06/20/five-telling-things-the-whole-foods-ceo-said-about-the-amazon-deal-in-an-employee-town-hall/?utm_term=.1e861128178f [Last accessed 11/7/2018].

2 (2017) Thomson Reuters Streetevents edited transcript WMT – Wal-Mart Stores Inc 2017 Investment Community Meeting, 10 October. Available from: https://cdn.corporate.walmart.com/ea/31/4aa1027b4be6818f1a65ed5c293a/wmt-usq-transcript-2017-10-10.pdf [Last accessed 19/6/2018].

3 Meyer, Robinson (2018) How to fight Amazon (before you turn 29), *The Atlantic*, July/August issue. Available from: https://www.theatlantic.com/magazine/archive/2018/07/lina-khan-antitrust/561743/ [Last accessed 11/7/2018].

4 McGregor, Jena (2017) Five telling things the Whole Foods CEO said about the Amazon deal in an employee town hall, *Washington Post*, 20 June. Available from: https://www.washingtonpost.com/news/on-leadership/wp/2017/06/20/five-telling-things-the-whole-foods-ceo-said-about-the-amazon-deal-in-an-employee-town-hall/?utm_term=.1e861128178f [Last accessed 11/7/2018].

5 Lovelace, Berkeley Jr. (2018) Amazon could double Whole Foods' customer base with Prime perks: analyst. CNBC, 25/6. Available from: https://www.cnbc.com/2018/06/25/mark-mahaney-amazon-could-double-whole-foods-customer-base-with-prime.html [Last accessed 11/7/2018].

6 Levy, Nat (2017) How Amazon's $13.7B purchase of Whole Foods is a 'blessing in disguise' for Instacart, *Geekwire*, 10 October. Available from: https://www.geekwire.com/2017/amazons-13-7b-purchase-whole-foods-blessing-disguise-instacart/ [Last accessed 11/7/2018].

7 Rovnick, Naomi (2017) Ocado dismisses fears of increased competition from Amazon, *Financial Times*, 5 July. Available from: https://www.ft.com/content/f48fecac-6151-11e7-8814-0ac7eb84e5f1 [Last accessed 9/7/2018].

8 Levy, Nat (2017) How Amazon's $13.7B purchase of Whole Foods is a 'blessing in disguise' for Instacart, *Geekwire*, 10 October. Available from: https://www.geekwire.com/2017/amazons-13-7b-purchase-whole-foods-blessing-disguise-instacart/ [Last accessed 11/7/2018].

9 Guest commentary.

10 Dawkins, David (2018) Marks and Spencer told to team up with Amazon to save retailer as stores close, *Express*, 20 June. Available from: https://www.express.co.uk/finance/city/977070/amazon-uk-marks-and-spencer-m-and-s-high-street-online [Last accessed 11/7/2018].

11 Key, Alys (2018) Iceland Food rules out deal with Amazon as Food Warehouse attracts new customers, *City AM*, 15 June. Available from: http://www.cityam.com/287618/iceland-sales-heat-up-food-warehouse-attracts-new-customers [Last accessed 11/7/2018].

12 Berg, Natalie (2017) 3 Predictions: Amazon and Wholefoods, *LinkedIn*, 21 June. https://www.linkedin.com/pulse/3-predictions-amazon-whole-foods-natalie-berg.

13 Ovide, Shira (2018) Amazon is still sorting out its grocery strategy, *Bloomberg*, 12 June. Available from: https://www.bloomberg.com/view/articles/2018-06-12/amazon-whole-foods-anniversary-sorting-the-groceries [Last accessed 11/7/2018].

A private label juggernaut: here comes the squeeze

08

Amazon has been quietly building up its own portfolio of brands as it spreads into new categories like grocery and fashion. However, many shoppers wouldn't even realize that these lines are exclusive to the retailer: of Amazon's 100+ own label brands,[1] only a handful bear the name 'Amazon' or 'Prime'. Devices like the Amazon Echo or Fire are exceptions to this rule.

> 'Your margin is my opportunity.'
> **Jeff Bezos**[2]

So why the big push into private label? To start, it will help Amazon inch closer to sustained profitability. With its own brands, Amazon can widen margins without raising prices. It gives them greater leverage over suppliers and allows them to sweeten the deal for Prime members, as many own label items are sold exclusively to them. With the sheer amount of customer data Amazon holds, no one is better positioned to understand customer needs and then develop ranges specifically for them.

Amazon is a disruptor and private label is no exception: SunTrust predicts that Amazon's own label sales could reach $25 billion by 2022.[3] But before we delve into Amazon's strategy, it's important to understand the context of own label development in the US and why it's only just catching on now.

The post-great recession mindset

Americans have historically had a strong affinity for national brands. The country's largest retailer Walmart regularly refers to itself as a House of Brands, and many household products today still go by their brand name – Kleenex, Tupperware, Q-tips, Band-Aids, Saran Wrap, etc.

Yet, as far back as half a century ago, retail analysts like Victor Lebow were warning retailers of the dangers of product sameness. In a *Journal of Retailing* essay in 1955, Lebow wrote:

> Quite a few studies have shown that a large proportion of shoppers, when questioned, cannot tell which of several competing variety chain stores, or supermarkets, they have just left. But this sameness of their merchandise, in stores that look like twins, provides the opportunity for different merchandise in stores that look different, individual, with a character of their own.[4]

Lebow was well ahead of his time: it would take over half a century for his advice to take hold. Private label in the US grocery sector has historically been slow to catch on due to a combination of market fragmentation and, up until relatively recently, the lack of grocery discounter presence. You only need to look across the Atlantic to see the opportunity for private label when a market is highly concentrated and swarming with Aldi and Lidl stores; in the UK and Switzerland, for example, own label can account for half of all grocery sales. In the US, however, own label products were traditionally the poor relation to the national brand, often confined to the bottom shelf. Cheap, but not cheerful. As such, growth of own label products was previously limited to periods of economic uncertainty. At the first sign of an upturn, shoppers would quickly abandon private labels and trade back up to national brands.

But something interesting happened at the end of the Great Recession in 2009. This time, many shoppers didn't revert back to their old ways; habits seemed to be permanently altered. Frugality went from being shamed to celebrated and the notion of 'smart shopping' took off. So, what was different this time compared to previous recessions? Technology adoption.

This was the beginning of the smartphone era – a technology development that would go on to become all-encompassing and, for many, indispensable. By the end of the Great Recession, consumers had access to information right at their fingertips, creating an unprecedented level of price transparency and therefore empowerment.

Meanwhile, a combination of media fragmentation and supermarket consolidation resulted in a shift in power away from national brands, making it more challenging for them to connect with customers. This was fertile ground for private label development. Many supermarkets saw this as an opportunity to deepen customer relationships by enhancing the quality and messaging behind their own ranges, taking them from generic knock-offs to brands in their own rights. At the same time, the notoriously less brand-loyal Millennials came of age during the Great Recession, creating additional opportunities for retailers to expand into new, higher-margin categories like organics and meal kits.

Amazon's private label ambitions

> 'We take the same approach to private label as we do with anything here at Amazon: we start with the customer and work backwards.'
> **Amazon, 2018**[5]

Amazon also recognized this change in behaviour and in 2009 launched its AmazonBasics range. At the time, Amazon had already begun dabbling in private label with a handful of other lines such as Pinzon kitchen gadgets, Strathwood outdoor furniture, Pike Street bath and home products, and Denali tools. But this was the first time Amazon would attach its brand to a product (hardware aside) so it made sense to start out in a low-risk, commoditized category and one that would complement its core product range – electronic accessories.

Priced approximately 30 per cent lower than major brands, the AmazonBasics line was initially limited to accessories like cables, chargers and batteries. But within just a few short years, the brand accounted for nearly one-third of Amazon's battery sales, outselling national brands like Energizer and Duracell.[6] Less than a decade after launch, AmazonBasics had been expanded to dozens of categories – home, furniture, pet supplies, luggage, sports, etc – and, by 2017, it was the third-best-selling brand overall on Amazon.com, according to One Click Retail.

This should hardly come as a surprise. Amazon is, as discussed throughout the book, in the enviable position of being the starting point for many product searches. From those searches, and indeed purchases themselves, Amazon can glean an incredible amount of insight into what shoppers want, allowing them to identify and prioritize own label investment in specific categories.

Keith Anderson, SVP of Strategy and Insights at Profitero explains:

> There's a huge difference in the intent signalled in searches on retailer sites versus searches on Google or traditional search engines. What we often find is the context of those searches on a retailer site is much more detailed. It tends to be product benefit or characteristic focused, and Amazon has the potential to analyse what people are searching for and either are finding, or maybe just as importantly, not finding in the selection that's available on the site.[7]

(Another) uneven playing field

So, Amazon already has a head start when it comes to understanding private label requirements. Another massive competitive advantage? Visibility.

In a physical setting, brands buy shelf space to guarantee exposure to the customer. The supermarket then tends to position its own label 'national brand equivalent' alongside the brand leader in a given category. The retailer's goal is to give the best possible placement to its own higher-margin goods for the highest chance of conversion.

The same principle applies to a virtual shelf. For many brands today, there's nothing more important than visibility on the world's most powerful retail platform. The problem is Amazon shoppers don't tend to search by brand; about 70 per cent[8] of all word searches made on the site are for generic items (ie shaving cream rather than Gillette). And for these unbranded or attribute-led searches, Amazon is becoming increasingly comfortable steering shoppers towards its own label items.

Brands can, of course, still pay for placement on Amazon and display their packaging and logos – and this is becoming a big business. Some large brands, according to the *New York Times*, spend six figures each month to advertise on Amazon's platform.[9] Unsurprisingly, advertising is Amazon's fastest-growing segment at the time of writing in 2018, with Wall Street analysts expecting it to scale very quickly from the current estimated $2–4 billion[10] to up to $26 billion by 2022.[11] Yet another spoke on the flywheel.

> 'I would say advertising continues to be a bright spot both from a product standpoint and also financially.'
> **Amazon CFO Brian Olsavsky, 2018[12]**

Today, if you search for coffee on Amazon, the first thing you see at the top of the page is a banner ad sponsored by Folgers. But you only need to scroll down slightly to find Amazon's equivalent 'Top-Rated from Our Brands' private label banner as well as items from its AmazonFresh and Solimo ranges listed on the first page of search results. It's also common for Amazon's private label products to feature a badge denoting that the item is a best-seller, sponsored product or 'Amazon's Choice' (meaning that the item is Prime-eligible, in stock and has a review rating of at least 4.0, among other criteria).

Amazon hold all the cards here. While generating revenue from digital advertising, they're simultaneously optimizing the placement of their private label products with the aim of maximizing the conversion of shoppers to their own brands. This is not unlike a brand paying a slotting fee to feature on a supermarket's shelf, only to find the private label equivalent sitting next to it.

But here's where Amazon differs – customer reviews. Imagine a grocery shopper at the shelf, trying to decide between a trusted national brand like Heinz or Coca-Cola and a less well-known own label. The shopper can see there is a cost advantage to buying the own label, but what's the quality like? Will it taste like the national brand? Will the kids turn their noses up at it?

Amazon can help to sway shoppers at this point thanks to its online customer reviews. If that same shopper can see that the own label item generates thousands of 4.5-star reviews, then they're probably going to feel more confident giving it a try. So, to build trust and awareness of its private label items, Amazon has been proactively utilizing its Amazon Vine programme to build up customer reviews of these new items. Under the invite-only scheme, Amazon's most active reviewers post opinions about new and pre-release items in exchange for free products. According to ReviewMeta, an analysis of over 1,600 private label products available on Amazon showed that approximately half had Vine reviews.[13]

'Private label is one of the highly underappreciated trends within Amazon, in our view, which over time should give the company a strong "unfair" competitive advantage', said SunTrust analyst Youssef Squali in 2018. '"Unfair" because it'll be very difficult to dislodge the company once it attains it; fair because it's earned, not bestowed.'[14]

At times, Amazon has resorted to more aggressive measures for driving private label conversions, for example by running own label advertisements on other brands' product detail pages. According to a 2018 Gartner L2 report, a whopping 80 per cent of product pages in the paper products (toilet paper) category featured an ad for Amazon's Presto range.[15] 'They have access to things other brands don't – like special templates for content and various merchandising placements',[16] said Melissa Burdick, an ex-Amazon executive, in a 2016 LinkedIn post. As an example, Burdick notes how on the Amazon Elements baby wipes detail page, the 'hot link' feature to see other items within the Amazon Best Sellers rank is disabled, making it more difficult for shoppers to find other best-selling alternatives.

And it's only going to get tougher for suppliers as voice-activated shopping takes hold: Alexa produces just two search results. 'When it comes to voice search you go first position or you go home because beyond the first or second place there is no future', says Sebastien Szczepaniak, former Amazon executive who now heads up e-commerce at Nestlé.[17]

We'll discuss how Alexa prioritizes search results in the coming chapters, but for now it's important to understand that in instances where the customer's shopping history is unknown, Alexa's recommendation will be an Amazon's Choice product. In a 2017 study, Bain & Co. found that for customers making a first-time purchase without specifying a brand, over half of the time Alexa's first recommendation was an Amazon's Choice product (over top search results). And for those categories that featured an own label item, 17 per cent of the time Alexa recommended the own label item even though such products account for just 2 per cent of volume sold.[18]

There is some good news for brands here. Voice works best when shoppers know exactly what they want, so if that brand loyalty already exists then Alexa will simply shorten the path to purchase and, crucially, remember the customer's preference for the next time.

Amazon has to maintain a delicate balance between driving private label sales and giving customers what they want. But for suppliers, the gloves are well and truly off. Many have succumbed to selling on Amazon because of its undeniable reach, but as own label becomes a greater focus so does Amazon's leverage.

A fashion powerhouse?

Amazon's own label efforts have, perhaps surprisingly, been largely focused on fashion. They have quietly built up a portfolio of highly targeted sub-brands – Lark + Ro, Ella Moon, Mae, Amazon Essentials, Buttoned Down, Goodthreads, Scout + Ro, Paris Sunday and Find (in Europe), just to name a few. In fact, clothing, shoes and jewellery make up 86 per cent of its own label lines, according to a 2018 Gartner L2 report.

It has the reach, but can Amazon convince shoppers that it's a credible fashion destination? Does its USP of convenience and choice really lend itself to fashion, a category where it's all about the product? Like grocery, the fashion sector is notoriously fickle. We don't doubt that Amazon can shift a boatload of clothes (remember, they're likely to be the largest clothing retailer in the US by the time this book is published[19]). But selling socks and t-shirts is not the same thing as selling fashion.

> 'The Amazon model is – you can get everything, and get it cheaply and conveniently. But it's very transactional. It's not the best proposition for fashion.'
> **Rubin Ritter, co-CEO of Zalando, 2017[20]**

Selling private label clothing helps to improve Amazon's overall margin mix, which will be further pressured as Amazon becomes more grocery focused, while crucially filling merchandise gaps when certain fashion brands are unwilling to sell on Amazon. 'For a long time people thought of Amazon as the place to get toilet paper or cat food', said Elaine Kwon, a former executive at Amazon's fashion business. 'In 2014, many brands were very hesitant to even let it be known publicly that they wanted to work with Amazon.'

But the balance of power is shifting. Online fashion is booming while sales at mall-based department stores are deteriorating. Amazon is ubiquitous today; it's become a sales channel that can no longer be ignored. But selling through Amazon isn't just about generating greater volumes – it also gives brands greater control of pricing and presentation of their products, since many are already being sold on Amazon via third parties.

'You can't disregard the fact that most of these platforms run a third-party marketplace, so, whether you like it or not, they're probably going to have a third-party marketplace for your brand; your brand's likely going to be on that site anyway.'
Chip Bergh, CEO of Levi Strauss, 2017[21]

Cracking down on such third-party sales was Nike's primary incentive for selling on Amazon – a decision that turned heads when it was announced in 2017. Nike had already been the number one clothing brand on Amazon, according to Morgan Stanley, even though it did not sell directly on the site. As part of the deal, Amazon agreed to monitor its site for counterfeits and no longer allow third-party vendors to sell Nike products.

Amazon's other top-performing clothing brands, according to a 2017 Morgan Stanley report, include, Adidas, Hanes, Under Armour and Calvin Klein. Its Amazon Essentials brand is the best-performing private label line and the 12th-most purchased clothing brand overall. 'The big challenge now is that Amazon is introducing their own private label apparel business and they're going to be massive in apparel over time', said Levi's Bergh in 2017.[22] It's no longer just third-party vendors that big brands have to worry about – it's Amazon itself.

But this won't happen overnight. It takes a long time to build a brand, and many question whether Amazon's utilitarian image will prevent it from being perceived as a fashion powerhouse. It needs both the big brands for credibility and own label for margins, but it also must find its USP in fashion. Near-infinite assortment is powerful, but also overwhelming – a search for a black dress will produce over 40,000 results.

Amazon may not be the go-to destination for browsing, but they are compensating for their weaknesses through innovations, as previously discussed, such as the launch of Prime Wardrobe and the Echo Look, as well as the Body Labs acquisition. Amazon has also been awarded a patent for an on-demand automated clothing factory designed to quickly produce clothing only after an order is placed – a move that would not only propel its own label fashion business but could reinvent the entire supply chain and shake up the entire apparel sector in the process. We're certainly not writing Amazon Fashion off just yet.

The branding conundrum: Amazon's mishmash of grocery brands

In 2014, Amazon launched its first major own label brand for the FMCG category – Amazon Elements. Many in the FMCG sector feared Amazon's premium range of nappies and wipes was the beginning of its long-awaited own label incursion. But within two months, the nappies were discontinued.

Feedback had been lukewarm, with Amazon citing the need for 'design improvements'. It was a hugely risky category in which to debut its first ever own label FMCG product; quality can be subjective at times but a nappy either works or it doesn't, and brands aren't given many second chances in a category like babycare. Nonetheless, Amazon maintained the Elements brand, using it exclusively for wipes before eventually extending it, somewhat bizarrely, to vitamins and supplements. But remember Amazon sees failure as an opportunity to iterate and improve, so it wasn't much of a surprise to see own label nappies resurface a few years later – this time under the Mama Bear brand.

The line, which also includes organic baby food, was one of several new FMCG ranges Amazon launched in 2016 prior to the Whole Foods acquisition. Others included: Happy Belly (trail mix, nuts, spices, eggs and coffee); Presto (paper towels, toilet paper, laundry detergent); and Wickedly Prime (gourmet snacks including potato chips, popcorn, soup, tea). Following the Elements fiasco, Amazon trod carefully and steered entirely clear of one big category – perishables.

That changed with the Whole Foods deal, when Amazon inherited its very well-regarded 365 Everyday Value and eponymous line of own label foods. Overnight, Amazon became a credible grocery operator with a compelling range of private label goods. Within four months, 365 took in $10 million in sales, according to One Click Retail, making it the second-largest private label available on Amazon.

In addition to all the benefits laid out earlier in the chapter, private label is particularly important for grocers because of the high-frequency/habitual nature of the category. Remember Amazon's goal is to take the chore of out grocery shopping by automating replenishment of everyday goods. That in itself is very powerful, but even more so when it's the retailer's own item that's being replenished. As of 2018, Amazon already has Dash buttons for a handful of private labels such as Amazon Basics, Amazon Elements and Happy Belly, and we expect to see additional expansion here once Whole Foods Market is fully integrated.

Since the Whole Foods deal, Amazon has quietly rolled out additional ranges including its own AmazonFresh brand (limited to coffee at the time of writing), Wag and Solimo in addition to exclusive brands like Basic Care and Mountain Falls. Amazon can be excused for being in experimentation mode but at some point they'll need to create a more unified and coherent message across their private label portfolio.

This brings up an important point about brand elasticity. Amazon is the king of diversification, but stretching into new sectors and services risks diluting their brand – or even worse, customer backlash. Would shoppers want Amazon-branded groceries along with their Amazon-branded Echos, Kindles, video and music streaming and, potentially in the future, bank accounts and healthcare services? In grocery, we believe that Amazon is destined to be a jumble of own brands, but that doesn't make them any less of a threat. Competitors should be prioritizing investment in private label while suppliers ensure they have strategies in place for defending market share. Deeper customer engagement will be essential and, where appropriate, own label production should also be considered.

Table 8.1 Amazon's FMCG own label ranges

Year launched	Brand		Category						
		Babycare	Beauty & grooming	Food & beverage	Health & personal care	Household supplies	Petcare	Vitamins & supplements
2014	Amazon Elements	X						X
2016	Happy Belly			X				
2016	Mama Bear	X						
2016	Presto					X		
2016	Wickedly Prime			X				
2017	AmazonFresh			X				
2017	Whole Foods Market*		X	X	X	X		
2017	365*	X	X	X	X	X		X
2017	Engine 2 Plant-Strong*			X				
2018	Basic Care**				X			
2018	Wag						X	
2018	Solimo		X	X	X	X		X
2018	Mountain Falls**	X	X		X			

*Acquired Whole Foods Market brands
**Exclusive to Amazon, but not Amazon-owned

Notes

1 Creswell, Julie (2018) How Amazon steers shoppers to its own products, *New York Times*, 23 June. Available from: https://mobile.nytimes.com/2018/06/23/business/amazon-the-brand-buster.html [Last accessed 29/6/2018].

2 Housel, Morgan (2013) The 20 smartest things Jeff Bezos has ever said, *The Motley Fool*, 9 September. Available from: https://www.fool.com/investing/general/2013/09/09/the-25-smartest-things-jeff-bezos-has-ever-said.aspx [Last accessed 29/6/2018].

3 Franck, Thomas (2018) Amazon's flourishing private label business to help stock rally another 20%, analyst says, *CNBC*, 4 September. Available from: https://www.cnbc.com/2018/06/04/suntrust-amazons-private-label-business-to-help-stock-rally-20-percent.html [Last accessed 29/6/2018].

4 Lebow, Victor (1955) Price competition in 1955, *Journal of Retailing*, Spring. Available from: http://www.gcafh.org/edlab/Lebow.pdf [Last accessed 3/9/2018].

5 Creswell, Julie (2018) How Amazon steers shoppers to its own products, *New York Times*, 23 June. Available from: https://mobile.nytimes.com/2018/06/23/business/amazon-the-brand-buster.html [Last accessed 29/6/2018].

6 ibid.

7 Anderson, Keith (2016) Amazon's move into private label consumables, *Profitero* (blog post) 28 July. Available from: https://www.profitero.com/2016/07/amazons-move-into-private-label-consumables/ [Last accessed 11/9/2018].

8 ibid.

9 ibid.

10 Anonymous (2018) Amazon worth a trillion? Advertising may hold the key to growth, *Ad Age*, 13 March. Available from: http://adage.com/article/digital/amazon-worth-a-trillion-advertising-hold-key-growth/312716/ [Last accessed 29/6/2018].

11 Spitz, David (2018) Wow, RBC's @markmahaney out with report forecasting Amazon AMS to hit $26 billion in revenue by 2022 – most aggressive projection I've seen (and I tend to agree). $AMZN [Twitter] 22 June. Available from: https://twitter.com/davidspitz/status/1010278559213084673 [Last accessed 29/6/2018].

12 Sparks, Daniel (2018) Amazon.com, Inc. talks advertising, Prime's price increase, and more, *The Motley Fool*, 29 April. Available from: https://www.fool.com/investing/2018/04/29/amazoncom-inc-talks-advertising-primes-price-incre.aspx [Last accessed 29/6/2018].

13 Creswell, Julie (2018) How Amazon steers shoppers to its own products, *New York Times*, 23 June. Available from: https://mobile.nytimes.com/2018/06/23/business/amazon-the-brand-buster.html [Last accessed 29/6/2018].

14 Franck, Thomas (2018) Amazon's flourishing private label business to help stock rally another 20%, analyst says, *CNBC*, 4 June. Available from: https://www.cnbc.com/2018/06/04/suntrust-amazons-private-label-business-to-help-stock-rally-20-percent.html [Last accessed 29/6/2018].

15 Smith, Cooper (2018) We've been doing a lot of analyses on amazon's private label marketing strategy and one of the starkest findings is the # of ads they run on other brands' product listings ... ex) 80% of product listing pages in the paper products (ie toilet paper) category have an ad for Presto! [Twitter] 25 June. Available from: https://twitter.com/CooperASmith/status/1011314597213634560 [Last accessed 29/6/2018].

16 Burdick, Melissa (2016) Should CPGs be worried about Amazon Private Label? *LinkedIn*, 27 June. Available from: https://www.linkedin.com/pulse/should-cpgs-worried-amazon-private-label-melissa-burdick/ [Last accessed 29/6/2018].

17 Chaudhuri, Saabira and Sharon Terlep (2018) The next big threat to consumer brands (yes, Amazon's behind it), *Wall Street Journal*, 27 February. Available from: https://www.wsj.com/articles/big-consumer-brands-dont-have-an-answer-for-alexa-1519727401 [Last accessed 29/6/2018].

18 ibid.

19 Thomas, Lauren (2018) Amazon's 100 million Prime members will help it become the No. 1 apparel retailer in the US, *CNBC*, 19 April. Available from: https://www.cnbc.com/2018/04/19/amazon-to-be-the-no-1-apparel-retailer-in-the-us-morgan-stanley.html [Last accessed 29/6/2018].

20 Chazan, Guy (2017) Zalando updates its look as it prepares for a new push by Amazon, *Financial Times,* 28 May. Available from: https://www.ft.com/content/2e9d7e80-3bc0-11e7-821a-6027b8a20f23 [Last accessed 29/6/2018].

21 Business of Fashion and McKinsey (2017) The State of Fashion 2018 report. Available from: https://cdn.businessoffashion.com/reports/The_State_of_Fashion_2018_v2.pdf [Last accessed 29/6/2018].

22 ibid.

Technology and 09
frictionless retail

'Even when they don't yet know it, customers want something better, and
your desire to delight customers will drive you to invent on their behalf.'
Jeff Bezos[1]

In Chapter 4 we began to explore the 'on-my-terms' shopper. We started to discuss the impact of technology on retail and how it is revolutionizing the way we shop – 'on my terms'.

The key to understanding what this really means every day, to the average consumer, starts with understanding how a shopper sets these 'terms' for their shopping journeys. Simply put, rapid technology development has given consumers the tools to shop on their own terms. The digitization of modern life not only underpins our increased appetite for, and ability to seek out, more 'fun' or informed customer experiences over the more functional, weekly grocery type of shop; the so-called 'consumerization' of technology is also fuelling heightened expectations of convenience, immediacy, transparency and relevancy among more and more consumers.

While any looming retail apocalypse may be overstated, fears for the future of the industry are founded on the fact that many familiar household retail chains have fallen by the wayside. But we contend that their demise was by no means inevitable. They failed to accommodate today's digitally empowered, on-my-terms shopper. This is why any focus on Amazon as a causative agent is unfounded. But, as more retail casualties fail to use technology to digitally transform and differentiate in response to the industry-wide challenge of the on-my-terms shopper, it is worth taking an in-depth look at how Amazon has seemingly been able to stay one step ahead of both the competition and the needs of its customers.

In the next two chapters, we explore how Amazon continues to use technology development in artificial intelligence (AI) and voice as two particularly strong areas of focus in combination with the underlying drivers of change such development responds to, and the next-generation expectations and demand for frictionless retail experiences on the part of today's on-my-terms shopper it helps to meet. Through this exploration, it becomes easy to see how not just Amazon's business, but more so the technology advantage that underpins its execution, will continue to weed out complacent players and push the entire retail industry towards the creation of customer experiences that make shopping instore as effortless as it has become online and turn the functional into something more fun.

Customer obsession

Retailers that do not understand, and adjust their propositions accordingly in response to, the on-my-terms shopper are the very ones whose complacency means they also fail to keep pace with the impact of the technology drivers of change; they fail to recognize how the internet, mobile and subsequent tech-enabled service innovations, such as click & collect or shoppable media, are changing the retail landscape forever.

Before getting into how the technology itself has developed, let's first examine its overall impact on the wider industry landscape and its role in empowering the on-my-terms shopper. We are about to reach a major tipping point, where over half of the planet has access to the internet. Widespread adoption of technology as it relates to retail has put the customer firmly in control of the terms of the buying process. This is where it becomes impossible to ignore the spectre of Amazon. We can see how the shifting balance of power from retailers to consumers has not only tracked closely against technology development, but how Amazon has also used this shift to support its growth and evolution. Acknowledging this shift is central to understanding how, just like Amazon, any successful business can use technology to both its own and its customers' advantage. But here, it is also Amazon's desire to 'delight' its customers, as Bezos has put it, that has allowed it to tap its technology advantage. It is also a lesson in putting the needs of the customer at the heart of innovation any business could learn from.

In the 2010 Amazon Annual Report, Bezos wrote:

> Look inside a current textbook on software architecture, and you'll find few patterns that we don't apply at Amazon. We use high-performance transactions systems, complex rendering and object caching, workflow and queuing systems, business intelligence and data analytics, machine learning and pattern recognition, neural networks and probabilistic decision making, and

a wide variety of other techniques. And while many of our systems are based on the latest in computer science research, this often hasn't been sufficient; our architects and engineers have had to advance research in directions that no academic had yet taken. Many of the problems we face have no textbook solutions, and so we – happily – invent new approaches...

So, how has Amazon's success tracked so closely against the rise of digital retail in the wake of consumer technology adoption? We strongly suggest that it is because Amazon is a technology company first and a retailer second, but it manages to successfully keep the customer it serves at the heart of the technology innovation it harnesses in support of its business strategy. For example, out of Amazon's 14 Leadership Principles, the first is 'Customer Obsession'. As referenced in Chapter 2, it is this customer-centric ethos that has served it well as consumers have begun to embrace digitally enabled or enhanced technology shopping tools. It cannot be underestimated, however, how much it helps that Amazon's core business is founded on technology innovation. Before looking at this innovation, let's take a step back here, as it wasn't always this way.

Going back to 2002, with necessity truly being the mother of all invention, Amazon Web Services (AWS) was first born of the need for sufficient number-crunching capacity and standardized, automated computing infrastructures on which to run its retail marketplace. Capitalizing on advances in networking, storage, compute power and virtualization, Amazon began reselling its cloud computing capabilities as services in 2006.

However, from 2014 to 2015, Amazon saw its stock price fall 20 per cent. During that intervening time shareholders would have been forgiven for wondering if the company would ever make a profit, and its dwindling share price reflected this. In relative terms, it was smaller than Walmart. Even Alibaba, which went public in the autumn of the same year also dwarfed Amazon's 2014 market cap. In the meantime, though, Amazon had quietly been consolidating market share in meeting the fast-growing demand for cloud computing services.

Then, in 2015, in what would be a pivotal year for the company, it first revealed just how profitable AWS had become, with margins to rival those of Starbucks, and investors started to see their Amazon stock start to rise in value. Today, its AWS customers include Netflix,[2] NASA[3] and retailers such as Nordstrom, Ocado and Under Armour.[4] But even back then, in that fateful year, AWS was responsible for two-thirds of Amazon's profits; by 2017, this had grown to 100 per cent. Don't forget this is why we said Amazon is not your average retailer. It is a technology company first.

The power of obsession

Thinking about the values that have gone on to define Amazon, when it comes to technology innovation, its third Leadership Principle – 'Invent and Simplify' – is the most significant.

Although AWS fulfilled its potential to power Amazon to the behemoth it is today, in the first instance it was not afraid in its quest to invent and simplify its own operations. It then went on to repackage and resell these efforts to businesses and consumers alike. So much so that, since 2015 – the year following that fateful stock dive – its market value had increased fivefold to its 2018 market cap. It also provided its retail business with a massive balance sheet and the vast amounts of computing power required to build out the sophisticated AI-based systems needed to power its extensive, global e-commerce, supply chain and fulfilment operations, as well as the next digital frontiers in retail – automation and voice.

As we discussed in Chapter 2, Amazon itself suggests it can afford to 'be misunderstood for long periods of time', according to its third Leadership Principle. If the story of how AWS came to fruition isn't clear enough illustration of the fact, then let's take a closer look at Prime Day as another worthy proof point.

The first year Amazon held its Prime Day was 2015, in the company's 20th year. By then, its Prime membership scheme was already 10 years old. While some reports from the inaugural discount day highlighted a lack of blockbuster deals, online retail marketplace IT provider ChannelAdvisor found it boosted Amazon's US sales by 93 per cent and its European sales by 53 per cent.

On the second Prime Day, Amazon's total orders during the 24-hour period increased 60 per cent from its debut, striking such a blow for bricks and mortar retail competitors everywhere that they now struggle to competitively keep up with the annual discount day. By 2017, Prime Day had expanded to 12 countries and was offering special incentives to Amazon customers using its Alexa voice assistant. We need to understand how Alexa has come to take such a prominent role recently and will delve into that later. Here we should pause to recognize that the 2017 Amazon Prime Day generated $2.4 billion. Even so, to put that amount in further perspective, its Chinese competitor Alibaba raked in some $25 billion during Singles' Day in the same year.[5]

Despite its Chinese counterpart making Prime Day look like small change, it does represent a great example of Amazon's phenomenal growth. Putting this in context, we need to go back to 2015 again – not only for AWS' profits and the first Prime Day, but also because it was the year that sales exceeded $100 billion for the first time. Delivering sales growth was the last of Bezos' 'three pillars', where AWS provided for its cost base, while Prime has gone on to power its customer acquisition and retention strategy. Breaking out sales, Amazon states there is a 50-50 split between the units shipped of its first-party wholesale merchandise and that of the millions of independent merchants who pay to use its marketplace as a store front and who can also pay to use its e-commerce and Fulfilment by Amazon (FBA) suite of supply chain and logistics services.

The power of innovation

It is easy to see why 2015 was a momentous year for Amazon, where its Leadership Principles began to bear fruit, and Bezos' 'three pillars' became stable enough to sustain its 'flywheel' ecosystem. The approach enabled it to offer more of what the on-my-terms shopper wanted.

The first technology trend Amazon has, therefore, taken advantage of is the rapidly growing number of individuals accessing the internet over mobile devices. According to mobile operators, the number of unique mobile subscribers will reach 5.9 billion, equivalent to 71 per cent of the world's population, by 2025.[6] Other internet- and mobile-enabled developments that have transformed the way we shop include payment, enabled via online banking and mobile wallets. Debit and credit so-called 'card-not-present' payments and PayPal, which saves time and adds extra security on entering payment information, introduced consumers to online shopping, in the same way as contactless credit and debit cards are paving the way for the rollout of mobile payment schemes instore.

Seamless experiences

The common denominator among such innovation is consumer demand for more immersive and portable experiences. This has led to the objective of eliminating 'friction' in customer experiences, as it relates to the speed, convenience, transparency and relevance throughout the shopping journey. This may be, for example, browsing online, using an app or visiting a store, only to find the item sought is out of stock, or having to join long queues at checkout. Eliminating such friction requires that the retailer enable that customer to perhaps order the desired product online for delivery to home; or, on finding the item, it then facilitates the looking up of reviews or offers to check on the best deal, right through to final, rapid checkout via mobile or express fulfilment. By contrast, anything that introduces friction into the customer experience, such as queues, delivery issues or poor sales service, is not compatible with today's on-my-terms shopper. In order to give customers more of what they want, the 'what' of frictionless retail is enabled through the use of digital to improve customer experiences, where the 'how' is provided by technology. This is where Amazon's technology business gives it an unprecedented advantage, and why it is wrong for both traditional and online retailers to compare themselves directly against it. They are traditional retailers; Amazon is a retail technology firm.

Technology drivers

Technology is not only transforming the way consumers interact with retailers in this way, it is blurring the physical and digital divide. To understand how Amazon has successfully harnessed its technology advantage to provide a digitally enabled, frictionless shopping experience, it is necessary to first break down the fundamental drivers of technology that underpin the frictionless objectives of the on-my-terms shopper. They are:

1 ubiquitous connectivity;

2 pervasive interfaces; and

3 autonomous computing.

We see the effects of the first of these drivers with the impact of mobile in and out of the home, as well as instore and in other public places. The more that connectivity becomes truly ubiquitous, with the development of fifth-generation (5G) mobile networks, alongside blanket Wi-Fi availability, wireless charging, and whatever device or means that enable us to be always connected and online at faster speeds, the more impatient we become for greater choice, more intuitive search and instantaneous response and fulfilment times.

The context for the second technology driver, towards more 'pervasive interfaces', requires that we go back to the early, pre-internet days of computing, where the idea of a handheld pointing device or 'mouse' was relatively new. For example, in 1984, reporter Gregg Williams wrote of the introduction of the first Macintosh computer that it 'brings us one step closer to the ideal computer as appliance'.

'The Lisa computer was important because it was the first commercial product to use the mouse-window-desktop environment. The Macintosh is equally important because it makes that same very same environment affordable.'
Gregg Williams, 1984[7]

A mere 30 years later, we're used to using trackpads and balls, pointers, pens and graphics tablets, not to mention other PC peripherals like headphones and microphones, and even smart glasses, watches and other so-called 'wearables'. The common theme linking all of this development has been the search for the means of interfacing with computing devices that is also seamless or frictionless. In this sense, use of the interface becomes so intuitive that it enables the technology itself to essentially 'disappear' into the background, allowing its functionality to come easily to the fore to serve the user's particular needs. Perhaps the most common modern example of a pervasive interface is the touchscreen; so much so that a child born after the launch of Apple's iPhone is more likely to claw at the screen of any computing device they are given to control it, than to look for a button to switch it on.

Autonomous computing

Where connectivity and interfaces have, to date, been hardware-based, the third global technology driver is predicated on the development of increasingly 'intelligent' software that can almost think for itself and come up with answers to questions without necessarily being programmed with the necessary information. Instead, autonomous computing systems can cross-reference and correlate disparate data sources, augment their own algorithms, and answer complex 'what if?' sorts of questions. As such, AI, including machine learning and deep learning techniques, could not exist without autonomous computing development as the last global technology driver. AI development is, in fact, responsible for many of the functional computing advances of the last 15 years, from search algorithms, spam filters and fraud prevention systems to self-driving vehicles and smart personal assistants.

We can trace the influence of these drivers throughout Amazon's rise to dominance, where it has capitalized on its technology development based on these drivers to bring greater digital capabilities to bear in the quest to provide more frictionless shopping experiences.

The power of foresight

In the case of each technology driver, Amazon's attempts to capitalize on developments outside of its core capabilities (ie cloud computing and retail) have met with varying degrees of success. It's perhaps good to know even Amazon can get it wrong sometimes (just as it did experimenting with own-label nappies). But, with Bezos encouraging his people to come up with ideas that will give customers that something better, whether or not they know it yet, Amazon has certainly not been afraid to fail in this quest. Also, the bets it places are big enough that when they come off, they are so wildly successful that they more than make up for the failures.

In this context, let's consider the developments by Amazon that have been driven by the quest for ubiquitous connectivity and pervasive interfaces first. There may be some who may remember its ill-fated foray into smartphone manufacturing, a key example we first touched on in Chapter 2. After unveiling the Amazon Fire phone in June 2014, the device was met with a swathe of negative reviews that dismissed the device as not only 'forgettable',[8] but also 'mediocre'.[9] In fact, one reporter who declared the device 'forgettable' went on to advise consumers to 'wait for the sequel'.

However, the Fire phone bombed so badly, a sequel was never going to be forthcoming. Just one month after launch and the damaging reviews, Amazon slashed the price of its phone from US $199 (for the 32GB version) to just 99 cents. As if that wasn't admission enough of the device's abject failure, the company also revealed in 2015 that it had taken a $170 million loss on its development, manufacture and splashy launch event. Amazon was, perhaps, lucky at the time that the stellar AWS numbers it also revealed that year, which we referenced earlier in this chapter, stole the spotlight.

For a book that aims to deconstruct the secrets of Amazon's success, it is worth taking a moment here to dissect how and why the Fire phone failed; more so because, since then, it has seemingly learned from its mistakes. Taking a consensus view, Amazon's attempts to launch a smartphone at the peak of popularity of Apple's iPhone, where only a handful of Android OS-based devices led by Samsung could compete, were doomed to failure. In a market dominated by two major mobile operating system (OS) players, Amazon needed to clearly differentiate its offering on either price or quality, but it did neither. At the same time, though, we've acknowledged that it quickly recognized this and took ameliorative action.

The Fire phone did, however, reveal Amazon's ambitions to expand its move into PC hardware beyond its first e-reader, the Kindle, which was launched in 2007. As Marcus Wohlsen wrote for *Wired.com* in 2015, 'The [Fire phone] project was doomed from the start, because the only one who really needs an Amazon phone is Amazon.'[10] Amazon might have felt it needed the Fire phone to get closer to its customers and add another spoke to its flywheel to lock those customers into its ecosystem. An application called Firefly, which shipped with the Fire phone, was intended to do just that. Firefly was a text, sound and object recognition tool designed to let shoppers identify over 100 million different products and then buy them online – friction-free, from Amazon, of course. But even after a series of price reductions, the mobile device was subsequently discontinued in mid-2015.

Mistakes learned

Amazon learned from the failure of the Fire phone, and the misstep certainly did not dampen its ambitions in regard to taking advantage of the rise of technology that could enable more ubiquitous connectivity and pervasive interfaces. After all, it did have the success of its Fire tablet (launched in November 2011) to save its hardware development credentials. The tablet, which was already on its fourth generation by the time the Fire phone was launched, built on Amazon's e-book sales and Kindle success and also offers users access to the Amazon e-commerce site directly from its home screen. But it did not enable connectivity beyond the functionality of connecting to the Amazon store, nor did its early versions use the latest touch interface technology, despite the fact that Apple had commoditized the touchscreen with the introduction of the iPhone four years earlier. Where Amazon has been more successful in applying the first two global technology drivers, though, is in its core retail business, where it has brought the concepts of ubiquitous connectivity and pervasive interfaces to bear with far more success.

One click to no click

Applying the first two global technology drivers to the Amazon timeline, it is possible to recognize just how important their application has been in facilitating the removal of friction from the online shopping experience it offers. Its '1-click' patent is the preeminent example, even though the patent expired in 2017. Many industry watchers have questioned whether its ability to register billing, payment and shipping information details in advance of being able to then add products to a shopping basket and checkout to buy those products with 'one click' should have been granted a patent at all. They argued that it stifled e-commerce competition because it gave Amazon an unfair monopoly, predicated on what amounts to little more than an efficient means of using what quickly became standard e-commerce technology. But, back in 1999, it was perhaps easy to understand how it was then seen as a cutting-edge innovation and a first hint at how Amazon would go on to make shopping friction the enemy while changing the status quo. So, on the patent being granted, Amazon then famously sued the US bookseller Barnes & Noble for having implemented a similar method to the one described in its patent for allowing its customers to make repeat purchases. (The two companies reached an undisclosed settlement in the case in 2002.)

Meanwhile, the patent, and Amazon's rigorous defence of it, afforded the company a significant advantage over its competitors for nearly 20 years, where competitors could either choose to add more clicks to their check-out processes or pay Amazon licensing fees to offer '1-click' checkout. The reason it was such a powerful piece of functionality for Amazon was that the friction it reduced was effective in helping to eliminate shopping cart abandonment.

Just like every e-commerce player in the early days, Amazon could see customers browsing and adding items into their shopping basket. But online retail cart abandonment rates, ie the ratio of the number of abandoned shopping baskets to the number of initiated and/or completed transactions, have always been high. Most recently, analysis of 37 different e-commerce sites in 2017 found the average shopping cart abandonment rate was 69.2 per cent.[11] Unsurprisingly, Amazon doesn't publish its abandonment rates. But merchants selling via Amazon's Marketplace who, understandably, want to remain anonymous, have reported that Amazon has managed to consistently maintain lower-than-average rates of abandonment. Another published estimate, which assumed the technology increased Amazon's sales by a relatively modest 5 per cent, put the value of the patent at $2.4 billion annually.[12]

Paying for the privilege

The advantage Amazon gained with its 1-click patent demonstrates just how much a source of friction the checkout process can be in retail, whether online or offline. We only have to think about the times we have been discouraged from completing a purchase in a physical store on seeing a long queue at the checkout – many of us 'just walk out' (we will come to explore the significance of this term later). But here, Amazon has again proved its ability to stay one step ahead of its competition, by not only leveraging its 1-click expertise, but also by developing the functionality required to facilitate payment as well as fulfilment services for the merchants that sell via its marketplace. In 2013, Amazon rolled out its 'Pay with Amazon' service to third parties. The feature allows e-commerce sites to give customers the option to check out using the credit card and shipping information they have stored with Amazon (in just the same way as Google or Facebook's single sign-on speeds website registration), shaving the purchase process down to just a few clicks by running on Amazon's e-commerce transactional rails – for a price and the cost of collaborating to compete, of course.[13]

The last, and perhaps the most important, example of how Amazon has defined the development of frictionless shopping and realized its 'Invent and Simplify' Leadership Principle takes us back to its Prime service. We have already examined how much of a barrier to conversion the checkout process can be. But delivery costs are an even greater barrier. Research carried out by the Baymard Institute in 2017 among US consumers (once those just browsing without any intention to buy were eliminated from the survey pool) found that high extra costs associated with shipping, taxes and fees were the top reason for abandoning a shopping cart.

Amazon has, with its Prime service, solved two key sources of friction in online shopping. By offering a flat monthly or annual fee for expedited shipping, it has eliminated both the hidden cost of shipping before checkout and the perception that shopping online is slower than shopping at retail stores. Prime Now, with its promise of one-hour delivery in urban areas, takes this offering to its ultimate extent, with immediacy and instant gratification that can only be beaten only by going to a store and buying the product oneself. Add into this the offer of streaming media – music, TV, films and music – on demand as part of the offering, and it is easy to understand why today the scale of Prime membership, at 100 million-plus globally, dwarfs some of the most popular other online subscription services, including Spotify (with 71m users), Hulu (17m) and Tinder (3m),[14] and has proven such a central, supportive pillar to Amazon's flywheel ecosystem of services.

The transparency of Prime's model and the friction it eliminates are the capabilities that characterize Amazon's most notable innovative digital shopping achievements. Prime also allows Amazon to beat many other e-commerce competitors over the so-called 'last mile' of fulfilment. Taken together with the simplicity and elegance of Amazon's recently expired patent for one-click purchases, these developments could also be said to have laid the groundwork for Amazon's Dash Buttons, as well as shopping by voice using its Alexa voice assistant – all of which pull the customer further into the Amazon flywheel ecosystem.

Easy auto-replenishment

As first referenced in Chapter 6, Amazon's Dash Buttons were first launched in – yes, you guessed it – 2015. In addition to laying the groundwork for its move from one click to 'no click' online shopping, Dash Buttons for the first time gave Amazon and its brand partners physical, branded real estate in consumer homes. Launched the day before April Fools, leading some analysts to think it was a prank, some mocked the relatively low-tech idea, which relies on a wireless internet connection to communicate the reorder command, by pressing the Dash Button, to the owner's Amazon mobile app. The customer still confirms the reorder in-app to avoid any accidental purchases. But it builds on and augments the subscription success of its Prime fulfilment scheme.

To date Amazon has Dash Buttons for more than 300 products and, in 2017, said that orders using Dash Buttons were placed more than four times a minute compared to once a minute the year before. Although that's only a small part of Amazon's sales overall, retail data firm Slice Intelligence found that it translated to Dash Button order growth of 650 per cent in their first year.[15] The company then built on its Dash success with the introduction of the Dash Wand – a battery-powered device with a speaker, microphone and barcode scanner that updated its static predecessor with more sophisticated voice capabilities.

Add into this mix the fact that Amazon is now the starting point for over half of US consumers searching for products, and it is easy to see why it has grown to the position of online dominance it commands today. Indeed, among Millennials (many of whom were born after the World Wide Web went live in 1991), Amazon was the number one app they could not live without on their mobile devices.[16] But Amazon has not been content to innovate and develop a business strategy predicated on the ubiquitous connectivity and pervasive interfaces that are revolutionizing the way we live, work and shop, it also has its sights set on making the shopping process even more rapid and intuitive by relying on autonomous computing capabilities.

Notes

1 Amazon Investor Relations (2017) 2016 Letter to Shareholders, 12 April. Available from: http://phx.corporate-ir.net/phoenix.zhtml?c=97664&p=irol-reportsannual [Last accessed 2/4/2018].

2 Amazon Netflix case study (2016) Amazon AWS. Available from: https://aws.amazon.com/solutions/case-studies/netflix/ [Last accessed 2/4/2018].

3 Breeden II, J (2013) The tech behind NASA's Martian chronicles, *GCN*, 4 January. Available from: https://gcn.com/articles/2013/01/04/tech-behind-nasa-martian-chronicles.aspx [Last accessed 2/4/2018].

4 Amazon retail case studies (2018), Amazon AWS. Available from: https://aws. amazon.com/retail/case-studies/ [Last accessed 2/4/2018].

5 Wang, Helen (2017) Alibaba's Singles' Day by the numbers: a record $25 billion haul, *Forbes*, 12 November. Available from: https://www.forbes.com/ sites/helenwang/2017/11/12/alibabas-singles-day-by-the-numbers-a-record-25-billion-haul/#4677e8b81db1 [Last accessed 24/4/2018].

6 GSMA Intelligence (2018) The Mobile Economy 2018, 26 February. Available from: https://www.gsmaintelligence.com/research/?file=061ad2d2417d6ed1ab0 02da0dbc9ce22&download [Last accessed 10/6/2018].

7 Dvorak, John (1984) The Mac meets the press, *San Francisco Examiner*, 2 February, quoted in Owen Linzmayer, *Apple Confidential 2.0*, p115. Available from: https://books.google.co.uk/books?id=mXnw5tM8QRwC&lpg =PA119&pg=PA119#v=onepage&q&f=false [Last accessed 24/4/2018].

8 Molen, Brad (2014) Amazon Fire phone review: a unique device, but you're better off waiting for the sequel, *Endgadget*, 22 June. Available from: https://www.engadget.com/2014/07/22/amazon-fire-phone-review/ [Last accessed 1/5/2018].

9 Limer, Eric (2014) Amazon Fire Phone review: a shaky first step, *Gizmodo*, 22 June. Available from: https://gizmodo.com/amazon-fire-phone-review-a-shaky-first-step-1608853105 [Last accessed 1/5/2018].

10 Wohlsen, Marcus (2015) The Amazon Fire Phone was always going to fail, *Wired*, 1 June. Available from: https://www.wired.com/2015/01/amazon-fire-phone-always-going-fail/ [Last accessed 1/5/2018].

11 Staff researcher (2017) 37 cart abandonment rate statistics, *Baymard Institute*, 9 January. Available from: https://baymard.com/lists/cart-abandonment-rate [Last accessed 1/5/2018].

12 Pathak, Shareen (2017) End of an era: Amazon's 1-click buying patent finally expires, *Digiday*, 13 September. Available from: https://digiday.com/market-ing/end-era-amazons-one click-buying-patent-finally-expires/ [Last accessed 1/5/2018].

13 Brooke, Eliza (2014) Amazon touts reduced shopping cart abandonment with newly expanded 'login and pay' service, *Fashionista*, 16 September. Available from: https://fashionista.com/2014/09/amazon-login-and-pay [Last accessed 1/5/2018].

14 Molla, Rani (2018) Amazon Prime has 100 million-plus Prime memberships – here's how HBO, Netflix and Tinder compare, *Recode*, 19 April. Available from: https://www.recode.net/2018/4/19/17257942/amazon-prime-100-million-subscribers-hulu-hbo-tinder-members [Last accessed 1/5/2018].

15 Rao, Leena (2017) Two years after launching, Amazon Dash shows promise, *Fortune*, 25 April. Available from: http://fortune.com/2017/04/25/amazon-dash-button-growth/ [Last accessed 1/5/2018].

16 Lipsman, Andrew (2017) 5 interesting facts About Millennials' mobile app usage from 'The 2017 U.S. Mobile App Report', *comScore*, Insights, 24 August. Available from: https://www.comscore.com/Insights/Blog/5-Interesting-Facts-About-Millennials-Mobile-App-Usage-from-The-2017-US-Mobile-App-Report [Last accessed 1/5/2018].

AI and voice: the new retail frontier

10

'With 30 per cent of search queries across all platforms predicted to be screenless by 2020, users will become more reliant on whatever Alexa deems best.'
Heather Pemberton Levy (2016)[1]

To recap what we've explored in regard to the pivotal role technology has had to play in Amazon and the wider retail industry's fortunes so far, we have seen how global technology drivers have helped to facilitate Amazon's growth, and how it would not have been possible for it to take advantage of these drivers were it not, first and foremost, a technology company. It is reliant on the fact the on-my-terms shopper has embraced the internet, touchscreens and mobile apps, among other technology innovations. We have also discussed how its technology capabilities then enabled it to apply its significant ability to innovate at the point of divergence in shopping between the functional and fun. These innovations include: AWS; Prime, Prime Now and Prime Day; its marketplace and merchant services; the 1-click patent; Pay with Amazon; and its Dash Buttons and Wand.

The technology drivers harnessed by Amazon have helped it develop the e-commerce shopping journey and introduce new shopping experiences, including one-hour delivery and automated replenishment. But we have purposefully left the most revolutionary of its innovations for last: that is, voice technology. Having also outlined the impact of the first two global technology drivers (ubiquitous connectivity and pervasive interfaces) on retail as an industry and Amazon's dominance within it, it is here, with voice, that the third driver – autonomous computing – comes into its own. In order to understand the significance of this third technology driver on

Amazon's fortunes, it is important to understand the distinction between technology systems that are programmed to 'automate' and digitize previously manually intensive and error-prone processes, and those technology systems whose programs enable them to solve problems without implicit direction, ie autonomously. These systems are also described as 'machines that learn', spawning the development of a branch of AI called 'machine learning'.

Autonomous computing development – moving beyond simple automation to eliminating the need for human intervention – would not have been possible without massively networked systems, such as the internet, plus having some means of accessing the information they store, such as desktop client PCs, as well as smartphones and tablets. The likes of cloud computing, also developed out of the drive towards ubiquitous connectivity and storage access, is also an essential building block of autonomous computing systems. Big Data, generated as the result of increasingly pervasive interfaces that encourage users to digitize more of their lives, from music and messages to memories, feeds these systems with varied and potentially unstructured data needed to derive insight from innumerable 'what if?'-type scenarios.

The most significant manifestation of the drive towards increasingly autonomous computing systems is AI. In turn, AI has made checkout-less stores, robotics, driverless cars, drones and voice assistants a reality, and we have only begun to tap its potential. Indeed, market research firm The Insight Partners has predicted that AI spending in retail will exceed US $27.2 billion by 2025, growing at 49.9 per cent CAGR from an estimated $712.6 million in 2016.[2] It is no accident, therefore, that AWS, the massive amounts of data Amazon already has on its customers, and its relentless pursuit of simplification in the name of innovation, has supported the company's dominance in the rapidly emerging area of AI and its application through voice systems.

The value of recommendation

Having identified AI as the culmination of the main drivers shaping technology innovation today (stemming from a need for more autonomous computer systems particularly) – and before diving straight into voice technology as its current apotheosis – it is necessary to undertake an examination of how Amazon capitalized on the development of AI systems across its business and not just in its customers' homes, as we have already done with the drivers of ubiquitous connectivity and pervasive interfaces. This examination adds to our understanding of how it has achieved its aim of removing friction from the average shopping journey and, in so doing, created a virtuous cycle that, in turn, generates even more sales and growth.

In fact, it is AI that underpins the power of its search and recommendation engines. Back in the 1990s, Amazon was one of the first e-commerce players to rely heavily on product recommendations, which also helped it to cross-sell new categories as it moved beyond books. It is a category of technology development that Bezos has described as 'the practical application of machine learning'. Amazon's search and recommendation machine learning capabilities also underpin its sophisticated supply chain proficiency, as well as its most recent voice shopping assistant functionality. In all of these applications, it can use the massive computing power of its AWS division to crunch billions of data points in support of testing a variety of options and outcomes to rapidly work out what will and won't cost-effectively work with customers. McKinsey estimates put the proportion of Amazon purchases driven by product recommendations at 35 per cent.[3] In 2016, it made its AI framework, DSSTNE (pronounced as 'destiny') free, to help expand the ways deep learning can extend beyond speech and language understanding and object recognition to areas such as search and recommendations. The decision to open source DSSTNE also demonstrates when Amazon recognizes the need to collaborate over making gains with the vast potential of AI.

On the Amazon site, these recommendations can be personalized, based on categories and ranges previously searched or browsed, to increase conversion. Equally, Amazon's recommendation engine can display products similar to those searched for or browsed in the hopes of converting customers to rival brands or products. There are also recommendations based on anything 'related to the items you've viewed'. Or they can depend on items that are 'frequently bought together' or by 'customers who bought this item also bought...' with the aim of boosting average order value. In these cases, 'if that, then this' AI-powered decision engines work in the background to match the items in your basket with other complementary products. For example, browsing for a gadget might prompt Amazon to recommend the right-sized cover for it, or a compatible peripheral accessory.

All of this sophisticated marketing is powered by AI-based machine learning algorithms that can match whoever is using the site dynamically with what they see. This can depend on myriad variables, such as the customer's purchase history and preferences, and what's in stock and what stock needs shifting quickly, in such a way as only AI-based systems are advanced enough to deliver in real time.

China's Alibaba Group uses AI-driven product recommendations for shoppers with no previous transaction data. According to Wei Hu, Alibaba Merchant Service Business Unit director of data technology, its engine can consider data points from other browsing and shopping data points to match new shoppers with relevant items. Return customers to the Group's Tmall and Taobao platforms are presented with product recommendations based not just on their past transactions, but also on browsing history, product feedback, bookmarks, geographic location and other online activity-related data. During the 2016 'Singles' Day' shopping festival, Alibaba said it used its AI recommendations engine to generate 6.7 billion personalized shopping pages based on merchants' target customer data. Alibaba said that this large-scale personalization resulted in a 20 per cent improvement in conversion rate from the 11 November event.[4]

Recommendations and personalization aside, Amazon's reliance on AI systems to orchestrate its vast business operations as well as its customer-facing ones is diverse. But, as far those that are the most significant in our exploration of best retail practice established by the company, we cannot discuss Amazon and AI without also touching on its supply chain and the launch of its Amazon Go store.

Supply chain complexity

Again, in order to understand the true significance of Amazon's AI advantage in its supply chain, it is necessary to first grasp what the industry-wide challenges are. Global research carried out in 2015 by analyst firm IHL Group found that, in order to cope with unpredictable peaks in demand, the cost to retail companies of overstocking in their supply chains was around US $471.9 billion, and of understocking, $630 billion.[5] By contrast, Amazon's AI algorithms enable it to predict demand for the hundreds of millions of products it sells, often as much as 18 months ahead. Even so, Ralf Herbrich, Amazon's director of machine learning, recently remarked that clothes are among the most difficult items to predict demand for.[6] The company must decide which sizes and colours to stock at which warehouses, depending on nearby buyers' shapes and tastes, as their demand is affected by shifting trends and changes in weather too.

It is easy, therefore, to see why Amazon has been pushing forward in this space for some time now – right to back when 'predictive analytics' defined the limits of early forays into AI. The 'anticipatory shipping' patent it filed in 2014 caused waves in the industry for signalling its intent to use AI in order to squeeze even more efficiency out of its supply chain by putting the stock closer to customers before customers even knew they would want to buy it. After all, it perhaps had more to lose than its competition, as it had been offering free, two-day delivery through Prime since its launch in 2005, all while constantly growing demand could have threatened to outstrip its supply chain and fulfilment capacity. According to the shipping patent, Amazon said it was looking to pick, pack and ship the products it expects customers in a specific area will want, before they are ordered – based on previous orders and other factors. The packages could wait at shipping hubs or on trucks until an order arrives. Even in 2014, Professor Praveen Kopalle could see the potential of such sophisticated analytics. 'If implemented well, this strategy has the potential to take predictive analytics to the next level, allowing the data-savvy company to greatly expand its base of loyal customers', she said.[7] Then, in late 2014, it quickly became clear why it had been pushing so hard in this area, when it raised the stakes in the race over the last mile of e-commerce fulfilment by launching one-hour Prime Now delivery in urban areas.

The rapid expansion of its Prime commitments has almost certainly been a catalyst for Amazon to bring the ubiquitous connectivity of its cloud services to bear on the development of increasingly autonomous, command-and-control operational fulfilment capabilities for many years. In this way, it has also entrusted robots in its warehouses and delivery drones with autonomous functionality to support growth. As previously discussed, in 2012, Amazon acquired Kiva Systems, the robotics company that had been supplying warehouse robots for Amazon to automate its order fulfilment processes, and which is now the backbone of the company's Robotics division. In 2015, *MIT Technology Review* noted some 2,000 of the orange Kiva robots that were helping humans keep shelves stocked during a tour of a New Jersey Amazon distribution and fulfilment centre.[8] Today, consensus estimates put its total robot fleet at over 100,000. This would mean its robotic fleet constitutes at least 20 per cent of the company's workforce, performing its roles with varying degrees of AI-enabled autonomy. Then, in 2016, Amazon started testing delivery drones in the UK and made its first package delivery using a semi-autonomous drone, with grand aspirations that 'One day, seeing Prime Air vehicles will be as normal as seeing mail trucks on the road.'[9] (We explore the impact of Prime Air in more detail in Chapter 14.)

Just Walk Out

While we also explore the significance of its checkout-less convenience store, Amazon Go, in other chapters, we must include it here as evidence of Amazon's technology-fuelled ambitions not just to embed itself in our homes, on the mobile devices that accompany us everywhere, or through its own supply chain and fulfilment operations, but that it also now has its sights set on conquering the physical retail space. If retailers felt under siege by the inexorable erosion of their store-based market share by e-commerce, then Amazon Go is tantamount to an existential threat to their core bricks and mortar businesses and the people who staff them.

Amazon's 'Just Walk Out' technology system detects which products customers take from or return to the shelves, keeping track of them in a virtual cart so that the customers are automatically charged for the items they leave the store with. Apart from its relevance here to Amazon's use of AI in pursuit of providing more frictionless retail experiences, it is also a great demonstration of how it has used the technology drivers of change to enable this experience, eliminating the function of the checkout process altogether.

Amazon Go capitalizes on technology drivers of change to serve the on-my-terms shopper:

1 *Ubiquitous connectivity*: view customer activity and attribute spend at every point in their shopping journey – online or offline.

   a. Customers are unable to even enter the Amazon Go store without first registering their personal and payment details with Amazon.

   b. Customers must identify themselves using the Amazon Go app on their mobile device to gain entry to the store, and which also helps to track their movements through the store.

2 *Pervasive interfaces*: remove any barriers to shopping, such as technical issues that may arise with scan-as-you-shop, self-service systems that rely on customers to use their own mobile phones or purpose-built handheld devices provided by the retailer, at that retailer's capital expense.

   a. The use of a mobile app is the most friction-free way to ensure a smooth Amazon Go experience when a customer enters the store.

   b. The removal of any human interface from the most friction-filled process of any store-based shopping journey, ie checkout, affords the customer unprecedented speed and simplicity.

3 *Autonomous computing*: AI-based computer vision, sensor fusion and deep learning technologies power Amazon Go's Just Walk Out technology.

   a. Just Walk Out technology operates without manual intervention, eliminating the need for checkout staff or hardware.

   b. It also eliminates shrinkage as a major source of loss for traditional brick and mortar retailers. Customers are charged with whatever goods they walk out with, even if they try to hide the fact from the store's extensive computer vision camera systems.

The untapped potential of voice

It's taken a while to get here. But now, within the context of Amazon's track record of capitalizing on technology drivers of change, it is clear to see quite how important a bet it has made on voice – especially when you consider that a consensus of industry estimates predicts a 40 per cent adoption rate of voice-enabled devices in the US and 30 per cent internationally by 2020. In fact, David Limp, Amazon Digital Devices SVP, predicted in 2017 that 'voice control in the home will be ubiquitous. Kids today will grow up never knowing a day they couldn't talk to their houses'.[10]

Amazon launched its first voice-enabled hardware device, Echo, featuring its AI-powered Alexa voice assistant in – surprise, surprise – 2015. Just as it did with AWS, 1-click, Prime, its mobile app, Pay with Amazon, Dash, drone delivery, robots and Amazon Go, Amazon is now attempting to define a new mode of pervasive computing interface using sophisticated AI systems that play completely to its strengths, feed its existing ecosystem and embed it further in the everyday functions of the home. OC&C Strategy Consultants predict purchases made through devices such as Google Home and Amazon's Echo will leap from US $2 billion in 2018 to $40 billion by 2022.[11] The aim of Amazon's Alexa voice assistant is not solely to increase Amazon.com sales per se, but to deepen the reliance on its ecosystem among the on-my-terms shoppers it has so far served so well, and suck them in further. This is why some have said that 'Amazon won by losing the smartphone war'.[12]

The argument follows that, if the Fire phone had been a success at launch in 2014, Amazon would have been bogged down in the complexity of updating mobile device hardware and its Fire mobile OS ever since. Perhaps Amazon's management realized it was never going to win the smartphone wars with Apple and Google, whose core businesses are founded on mobile software and hardware development, not retail. Either way, the initial launch of the Echo voice-enabled device, followed by the revamped and expanded line of Echo devices it unveiled at the end of 2017, demonstrate a real differentiator for Amazon as well as the culmination of its flywheel strategy, which is based on its three pillars that are, in turn, built on the three global drivers of technology development, and which facilitate more and more frictionless retailing experiences.

First-mover advantage

While the voice assistant device market is still in its early stages of development, Amazon has already consolidated its first-mover advantage, enabling its users to watch web videos (with Fire TV), turn on kitchen timers, listen to music, check the weather and, of course, shop on Amazon – all using just their voice. It also cut the cost of its premium Echo device to $100 from $180 at the end of 2017 – all with the aim of positioning its voice devices as so indispensable that it is able to embed itself ever more firmly into its customers' homes. It's also worth mentioning here that Black Friday and Prime Day have certainly helped Amazon sell more Echo devices. It also uses these artificial promotional events to offer exclusive discounts on orders placed through Alexa in order to get shoppers comfortable with the idea of voice-activated shopping.

Harking back to its Fire phone misstep, Bloomberg's Shira Ovide correctly observed at the time: 'Amazon is building a future untethered from the smartphone, but with all the software intelligence of that gadget and more – with the company at the centre. Amazon can embrace this future because it lost the recent past.'[13] Every Alexa-embedded device sale sucks that customer further into Amazon's flywheel ecosystem, as it is very hard not to interact with Amazon when using one, much in the same way as Google and Apple funnel their customers into their respective ecosystems and maximize lock-in by removing friction to ensure the seamless interoperability between their different proprietary products. 'The default option for buying stuff through the Amazon devices is Amazon', Ovide added.

Amazon's ecosystem play lies at the heart of its voice development, and so, perhaps unsurprisingly, it has emerged that shopping is not the main use case for Alexa in most households. In fact, it's the least popular use case for Alexa, as Clavis Insight discovered. The e-commerce analytics firm harvests over 10,000 search terms per day from Amazon US alone and also tracks the growth indicators in customers' use of Amazon's Alexa voice assistant to initiate these searches, as well as what other kinds of tasks people are asking Alexa to do.

> **Top Alexa-enabled commands**
>
> 1 Tasks and music.
>
> 2 Home automation.
>
> 3 Skills and shopping.
>
> compiled by Clavis Insight, 2016–2018.

These findings were supported by research carried out late 2017 by Amazon e-commerce analytics firm and Clavis partner, One Click Retail, which found 71 per cent year-on-year growth in sales of home automation devices via Amazon.com that are capable of connecting with Alexa. However, the top device sold via Amazon during that period to shoppers looking to connect to and control the likes of lighting, security and heating systems in their home via Alexa was its rival, Google's Nest heating thermostat controller. Amazon subsequently withdrew Nest devices for sale from its site in March 2018, clearly demonstrating how ruthless it is in not being afraid to kill the competition.

Voice as the next frontier

The main question on every retailer and brand owner's lips is whether voice will add to or cannibalize sales made in other channels. One Click Retail found that only 32 per cent of Alexa owners have ever used their voice assistant to purchase a product once, much less to make repeat purchases. In fact, it discovered that the numbers using Alexa to buy products drops off dramatically after the first purchase, ie customers are not using it for repeat purchases. But again, that might not worry Amazon as much as individual brand owners and retailers if every sale, regardless of what is purchased, goes through Amazon.com.

In fact, a study conducted by Alpine.AI, in partnership with InfoScout, revealed that while the average Amazon customer made about 19 purchases over the course of the year, Echo owners bought items nearly 27 times, showing that the device encourages shoppers to make additional impulse buys. Of those shoppers who are using Alexa for repeat purchases, the categories most likely to win with voice emerged as those in brand-heavy categories that must be replaced more frequently such as pet food and treats, baking and cooking items, shaving and grooming supplies, and oral hygiene items. The products bought most often were from the health and beauty category, which were purchased 53 per cent more often over the 12-month timeframe.[14]

The other question worrying retailers and brands with voice is how it will affect the discoverability of their products when the billions spent on marketing and advertising are not transferable to the voice platform. This is why Alexa will only return two results to a search query, as opposed to the pages of results returned when using mobile or desktop Amazon search (along with the ads, recommendations and various other marketing tools that subsume the shopping experience). Based on a consensus of research to date, there are a number of factors that determine which of those two results are returned via voice (Source: One Click Retail):

1 Purchase history – Alexa will offer to reorder exactly the same item if purchased before.

2 If there is no prior purchase history for Alexa to revert to, it will then offer an 'Amazon Choice' – a dynamic tag assigned to certain items based on a number of factors introduced with the launch of its first Echo device. These include that the product has to be available via Prime, and so will be shipped via its Fulfilment by Amazon service (from Amazon itself or an Amazon seller); it has to be in stock and replenishable; and it has to have a review rating of 4.0 or higher.

3 In the absence of prior purchase history or an Amazon Choice, Alexa will return the same top two organic search results that Amazon's search would serve on via mobile or desktop PC.

This means that, to win with Alexa for shopping, the fundamentals of search – keywords, title and product feature bullets and description – still apply. Put another way, it is the same content and attributes used to describe a product that drives both higher click through, and then sales conversion rates, from both traditional and voice search results that will determine how high up the search ranking that product appears.

Companies have also rushed to develop so-called Alexa 'skills' to integrate with their offerings, not unlike the rush to develop mobile apps for Apple and Android app stores in the early days of consumer smartphone adoption. In fact, online grocers like Ocado and Peapod were among the first to integrate Alexa globally, overlooking the fact that AmazonFresh is a growing threat to their business. Voice is a natural next step for grocery e-commerce. For example, in 2017, Peapod developed an 'Ask Peapod' skill for Alexa that allows consumers to voice order items, which are then added to the shoppers' weekly grocery carts.[15] As we have already said, Peapod is by no means the first company to tap into the ordering capabilities of

Alexa – beer lovers, for example, can order Miller Lite in some circumstances on Alexa by saying, 'Alexa, start Miller Time'. But Peapod sees its skills investment as worthwhile because it enables consumers to immediately add an item to their grocery list, putting the online grocer or its parent company Ahold Delhaize in the best position to fill the order. Otherwise, the shopper may decide later to purchase it elsewhere, or forget to add the item to their online basket altogether.

Similarly, in 2018, Google introduced a rival programme called Shopping Actions, offering a universal shopping cart for shopping on mobile, PC or via a voice-enabled device. Major retailers, including Walmart, Target, Ulta Beauty, Costco and Home Depot, have signed up to the programme to list products across Google Search, in its Google Express shopping service, and in the Google Assistant app for smartphones and on smart speakers like the Google Home.[16]

For Millennials and other shoppers increasingly turning to the web to buy their groceries, Peapod says its Ask Peapod function is a great way to attract customers who may use the technology as their preferred way of ordering many of their groceries. With Amazon making bigger inroads in the grocery space – highlighted by its recent acquisition of Whole Foods and competitors like Instacart (which was still a grocery delivery partner of Whole Foods at the time of writing, in spite of rival Amazon's acquisition) – rapidly expanding operators like Peapod are likely under so much competitive pressure that they can ill afford not to participate in the different methods used by consumers to stock their fridges and cupboards, regardless of how often or little customers may use voice ordering. Ocado was the first UK grocer to embrace it, demonstrating the power of voice to drive 'co-opetition' and the importance of capitalizing on voice as quickly as possible for online-only grocers. Feeding further into Amazon's flywheel ecosystem, Alexa is just the latest technology-based competitive tool that forces rivals such as Peapod to build on it in order to fulfil the need to remain relevant against a competitor that is helping to drive unprecedented, technology-fuelled change in the retail space.

'You do not survive in this industry without being a little paranoid and looking over your shoulder', Carrie Bienkowski, Peapod's chief marketing officer, said in an interview just before the launch of its Ask Peapod skill. 'Ten years ago, just getting your groceries delivered – that was convenient. But one of the things we're really internalizing is the fact that we've got to continue to evolve beyond just the delivery of groceries.'

While Peapod could be applauded for embracing 'co-opetition' and developing for Alexa, it is likely that the real winner as a result of its efforts is not the consumer, but Amazon. As Danny Silverman, Clavis Insight chief marketing officer, points out, 'The reality is that, out of some 30,000 skills that are now available, only a tiny percentage are actually being downloaded and even less are being used more than once.'[17] This explains why Amazon has invested to build out its Alexa hardware beyond just facilitating online shopping, adding calling facilities and even, most recently, a screen (which may seem to run counter to the idea of increasingly pervasive computing interfaces that 'disappear' into the background). The extension of the Home Skills API in 2018 to control more smart devices, from ovens to TVs, adds to the 800-plus skills and more than 1,000 devices that Alexa can control in the home today.

Spencer Millerberg, One Click Retail managing partner, therefore advises that deciding how much investment to put into Alexa voice search is 'all about prioritization. 'If you're the CEO of a music business, then absolutely, this has got to be one of your first [strategic development] priorities. If you're the CEO of a consumer brand, it's going to end up becoming a little bit less [of a priority], because shopping is not a top Alexa use case; whereas if you're in home automation, maybe it's the middle ground you have to work in. The main thing we have to focus on is the fundamentals.'[18]

Silverman adds: 'At the end of the day, [the fundamentals are that] the same things that drive voice search are what drive search on desktop and mobile. If you have the data and insights to understand what's working or not [as regards search rankings on Amazon.com], and you optimize against those for desktop and mobile, you will win with voice at the same time.'

So, while it's hard to chart the evolution of frictionless retail against the drivers in technology development that have enabled it without including Amazon on the map, it is also impossible to envisage its growing influence on this evolution abating.

Retail technology smarts

But where does this journey of innovation towards truly frictionless retail experiences leave the rest of retail? Indeed, with the retail market reeling from the latest round of profit warnings and administrations in the sector, many retailers will be looking towards digital technology differentiation to ride out challenging times and futureproof their businesses. Uwe Weiss, Blue Yonder chief executive, argued that the 'Amazon Effect' – in the sense of ongoing disruption and evolution of the retail market caused by the consumerization of technology and the on-my-terms shopper – will now increase its influence as retailers fight to retain market share and customer loyalty. When it comes to its impact on brands, for example, the industry is anxiously waiting to see if voice has a tangible impact on brand loyalty and marketing strategies – particularly if voice systems remain ad-free. The need for sophisticated content and attribute-led management to top search rankings could require some drastic reorganization in some companies.[19]

Weiss pointed out that, with Amazon already using AI to deliver personalized shopping recommendations and optimize their supply chains, traditional retailers must be all the more aggressive in their adoption of next-generation technologies if they are to retain market share. 'With the likes of more traditional retailers facing closures, innovation needs to be in the spotlight more than ever', he said. He rightly highlighted that the field of AI is developing incredibly quickly. Amazon's recommendation system runs on a totally machine learning-based architecture, so its suggestions on what to buy, watch or read next are 'incredibly smart', and Google's DeepMind division is now giving its AI algorithms an 'imagination' so that it can predict how a certain situation will evolve and make decisions. 'This leads to more conversions and upselling across the business, as well as giving Amazon insight on how to price its products for its customers, and how much stock to hold', he added.

Rightly so, though Weiss warned against using technology for technology's sake, especially in areas where Amazon's advantage of being a technology company first is insurmountable. While it is clear that the potential of AI to boost levels of productivity, efficiency and personalization in the retail industry is promising, he advised retailers to also be realistic about what they can expect from AI and machine learning. 'AI in retail doesn't predict the future – at least not yet!' he stressed. 'It analyses reams and reams of intricate behavioural and circumstantial data to identify patterns and trends. These trends enable retailers to make informed decisions that result in more accurate stock levels, and pricing that better suits product lifecycles.'

Weiss also rightly pointed out that, if traditional retailers, particularly in the grocery sector, are to survive and compete with online giants such as Amazon, they will need to radically adjust their approach to technology and data. 'Retailers need to begin thinking of data as one of their most important assets, and as the key that can enable them to build better relationships with their customers, optimize their supply chain and pricing, and compete against online competitors', he concluded. For example, research has shown that over half of all Amazon Echoes are located in the kitchen, meaning the opportunity for greater category-specific engagement around recipe preparation and ad hoc basket building for household goods and grocery could initially be higher for operators with relevant businesses and brands. Voice expands on the 'in the moment' shopping trend and may even become the gatekeeper to the shopper, particularly for grocery retailers and FMCG brands from a retail volume point of view.

It's perhaps not surprising that those grocers that still don't want to join Amazon have formed an 'anti-Amazon' alliance with Google over its voice assistant, and the internet giant has been more than happy to oblige. Unsurprisingly, Walmart, Tesco and Carrefour have signed up to develop capabilities for their customers to order goods online using Google Assistant via its Google Express shopping service. Carrefour, for example, announced in 2018 that it was partnering with Google to create an online voice assistant called 'Lea' as part of the French retailer's five-year, $3.5 billion digital transformation plans. 'Lea has been designed to make day-to-day life easier for our customers – they can use it to manage their shopping lists... using just their voice', the French retail giant stated at the time.

Competitive landscape

Google is currently the only viable alternative voice platform to Alexa for shopping. Even so, Google trails a distant second to Amazon, with Echo accounting for over 70 per cent of sales during 2017 in the smart speaker category. But the Google Assistant itself can claim far higher penetration levels, and Google has said it is now accessible on more than 400 million devices including home appliances from LG, headphones from Bose and a range of speakers from 15 different companies, as well as all devices running its Android OS. But the supporting Google Express shopping platform is relatively small in scale, scope and fulfilment speed in comparison to Amazon's Marketplace, Fulfilment by Amazon and Prime Now services.

Other players are also entering the fray. In 2018, Starbucks entered a joint partnership with Shinsegae Group in South Korea to integrate voice recognition ordering with Bixby, Samsung's voice assistant, which is available on select Samsung Galaxy devices. These features are an extension of Starbucks' mobile order-ahead-and-pay technology. Apple's Home Pod device, which was launched early in 2018 and features its voice assistant Siri, has met with lukewarm reviews. While it offers voice-activated smart home and audio-visual control and device integration, as well as news, weather, calendar and mapping functionality, where you can ask it, 'what's the best vegetarian food nearby?' for example, Apple hasn't yet forged the partnerships or ecosystem required for consumers to do any shopping with it.

Whether consumers come to trust Alexa and its counterparts to delegate shopping tasks, however, is another matter entirely, given the nature of their operation means some are by design always on and listening, while others require a separate physical interaction with the device before listening for a voice prompt – think Apple and the long home-button press to activate Siri on an iOS device. Instead, a number of reports have suggested that Alexa can mishear words in conversation or even on the TV that it thinks are a cue to leap into action. Such accidental activation has led to reports of Alexa uttering random creepy laughter, or even thinking it had been prompted to record a man and his wife's conversation and then send the recording to one of his employees.[20]

The other unknown is how the use of voice may play out in the store, which we explore in greater depth in the next chapter. Meanwhile, Amazon struck a deal with BMW to integrate Alexa in its cars starting in mid-2018 and already has a similar partnership with Toyota. Even satellite navigation manufacturers are getting in on the act, like Garmin, whose Speak Plus is a 1.5-inch dashboard camera that also comes with Alexa integration. Users will be able to use voice commands to get directions, play music, make phone calls, control smart devices in their Connected Car, and place orders for products and services, like takeaway delivery or collection. But here, Amazon must compete with car manufacturers' own voice prompt systems, as well as the significant traction that Apple has gained with its CarPlay system to connect Apple's iOS devices to a car for navigation, music and voice prompt-based integration.

If we have learned anything from our study of Amazon's pivotal role in the development of AI and voice in the pursuit of a more frictionless retail experience, it is that AI holds the ability to improve return on investment both instore and online, by simplifying shopping journeys, improving inventory accuracy and optimizing the supply chain in order to support growth. It is the culmination of development of the technology drivers of change with the use of data generated by the digital shopping tools that technology innovation and development has enabled. The reason AI has become so important in this way is because the likes of Amazon are using it to provide greater convenience, immediacy, transparency and relevancy for today's on-my-terms shopper, who is seeking to make the functional expedient and the bring the fun parts of shopping to the fore. It is clear that retailers should see technology, specifically AI and digital tools and data, as critical in helping them keep pace with online disruptors in the race to adapt to today's

Table 10.1 Amazon technology hardware launches, 2011–2018

Amazon device	Launch date	Price at launch	Functionality
Kindle Fire	November 2011	$199	Tablet computer
Fire TV	April 2014	$70	Smart TV streaming media device
Fire Phone	July 2014	$199	Smartphone
Dash Button	March 2015	£4.99 (redeemable against first purchase)	One click, auto-replenishment device
Echo	June 2015	$100	Smart speaker and voice assistant
Echo Dot	March 2016	$50	Mini version of smart speaker and voice assistant
Amazon Tap	June 2016	$80	Smart, battery-powered speaker and voice assistant
Echo Look	April 2017	$120	Smart speaker, voice assistant and handsfree camera
Echo Show	June 2017	$230	Smart speaker and screen, voice assistant and videoconferencing system
Dash Wand	June 2017	$20	Battery-powered, voice assistant-enabled grocery scanner
Cloud Cam	September 2017	$120	Home security camera
Blink	September 2017	$100	Smart home security camera and door bell
Echo Plus	September 2017	$150	Smart speaker, voice assistant, and connected home device hub
Echo Spot	December 2017	$130	Smart speaker, voice assistant and digital alarm clock
Echo Connect	December 2017	$35	Telephony connector to Echo devices
Echo Buttons	December 2017	$20	Gaming control extensions to Echo devices
Amazon Fire Cube	June 2018	$119	Voice assistant-enabled 4K TV streaming set-top-box

digitally enabled consumer expectations. In the meantime, it should now be easy to understand why Amazon has, so far, shown them the way.

Notes

1 Pemberton Levy, Heather (2016) Gartner predicts a virtual world of exponential change, *Gartner*, 18 October Available from: https://www.gartner.com/smarter-withgartner/gartner-predicts-a-virtual-world-of-exponential-change/ [Last accessed 27/6/2018].

2 Staff researchers (2018) Artificial intelligence in retail market 2025 – global analysis and forecasts by deployment type, retail type, technology and application [Report] *The Insight Partners*, February 2018, Available from: http://www.theinsightpartners.com/reports/artificial-intelligence-in-retail-market [Last accessed 1/5/2018].

3 Mackenzie, Ian, Meyer, Chris and Noble, Steve (2013) How retailers can keep up with consumers, *McKinsey & Company*, October. Available from: https://www.mckinsey.com/industries/retail/our-insights/how-retailers-can-keep-up-with-consumers [Last accessed 9/7/2018].

4 Erickson, Jim and Wang, Susan (2017) At Alibaba, artificial intelligence is changing how people shop online, *Alizila*, 5 June. Available from: https://www.alizila.com/at-alibaba-artificial-intelligence-is-changing-how-people-shop-online/ [Last accessed 9/7/2018].

5 Buzek, Greg (2015) REPORT: Retailers and the ghost economy: $1.75 trillion reasons to be afraid, *IHL Group*, 30 June. Available from: http://engage.dynamicaction.com/WS-2015-05-IHL-Retailers-Ghost-Economy-AR_LP.html [Last accessed 1/5/2018].

6 Staff writer (2018) In algorithms we trust: how AI is spreading throughout the supply chain, *Economist* Special Report, 31 March. Available from: https://www.economist.com/news/special-report/21739428-ai-making-companies-swifter-cleverer-and-leaner-how-ai-spreading-throughout [Last accessed 1/5/2018].

7 Kopalle, Praveen Prof (2014) Why Amazon's anticipatory shipping is pure genius, *Forbes*, 28 January. Available from: https://www.forbes.com/sites/onmarketing/2014/01/28/why-amazons-anticipatory-shipping-is-pure-genius/#4011e6ba4605 [Last accessed 1/5/2018].

8 Knight, Will (2015) Intelligent machines: inside Amazon, *MIT Technology Review*, 23 July. Available from: https://www.technologyreview.com/s/539511/inside-amazon/ [Last accessed 1/5/2018].

9 Amazon (2018) Amazon Prime Air, *Amazon.com*. Available from:
   https://www.amazon.com/Amazon-Prime-Air/b?ie=UTF8&node=8037720011
   [Last accessed 1/5/2018].

10 Harris, Mark (2017) Amazon's latest Alexa devices ready to extend company's
   reach into your home, *Guardian*, 27 September. Available from:
   https://www.theguardian.com/technology/2017/sep/27/amazon-alexa-echo-
   plus-launch [Last accessed 12/11/2018]!]

11 OC&C News (2018) Alexa, I need … everything. Voice shopping sales could
   reach $40 billion by 2022, *occstrategy*, 28 February. Available from:
   https://www.occstrategy.com/en-us/news-and-media/2018/02/voice-shopping-
   sales-could-reach-40-billion-by-2022 [Last accessed 10/6/2018].

12 Ovide, Shira (2018) Amazon won by losing the smartphone war, *Bloomberg*,
   28 September. Available from: https://www.bloomberg.com/gadfly/
   articles/2017-09-28/amazon-leaped-ahead-on-gadgets-by-losing-the-
   smartphone-war [Last accessed 1/5/2018].

13 ibid.

14 Marchick, Adam (2018) Strong signals that the Amazon Echo is changing
   purchase behaviour, 30 May. Available from: https://alpine.ai/amazon-echo-
   changing-purchase-behavior/ [Last accessed 24/6/2018].

15 Peapod (2017) Ask Peapod Alexa Skill, *Amazon.com*, 25 June. Available from:
   https://www.amazon.com/Peapod-LLC-Ask/dp/B072N8GFZ3
   [Last accessed 1/5/2018].

16 Blog (2018) Help shoppers take action, wherever and however they choose
   to shop, *Google Inside Adwords*, 19 March. Available from: https://adwords.
   googleblog.com/2018/03/shopping-actions.html [Last accessed 24/6/2018].

17 Clavis Insight (2018) One Click Retail: the double click episode
   (video podcast), 15 March. Available from: https://www.youtube.com/
   watch?v=218LelVkGDQ&t=11s [Last accessed 13/9/2018].

18 ibid.

19 Blue Yonder (2018) Media alert: 'Amazon effect' will grow as retail
   challenges increase, say Blue Yonder, 16 April. Available from:
   https://www.blueyonder.ai/sites/default/files/media-alert-amazon-effect-will-
   grow-as-retail-challenges-increase.pdf [Last accessed 11/9/2018].

20 Chokshi, Niraj (2018) Is Alexa listening? Amazon Echo sent out recording of
   couple's conversation, *New York Times*, 25 May. Available from:
   https://www.nytimes.com/2018/05/25/business/amazon-alexa-conversation-
   shared-echo.html [Last accessed 10/6/2018].

Store of the future: how digital automation will enrich the customer experience

11

> 'It's data with heart. We're taking the data we have and we're creating physical places with it.'
> **Jennifer Cast, vice president of Amazon Books, 2015[1]**

We've seen how Amazon's technology innovation and first-mover advantage have given it the edge online with the development of its e-commerce services and functionality, as well as in the home, through its various hardware devices and Alexa voice assistant. Here, Amazon has used digital shopping tools applied with AI-based capabilities to remove the friction from online shopping and personalize the experience with tailored recommendations. So much so, that the ease with which Amazon can enable shopping online and delivery right to you for free the next day, or within two hours with Prime Now, has fuelled constant debate over its role in the impending death of the store. We've already declared our view that physical retail is far from in terminal decline, and the majority of sales are still being completed in stores.

We would, however, contend that over two decades on from Amazon's Day 1, chain retailers have as much to learn from the way Amazon is bringing its digital automation and innovation skills to bear to bricks and mortar retailing as Amazon has to gain by mastering the physical sales territory that traditional chain retail has dominated for over 40 years. We will argue that the lessons Amazon still has to learn about retail are based on the very advantages of the physical store it has tried to overcome online: the ability to touch, feel and try; the instant gratification of being able to walk out with purchases immediately; and the chance of human interaction delivered by competent customer service specialists and knowledge experts. These physical advantages are precisely why so many sales are still fulfilled instore, even if ordered online, and it is the major reason why Amazon has had to make the inevitable move offline with its bookstores, Whole Foods purchase, Amazon Go and Amazon 4-Star, if it is to sustain anything near its current levels of growth into future. The impact of blended online-to-offline services also features heavily in our examination of Amazon's fulfilment strategy in Chapter 13. But for the purposes of our look at how the store of the future may develop, its operators could certainly learn a thing or two from Amazon and its e-commerce counterparts about making the physical shopping experience a more attractive one that is not fraught with crowds, queues or empty shelves.

Ironically, Amazon's move into bricks and mortar also reveals the skills it so desperately needs that are prized by physical retailers: marketing and merchandising a brand or multiple brands within a finite space and the art of curation through seasonal and sale events, as opposed to the 'endless aisle' search results associated with the Amazon.com shopping experience; the buying, planning and forecasting required to maximize product and staff availability while minimizing inventory exposure and customer throughput time; and the ability to surprise and delight through the overall experience instore. It is these inherent physical store advantages, applied with skill, that retailers need to channel and develop to compete with Amazon, and which can all be blended, enhanced or augmented by digital automation.

As we shift our focus into the store, we see both how Amazon is taking a lead in bringing digital automation and innovation to bear on common tangible retail friction points, such as product selection and checkout, and how its competitors are exploiting their bricks and mortar presence through technology deployments that can also enrich the customer experience to overcome the Amazon effect. In this context, we will look at how Amazon has influenced the search, browse and discovery stages of the typical shopping journey and, in this way, where other retailers can use similar blended digital tools in their stores to learn from and capitalize on both Amazon's e-commerce and burgeoning physical retail impact.

Research online, buy offline

We need to take a step back to understand why the traditional store, with its purely transactional focus, is under threat. Many consumers in the first wave of e-commerce development discovered the internet and online shopping via PCs and laptops with the effect that e-commerce sales have grown and eaten into traditional stores and their footfall. A 2017 US survey[2] found consumers split into three groups: those who prefer to shop online (32.5 per cent), those who prefer instore (29.70 per cent), and a combination of both (37.8 per cent). Over half (52 per cent) said their main reason for shopping online was convenience and the ability to price compare, as well as a wider choice of merchandise, free delivery and returns, and access to more detailed product information and customer reviews. But they don't like the fact they can't interact with the merchandise to assess size and fit or quality and freshness, and that they have to wait for delivery, which may be missed or unsuccessful.

All over the world, though, the current and next waves of consumers are discovering e-commerce via mobile first, where there are no physical boundaries to where you can shop online. When you add social media, mobile payments and apps into the equation, retailers have had to develop – some say transform – their digital presence in order to compete. They have certainly been sure to capitalize online by launching their own e-commerce channels. Some have even begun to join these up with online-to-offline services, such as click & collect. But this is why mobile apps and other mobile-enabled areas of digital automation also have a central role to play in the store of future, for their ability to bring the speed, convenience, transparency and relevance associated with the online shopping journey in customers' hands directly into the store.

Yet again, though, when it comes to mobile, Amazon has a head start; nearly half of all Millennials have their Amazon app accessible on their home screen, according to a 2017 survey conducted by a US media analytics company.[3] Further research conducted among consumers in the US, UK, France and Germany in 2017 found:

- 72 per cent use Amazon to find information on products before making a purchase; and,
- 26 per cent will check prices and information on Amazon if they are about to buy something in a store.[4]

Amazon's online dominance in the markets where it operates will continue to exert heavy influence on the online research phase of any shopping journey, regardless of where the shopper's search takes place, as well as potentially stealing that sale from a physical rival. However, thinking about the two-thirds of shoppers who like to shop exclusively instore or in combination with online, the popularity of ROBO – research online, buy offline – or 'webrooming' as it is also known, favours the physical retailer. Nearly half (45 per cent) of consumers that bought a product instore in 2018 said they had first researched it online. The same survey, conducted by Bazaarvoice, revealed the product categories most impacted by ROBO were appliances (59 per cent), health, beauty and fitness (58 per cent), and toys and games (53 per cent). These were followed closely by electronics (41 per cent) and baby merchandise (36 per cent).[5] So, it could be said that a retailer may lose as many sales online to Amazon in the search phase as it may win instore via the ROBO trend.

'webrooming'
noun, informal
Definition: When shoppers research items online so they can check out and compare lots of options, but then head to a physical store to complete their purchase, leading it to also become known through the practice of researching online to buy offline (ROBO). Often, consumers will use this method when they want to see exactly what the product looks like in real life before they make the final purchase.

With ROBO, the retailer must win during the search phase of the shopping trip, by beating Amazon on either price, product range and information or location – the first of which we already know, given the online giant's dominance, is far easier said than done. Playing to the ROBO trend, Amazon established an early advantage when it came to price in 2010 with the introduction of its Price Checker barcode scanning app. It even offered a one-off 5 per cent discount (up to $5) on each of three items for a total of $15 off purchases for one day at the end of 2011 to encourage shoppers to use the app. It also asks customers to report advertised instore price and location information back to Amazon to ensure it is offering the most competitive deals.

Amazon's early-mover advantage in recognizing the power of customer ratings and reviews to enhance available product information has also informed the company's move offline. According to the Bazaarvoice study, 45 per cent of bricks and mortar shoppers read customer reviews online before purchasing products, marking a 15 per cent year-on-year increase through to 2018. Being a forerunner in its pre-eminent use of customer product and marketplace seller reviews as a determining factor in how high a product appears in its search rankings, Amazon has an obvious advantage over retailers with less well-developed equivalent e-commerce features. But a retailer can still exploit online reviews to their own advantage. One e-commerce systems provider has suggested that 50 or more reviews per product can generate a 4.6 per cent increase in online conversion rates, while a customer is 58 per cent more likely to convert after interacting with a review.[6]

It's easy to see understand why, then, Amazon put its customers' ratings and reviews front and centre of its first foray into physical retail with the 2015 debut of Amazon Books in its home town of Seattle. As we touched on in Chapter 5, each title is accompanied by a label, or 'shelf talker' in bookseller parlance, that features an Amazon.com customer review and its star rating, alongside a barcode. The absence of shelf-edge pricing forces customers to scan the code via Amazon's app to access the price and other information, or store associates equipped with handheld devices can scan items for you.

Having been accused of killing off the traditional bookstore, however, some in the industry were quick to point out that Amazon's move into their territory betrayed a lack of experience in physical retail spaces. The store was criticized for shelving positioned too close together, with an illogical configuration that paid no mind to arranging titles in alphabetical order, and rival booksellers questioned how it could only stock a very limited selection of 5–6,000 titles displayed in the most wasteful way as regards space, facing cover out and not spine out.[7] In addition, the first store was not a location to pick up Amazon orders, and Amazon Books also didn't offer preferential pricing for Prime customers until it had opened its third store at the end of 2016. Some described the debut location as a 'store without walls', for the fact that customers can browse endless online aisles in the store and place orders to have them delivered. Others called it a 'marketing expense',[8] in the same way as Apple focuses the role of its stores on showcasing its hardware – Amazon Books also sells its Kindle reader and Echo smart speaker ranges among other Amazon devices – but, in comparison to Apple's expansive and glass-lined 'Town Square' stores, commentators also highlighted the first Amazon Books store's relatively utilitarian look and feel.

Further supporting the view of Amazon Books as having more value as a marketing showcase for Amazon than a book store, when it broke out its physical store sales for the first time towards the end of 2017, it emerged that its relatively small store estate generated almost no revenue.[9] In its wider marketing context it is easy to see how Amazon Books' objective was not necessarily to make money, but to test how it could transfer the best of its online experience offline and start building out physical spokes on its flywheel. Here we see how mobile is key to this, unlocking the wider Amazon range for customers in the store, at the same time as getting registered Amazon and Prime app users to associate their online preferences and purchase history with their physical store visit, giving Amazon visibility across its customers' entire shopping journey so it can accurately measure attribution, across both online and the store.

This instore, mobile-enabled view of the customer, which we will come to understand as a major enabler of Amazon's customer-centric proposition, is in fact the real Amazon Books differentiator – not the books or the Amazon gadgets. Just as it allows Amazon to match a customer identified instore by their purchase history and preferences to the offers and recommendations it gives them online, so it can refine its physical offer according to how customers actually shop the store, as well as what it can offer each individual store customer in terms of pricing, product information and promotions. Amazon's aim has been to create a physical retail environment where customers readily identify themselves, so it can iteratively use the data they then share to personalize their experience and tailor it, so it complements whatever stage they're at during their shopping journey. By pushing pricing and other such information to an app that lives on a customer's own personal device, Amazon can potentially personalize every offer, recommendation and price to each customer in real time, whether they are in an Amazon or a rival store, to optimize conversion and every transaction.

Location as a proxy for relevance

Even though ratings and reviews had been the preserve of the e-commerce pureplay to inform the research phase of the shopping trip, we can see how Amazon has transposed them via mobile into its Amazon Books store environment to personalize and so enhance the customer experience. But it has also used the data its customers generate from their shopping activities online to inform every aspect of these stores – from ranging and merchandising, to pricing and promotions – so it can then tie the offline results back to its online execution and vice versa in what should become a virtuous loop of constant refinement and improvement.

Bear in mind that under the influence of digital, marketers now view the research phase of the shopping journey as a 'zero moment of truth' (or ZMOT, a term coined by Google in 2011).[10] By virtue of the fact that shoppers can look for products anonymously online, just as they can do instore, it should come as no surprise to see Amazon exporting such features, which can positively influence this ZMOT by promoting conversion, offline. When it comes to exploiting the store's physical advantage at the ZMOT – to potentially aid a ROBO sale for example – location-based or 'near me' search is a powerful tool at the bricks and mortar retailer's disposal that capitalizes on the store's physical advantage of being able to provide instant gratification (if the sought-after product is in stock). This is because, in the days before Amazon even existed, location has always been a powerful proxy for relevance and why, therefore, the world's largest retailers have such extensive and, in some cases, densely located store networks.

As Google itself has suggested, 'near me' search is no longer just about location; it is about connecting people to things in a timely manner as much as it is about finding a place in and of itself. In 2017 the search giant called out the fact that 'near me' searches containing variants of 'can I buy?' or 'to buy' terms had grown by 500 per cent within two years.[11] This is because shoppers will often use searches to find answers to an immediate need. But when it comes to immediacy, the store will trump online nearly every time – especially if the retailer also offers the opportunity to 'save the sale' on out of stocks by making store inventory available to order online. This is another reason why customers expect to see the same range and have an equivalent experience instore as is on offer online – the digital experience enables it, so why doesn't the retailer?

It is also why the digital presence of a physical store must not neglect basic search engine optimization (SEO) requirements to ensure it and its inventory can be found. Other Google features, such as its patented Knowledge Panel feature that appears to the right of its search results, are designed to help discover brands or locate businesses; and, like Amazon, its paid search and Shopping and Express platforms can make a bricks and/or clicks business discoverable in the moment, where Amazon's two-hour delivery range does not yet stretch. We explore how Google is further capitalizing on its 'What Amazon Can't Do' (WACD) advantages through fulfilment in Chapter 13.

Ramping up this pressure on Amazon and other retailers whose businesses are online first or online only, in 2018 Google introduced shoppers to the power of local store inventory search with a new tool called See What's In Store (SWIS). Shoppers can search for a specific product and discover which local stores have that item in stock, or search a single store's entire inventory when using Google's main search bar or Google Maps. Selecting the closest store location will generate a second search bar in the Google Knowledge Panel where shoppers can search that store's inventory, a feature that Google currently offers for free. Shoppers can also type the name of a specific product into the Google search bar, and the results will show which local stores have that item in stock. However, stores must pay to show up in these Local Inventory Ads results.

> 'E-commerce wins a lot because people don't know where to find stuff. That's a major disadvantage local stores have to Amazon. If you knew something was available one block away, or that you could pick it up in a local store without having to wait for shipping, you might not choose to order it online.'
> **Mark Cummins, CEO of Pointy, a Dublin-based tech firm partnering with Google to power SWIS**[12]

Amazon may not yet have an extensive store network to match the physical network of its global grocery and general merchandise rivals, but in spite of Google's efforts to level the playing field with features like Local Inventory Ads and SWIS, Amazon is still dominant when it comes to product search. As previously stated, nearly half (49 per cent) of consumers turn to Amazon first when searching for products online, with search engines taking 36 per cent and retailers coming in third, at 15 per cent. When asked why, though, price was not the stand-out reason (Figure 11.1), suggesting again that there are more ways to compete with Amazon in the ROBO wars.[13]

When it comes to winning the ZMOT, we cannot think about the research phase of the journey without considering the advent of visual search. Technology provider Slyce delivers visual search engine image recognition for numerous retailers including Home Depot, Macy's and Tommy Hilfiger in the US and UK, for example. The company says the quality of its image recognition is superior to the likes of Amazon and Google as it builds classifiers and detectors, which are the initial level of recognition. Machine learning is employed to train the software to recognize user-generated photographs of variable quality. It claims retailers see average order values increase by 20 per cent and conversion rates are 60 per cent higher when integrating the technology with their own e-commerce website or mobile app searches.

Figure 11.1 The top reasons why US consumers begin their product searches on Amazon[14]

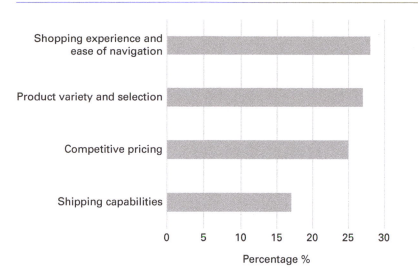

Here, Amazon had a head start back in 2009 when it used its image recognition and machine learning AI capabilities to launch a visual search solution in its app, Amazon Remembers, aimed at scanning the barcodes of books, debuting it in-app as an additional camera search feature called Flow in 2014. It then integrated it as an app called Firefly with its ill-fated Fire phone later that year before also introducing it to its Kindle Fire HD device, and expanding the visual capabilities of the Amazon app to recognize almost any item in 2016.[15] This visual search app functionality has continued to grow thanks to a 2017 partnership with Samsung to embed the functionality into one of the handset maker's flagship smartphone models, the Galaxy S8. Using the S8 camera with the Samsung assistant Bixby, shoppers can snap a photo of an item or barcode to reveal relevant results from Amazon's catalogue of products.

Features like visual search can help bridge the offline-to-online gap both remotely and instore to enhance the customer experience, introducing the opportunity to browse a selection of similar products according to their visual attributes. It's no surprise then that Microsoft's Bing search engine has its own Visual Search capability and even Pinterest got in on the act in 2017 with the launch of Lens. The point here is that the store retailer must now consider how to use such digital tools to make them discoverable in the online world, where their location, range and availability, in combination with price, may be enough to steal a potential Amazon sale.

The store as a showroom

All of the developments we have so far explored can take place anywhere outside, as well as inside a store. The significance of mainstream mobile adoption means that search can take place anywhere, but it also has a significant influence on the shopper's purchasing decision while they are inside a store. Whereas ROBO refers to the search and purchase phases of a shopping journey, where browsing is a purely virtual experience, the idea behind the concept of 'showrooming' places the browsing phase squarely inside the store. Unlike ROBO, though, it is the store that loses out on the sale.

> 'showrooming'
> noun, informal
> **Definition:** When customers visit a shop to check out a product, but then actually complete the purchase online, sometimes at a lower price. Essentially, the store acts as a product showroom for online shoppers.

It should come as no surprise, then, due in part to its prevailing online dominance, that even as far back as 2013, Amazon was used twice as much as Google for showrooming.[16] Even back then, it also found 58 per cent of smartphone owners, or one-third of all US shoppers, showroom regularly. Of those, 56 per cent had bought items on their mobile while in the store's aisles. Interestingly, 46 per cent of showroomers were also users of Amazon Prime. The study concluded that Amazon is smart at working around exclusive SKUs and merchandise by serving up comparable, competitive items, powered by its recommendations engine. You can imagine this works particularly well with functional items, in books or grocery household categories, for example, which can easily be matched by brand or description, compared to sectors such as fashion or electronics, where the look and feel of the item are more important.

Amazon also recognized this limitation with its timely anti-showrooming patent, granted the month before it announced its Whole Foods acquisition in 2017.[17] Having exploited the trend to its own ends, its patent is designed to prevent customers from showrooming in its own stores. It describes a mechanism to identify what content a shopper is accessing via a browser connected to the retailer's Wi-Fi network. If the content is deemed as product or pricing information from a competitor's website, Amazon can take any number of actions, from comparing the product searched for to what's available instore and then sending price comparison information or a coupon to your browser, to suggesting a complementary item, or even blocking content outright. Of course, it also means Amazon stands to bene-fit from any future attempts by technology providers or retailers to develop similar systems, serving as a reminder of its aggressive competitiveness.

The same visual search capabilities of mobile apps and devices that contain image recognition functionality and features can be used to win the sale at that 'zero moment' (ZMOT) in both 'research online, buy offline' (ROBO) shopping journeys, as well as in response to showrooming inside the store. Augmented reality (AR) relies on similar image recognition and machine learning AI capabilities that shoppers use for image searches in combination with additional computer vision and geolocation develop-ments. It is so-called because, in comparison to the complete immersiveness of virtual reality (VR) headsets and controllers, AR overlays images, text, video, graphics and other media onto the view that a smartphone camera sees of the real world. AR is an area that retailers and brands have so far only dabbled in, but in the store of the future, it has the potential to really enhance marketing and merchandising during the browsing phase of the shopping journey both inside and outside the store.

Ikea, for example, was one of the first to apply mobile AR in the home sector. It launched an AR app in 2013 for visualizing 3D models of its furni-ture in customer homes. In 2014, it combined the app with its globally pre-eminent catalogue by allowing customers to put the catalogue where they wanted to overlay the app view and see the actual product in its place. In 2017, Ikea then made use of Apple's just-released AR software develop-ment kit (SDK) for its iOS mobile operating system (OS) to launch the Ikea Place app, which upgraded the view of furniture models to 3D renderings of over 2,000 products that can be viewed from different angles. It also enables customers to reserve the ones they want in the app, which directs to the Ikea site to complete purchases. The home furnishings giant is now considering combining its three apps – for planning store visits, browsing its catalogue and virtually planning décor – into one, after Ikea Place received over 2 million downloads within its first six months on Apple's App store.

JD.com's Yihaodian, China's largest online grocery store, has experi-mented with the idea of AR convenience stores, allowing customers to use its mobile app to shop virtually at the designated locations. Lego first installed AR kiosks in its stores in 2010 to allow customers to see how a finished model would look like superimposed on its box when held up to the kiosk screen and, in 2015, launched a Lego X app for enthusiasts to build 3D brick models on their phone. Japanese apparel retailer Uniqlo worked with AR specialist Holition in 2012 to introduce a 'Magic Mirror' to some of its stores to let customers see how they would look wearing an item they have tried on, but in different colours. In 2016 cosmetics brand Max Factor worked with Blippar, another AR provider, to make all of its 500 products interactive and enable shoppers to reveal multimedia content tailored to each product using the Blippar app.

The digital customer experience

Even if they're not showrooming using the Amazon app, or 'blipping' products at the shelf edge to access AR content, consumers are developing ever more sophisticated expectations around the level of digital interaction or self-service available when instore, set by their shopping experiences online. Here, Wi-Fi is the prerequisite enabler for meeting these expectations. Yes, admittedly, it facilitates showrooming, but so does the shopper's own mobile data plan if coverage is available in the store. The difference is that Wi-Fi is also the essential connectivity required by retail store owners looking to maximize returns on investment from any customer-facing digital touchpoints instore. Recalling the reasons why retailers have adopted Wi-Fi in their stores, one once (anonymously) commented that the inability of mobile data signals to penetrate the depths of their wireless network-unfriendly store sites meant that, if they didn't offer Wi-Fi, they'd lose the sale to Amazon anyway because the customer would leave the store to get a mobile data signal, perform their price check and then never come back.

Also, although mobile data coverage and speeds will continue to increase as new networking protocols and spectrum for bandwidth develop, a key driver for instore Wi-Fi adoption has been to facilitate more digital touchpoints that can enhance the physical shopping journey and dissuade the shopper from completing their purchase elsewhere. At least with Wi-Fi, the retailer can ensure ZMOT can be anywhere in the store, including the shelf edge, where the retailer can exert the most influence. We've already talked about how the in-built camera function of a mobile device can help shoppers find similar products they are looking for in the offline world online. But the geolocation features in these devices mean mapping functionality has come a long way too.

Accurate real-time, location-based and mobile-optimized information about the store and its offer can persuade consumers to pay a visit but, once inside, retailer mobile-optimized websites and apps that include 'wayfinding' can help them quickly navigate their way to the right shelf edge and find the products they are looking for more quickly. French grocer Carrefour has trialled an in-app service that allows shoppers to receive directions, via their mobiles, to promotions in a store – often linked to individual preferences. It has used 600 Bluetooth Low Energy (BLE) beacons in its 28 Romanian hypermarkets to connect to an app on shopper smartphones or retailer-supplied shopping carts equipped with Samsung tablets. Carrefour's Euralille hypermarket in Lille, France also installed 800 programmable Philips LEDs as part of a major refit not only to save energy but to also use Philips visual light communication (VLC), which encodes light waves with data about products and promotions and transmits the information straight to the camera on a shopper's smartphone. An app then displays the directional information, which helps to guide the consumer to a product location.

Intelligent space

The benefit of owning the network connectivity instore is the intelligence it can provide from the data it generates. For example, retailers have traditionally relied on people counting systems that tracked footfall based on infrared camera imagery or the numbers of shoppers entering or leaving the store as they cross its threshold. The store of the future will use data garnered from Wi-Fi and mapping systems alongside other footfall-monitoring technologies to improve store design and layout in line with how their customers shop, particularly in stores with regularly updated assortments and ranges.

In 2017 Apple introduced an AR software development kit (SDK) for its mobile OS – ARKit for iOS – to add immersive virtual and 3D features to its mapping functionality and make up ground on rival Google Maps. Taken with developments like VLC and visual search, AR mapping could also be used to gamify shopping. Shopkick was an early pioneer in this regard, working with US retailers Best Buy, JCPenney, Target and Macy's from 2012 to make location-based rewards and offers available to shoppers for checking in at participating stores and scanning barcodes of specific items. At the end of 2016, Starbucks and telco retailer Sprint collaborated with Nintendo to add Pokémon Go AR 'lures', called PokéStops, and drive footfall by enticing players into their stores.

When it comes to digitizing every instore experience, electronic shelf labels (ESLs) are not new technology. But they do typify the reason Wi-Fi should be basic hygiene in a store of the future that employs technology to build digital touchpoints into the customer experience at the ultimate ZMOT in the discovery phase of the shopping journey. Apart from the fact that a 2018

ESL study found that for 80 per cent of consumers, price has the greatest influence on buying decisions at the shelf edge, for 67 per cent of retailers the cost of manually managing labelling or signage changes related to pricing and promotions instore amounts to 1–4.99 per cent of average monthly store turnover, representing a whopping \$104 billion of sales during 2017.[18]

Coupled with the costly inefficiencies of swapping out paper shelf-edge price labels, which include a band of store associates armed with the pre-printed labels or belt-worn label printers, the inaccuracies that are more liable to occur with old-fashioned pricing methods may also lead to breaches of regulations around the accuracy of pricing[19] and product information[20] if the store is located in the European Union, for instance. But the time it takes to manually change prices also means the traditional store's ability to react quickly to competitor discounts is severely limited, putting it at a disadvantage to the might of Amazon's AI-driven dynamic pricing algorithms that mean it can change prices on millions of items a day. This is compared to 50,000 total price changes made by Best Buy and Walmart in an entire month.[21]

Given that the ESL study also found accurate pricing is the main type of information shoppers wish to see displayed (82 per cent), with only 43 per cent always trusting that the prices on display will be the same paid at the till, ESLs can enhance the customer experience by also increasing shoppers' confidence in the accuracy of shelf-edge pricing. Coupled with the improved capabilities of AI computer vision software, facial recognition at the shelf can even help to personalize the experience. Intel showcased its RealSense technology for ESLs at an industry event in 2018, supporting AMW Smart Shelf and Automated Inventory Intelligence software being trialled by Walmart, The Hershey Company and Pepsi across five stores. The software enables digital shelf labelling to recognize when people are passing by the shelves and to display pricing. When nobody is close by they show promotional imagery instead. Kroger was also on hand at the same event, demoing its smart shelf solution. It said that its digital shelf signage allows the retailer to seamlessly change prices and offer a personalized experience to shoppers. The tech was live in 17 stores at the time of writing, and Kroger said it planned to roll it out to 140 stores by the end of 2018.

The bi-directional, wireless communication capacity required to update ESLs can also be turned towards the customer to connect with their mobile devices via Wi-Fi, Bluetooth beacons or the same near-field communications (NFC) technology used by mobile wallets and contactless credit and debit cards. In future, harnessing this connection at the shelf edge to deliver complementary product recommendations, reviews and offers to inform the customer experience will become more important. An ESL can drive further positive engagement by offering more detailed pricing, origin and allergy information, etc than is possible to display on a traditional shelf-edge label. Some retailers have already deployed large-sized ESLs for their capacity to present more information, accompanied with QR codes that direct customers to more information online. European home improvement retailer Leroy-Merlin deployed ESLs to solve the accuracy, productivity and pricing velocity challenges already associated with paper-based labels. But it also used its ESLs to offer customers automatic and real-time geolocation of products inside the store.

Digital points of purchase

Wi-Fi, beacons, VLC, ESLs and AR can all turn various elements of the store into digital points of purchase. House of Fraser and Ted Baker in the UK have tested mannequins fitted with beacons that can send out promotions. OfferMoments uses them to make digital billboards change to display the face of a shopper as they pass alongside offers tailored to their preferences. Its micro-location app allows shoppers to accept and then redeem offers at nearby outlets. Meanwhile beacons have also been used in the drive-through space. Diners can use voice control technology in their car to place a Pizza Hut order, and the restaurant receives an alert of their impending arrival using beacons. Payment is completed via Visa, whose system is integrated into the car dashboard.

Another key area is interactive digital signage. In 2018 Samsung unveiled its Nexshop cloud-based digital store software platform with real-time behavioural sensing using IP and mobile devices. In addition to analysis capabilities, the solution allows store associates to interact with shoppers using cloud-based content via tablets or interactive displays, for a more engaging customer experience. Finish Line and Elo in the same year demonstrated MemoMi smart mirror technology that allows customers to take a photo of themselves wearing new clothing items and superimpose the image on a variety of backgrounds. The screen can text the image to the customer, allowing for easy social sharing of the image.

US-based 1-800-Flowers recently added conversational commerce powered by AI to its instore innovation, telephone ordering, e-commerce, and mobile and social media. It was the first retailer to launch a Facebook Messenger purchasing bot, has an AI-powered concierge named GWYN ('Gifts When You Need'), and it has partnered with Amazon and Google to allow customers to make purchases with just their voice. But use of voice in the store of the future is coming, and Amazon and its Alexa voice platform could have a substantial play.

In 2017, independent German retailer HIT Sütterlin, based in Aachen, tested an Alexa-based store customer service system to communicate with its customers, offering information on offers and products, in conjunction with digital displays, based on a customer's voice prompts. The 'Alexa Shop Assist' concept developed just for the TechCrunch Disrupt 2017 Hackathon, using Alexa-powered hardware, the Alexa Skill Set and Voice Service, AWS Lambda platform and an iOS app, enabled customers to ask where a certain item is and be told which aisle to go to. It also aimed to track a customer around the store based on where questions are asked.

The store of the future will certainly offer digitally empowered assistance. But, with an emphasis on self-service, where does this leave most retailers' frontline staff? One retail IT director, who shall (for obvious reasons) remain unnamed, was at a corporate event a few years ago lamenting that 'the customers were coming into the store armed with more information on their mobile than our store associates'. Here, the digital version of a 'Black Book' system used in luxury retail to serve high-value customers, called 'clienteling', can empower store staff with digital devices to assist in high-value, high-touch, consultative sales in sectors including health and beauty, consumer electronics, automotive and luxury. In 2016, for example, Boots launched the MyBeauty app to help associates show product information, ratings and reviews, look up inventory online and make personalized customer recommendations based on online analytics.

The importance of the human touch

The role of staff in the store of the future will therefore be to facilitate more digitally enabled consultative than transactional services. They must become proper brand ambassadors. Like clienteling, staff can also be deployed with queue-busting capabilities, using integrated handheld product barcode scanners, card payment and PIN entry machines particularly for cashless sales. But practical consideration must be paid to the bagging and security de-tagging process. More widely used in grocery particularly are self-scan and checkout systems. While they increase customer speed and throughput at checkout, they also shift the entire burden of the shopping journey onto the customer, compounding the fact by asking customers to scan loyalty cards as part of the payment process, just before they leave the store! Indeed, the refrain, 'unexpected item in bagging area', has spawned many an internet meme, betraying a strong dislike among consumers for the systems, while retailers have had to accept the increased risk of theft their use carries with them. Walmart dumped its 'Scan & Go' mobile app in 2018 due to low take-up, while rumours had it that it was also subject to high levels of theft. However, Sam's Club and Costco still offer similar instore scan and payment apps, and Starbucks enables payment using the stored value card functionality of its app, customers can also order ahead for quicker pickups.

So, the final phase of the shopping journey focuses on checkout and payment, where the next stage of development is from unmanned checkout to unmanned stores, and 'checkout-less' or 'checkout-free' shopping. Here, China leads the way. The F5 Future concept store in Guangzau, China uses mobile payment and robotic fulfilment. Customers order and pay for products at a special terminal or wirelessly with their smartphones. The retrieval of goods and cleaning of tables is done solely by robotic arms attached to the appliances. Other unmanned prototypes include Auchan China's Minute and BingoBox stores and the self-driving Wheelys MobyMart, which rely on the customer using an app to access the store and pay for goods by scanning QR codes, or computer vision that debits the customer's account on exit. There's also the 7-Eleven Signature concept in South Korea.

These rivals to Amazon are setting the standard, but it is unlikely we will see the store of the future dominated by unmanned, robot-run boxes. The high cost of the technology involved limits them to small-footprint, convenience formats, and the human touch will always be most prized in sectors that require more consultative sales. But Walmart and Portugal's Sonae have also both tested autonomous shopping carts for shoppers with limited mobility.

When it comes to the role of robots in the store, examples such as Simbe's Tally, tested by Target, may take over the repetitive and laborious task of shelf auditing to identify out-of-stock, low-stock and misplaced items, and pricing errors. Others, like the LoweBot, trialled by US home improvement retailer Lowe's, are capable of limited customer interaction. LoweBot can understand multiple languages and uses a 3D scanner to detect people in the stores. Shoppers can seek the robot's help to search for any product, either by talking to it or by typing items into a touchscreen on its chest. The robot then guides them to the products using smart laser sensors. Softbank's Pepper robot has been deployed in multiple customer-facing situations, including taking Pizza Hut orders in Asia, and electronics retailer MediaMarktSaturn has deployed a robot called Paul to greet and guide customers. The German retailer is also among those around the world testing autonomous robotic delivery vehicles developed by Starship, a start-up owned by Skype founders Ahti Heinla and Janus Friis. Even so, robots won't be replacing humans altogether anytime soon.

From self-checkout to no checkout

So, we come to Amazon Go, which first opened its doors in Seattle in 2018. The computer vision-equipped, AI-powered store uses Amazon's patented 'Just Walk Out' technology to enable customers to literally walk out with their goods without having to go through any checkout process at all. Customers have to scan their Amazon Go app to gain entry and register a form of payment that is charged when they leave according to what the computer vision systems detect they have taken from the shelves. Its beauty is Amazon knows precisely who is in its store and what they do at every move, while the technology eliminates shrink. The success of the checkout-free model, particularly in attracting repeat custom, according to Amazon Go vice president Gianna Puerini,[22] means more stores are likely planned for San Francisco, Chicago and London. But it is hardly unmanned, as staff are on hand to restock shelves and prepare fresh items, and it relies heavily on densely populated, high-traffic locations to make its higher-margin convenience format offset the high-tech costs.

Nevertheless, Amazon Go has raised the game for rival retailers. Ahold Delhaize also announced in 2017 it was trialling a checkout-less concept, where purchase is made by tapping a contactless card against ESLs to verify transactions. Meanwhile, Sainsbury's tested the ability for customers to bypass the till and pay for goods using their mobile phone, and UK rival Tesco is trialling 'scan and go' technology to enable customers to pay for groceries via the retailer's Scan Pay Go smartphone app in its Express convenience store at its own Welwyn Garden City HQ, and tech giant Microsoft is working on a checkout-less store concept that works by attaching cameras to shopping carts in order to track purchases as customers walk the aisles. JD.com actually beat its US rival to open the already-referenced BingoBox as the first automated, unmanned store in partnership with Auchan, in 2017 (although remote customer service is available, and the store is manually restocked daily). The first unmanned and checkout-less D-Mart c-store opened at JD's company headquarters in the same year. This so-called Smart Store is equipped with an Intel-based responsive technology suite that includes smart shelves, intelligent cameras, gateways and sensors, smart counters for checkout-free shopping and smart digital signage. The JD solution offers low-cost wholesale or incremental customization flexibility to allow traditional retail store owners to upgrade their operations in a 'low touch' and cost-effective way. It also supports JD.com founder and chief executive Richard Liu's ambitions to open a modern convenience store in every village in China within the next four years.[23]

Both JD.com and Alibaba's offline moves arguably deserve more credit than that afforded Amazon Go for the fact that they offer more accessible digitally enabled experiences. With a focus also on fresh, convenience and food service, JD.com's 7fresh concept and Alibaba's Hema Supermarkets also blend the best of the physical with QR codes, app-based digital touch-points including ESLs, and payment. Again, mobile payment will play a key role in enabling the store of the future where – if retailers are serious about automating this final, most friction-filled part of the shopping journey – they also get to tie the customer's identity back to the final transaction and basket. Both Visa and MasterCard have recently showcased biometric payments to enable customers to bypass queues at the checkout. KFC in China, in cooperation with Alibaba-owned Ant Financial Services, recently launched the first 'smile-to-pay' payment system in China. Alipay customers can authenticate their payments through a combination of facial scanning and inputting their mobile phone numbers, which means they need not reach for their wallets – or even smartphones – anymore. 7-Eleven's Signature store in Seoul uses 'HandPay', a biometric verification system that scans palm vein patterns.

While many established store-based retailers are facing the reality of slowing sales and being overspaced, other digital-first players have recognized the critical importance of gaining a physical presence. Stores help support the omnichannel proposition by providing extra flexibility in terms of order collection, returns, service and a physical environment to showcase the brand. So, retailers should bring pervasive tech interfaces, ubiquitous connectivity, and autonomous computing of digital and mobile to bear so the store can support every stage of the shopping journey, off- and online, from browse and search through to discovery and payment phases in ways that match the speed, accessibility and availability of online.

Stores for digital players play a different role from the primary role of the traditional store simply selling products. We believe that these players, with their strong skills and capabilities in technology, are the ones that will really push forward the vision of the digitally enabled and automated store of the future to enhance its role as a powerful, tangible engagement point within their wider customer ecosystems.

Notes

1   Greene, Jay (2015) Amazon opening its first real bookstore – at U-Village, *Seattle Times*, 2 November. Available from: https://www.seattletimes.com/business/amazon/amazon-opens-first-bricks-and-mortar-bookstore-at-u-village/ [Last accessed 25/6/2018].

2   Press Release (2017) The shopping habits of today's consumers: ecommerce vs. in-store, *Imprint Plus*, 16 October. Available from: https://www.prnewswire.com/news-releases/the-shopping-habits-of-todays-consumers-ecommerce-vs-in-store-300535550.html [Last accessed 25/6/2018].

3   Lipsman, Andrew (2017) 5 interesting Millennials' mobile app usage from the '2017 mobile app usage report', *comScore*, August 24. Available from: facts about https://www.comscore.com/Insights/Blog/5-Interesting-Facts-About-Millennials-Mobile-App-Usage-from-The-2017-US-Mobile-App-Report. [Last accessed 6/9/2018].

4   White Paper (2017) Amazon: the big e-commerce marketing opportunity for brands, *Kenshoo*, 13 September. Available from: https://kenshoo.com/e-commerce-survey/ [Last accessed 20/6/2018].

5   Bazaarvoice (2018) The ROBO Economy: how smart marketers use consumer-generated content to influence omnichannel shoppers [E-book] January. Available from: http://media2.bazaarvoice.com/documents/robo-economy-ebook.pdf [Last accessed 6/6/2018].

6   Cullinan, Emily (2017) How to use customer testimonials to generate 62% more revenue from every customer, every visit, *Big Commerce*, 2 April. Available from: https://www.bigcommerce.com/blog/customer-testimonials/ [Last accessed 20/6/2018].

7   Kurst, Dustin (2015) My 2.5 star trip to Amazon's bizarre new bookstore, *New Republic*, 4 November. Available from: https://newrepublic.com/article/123352/my-25-star-trip-to-amazons-bizarre-new-bookstore [Last accessed 26/6/2018].

8   Gobry, Pascal-Emmanuel (2015) Why Amazon built a bookstore, *The Week*, 4 November. Available from: http://theweek.com/articles/586793/why-amazon-built-bookstore [Last accessed 25/6/2018].

9   Kim, Eugene (2017) Amazon is getting almost no revenue from its bookstores, *CNBC*, 26 October. Available from: https://www.cnbc.com/2017/10/26/amazon-is-getting-almost-no-revenue-from-its-bookstores.html [Last accessed 25/6/2018].

10 Lecinski, Jim (2011) Winning the zero moment of truth ebook, *Google*, June. Available from: https://www.thinkwithgoogle.com/marketing-resources/micro-moments/2011-winning-zmot-ebook/ [Last accessed 25/6/2018].

11 Gevelber, Lisa (2018) How 'Near Me' helps us find what we need, not just where to go, *Think with Google*, May. Available from: https://www.thinkwithgoogle.com/consumer-insights/near-me-searches/ [Last accessed 26/6/2018].

12 Peterson, Haylet (2018) Google now lets you see what's on shelves at stores near you, and it's a powerful new weapon against Amazon, *Business Insider UK*, 12 June. Available from: http://uk.businessinsider.com/google-see-whats-in-store-vs-amazon-2018-6 [Last accessed 20/6/2018].

13 Murga, Guillermo (2017) Amazon takes 49 percent of consumers' first product search, but search engines rebound, *Survata*, 20 December. Available from: https://www.survata.com/blog/amazon-takes-49-percent-of-consumers-first-product-search-but-search-engines-rebound/ [Last accessed 25/6/2018].

14 ibid.

15 Press release (2016) Three, Two, One…Holiday! Amazon.com launches Black Friday deals store and curated holiday gift guides, *Amazon*, 1 November. Available from: http://phx.corporate-ir.net/phoenix.zhtml?c=176060&p=irol-newsArticle&ID=2217692 [Last accessed 25/6/2018].

16 Mason, Rodney (2014) Dynamic pricing in a smartphone world: A shopper showrooming study, *Parago*, 4 January. Available from: https://www.slideshare.net/Parago/dynamic-pricing-30010764 [Last accessed 25/6/2013].

17 Amazon Technologies, Inc. (2017) Physical store online shopping control, US Patent No. 9665881, 30 May. Available from: http://patft.uspto.gov/netacgi/nph-Parser?Sect2=PTO1&Sect2=HITOFF&p=1&u=/netahtml/PTO/search-bool.html&r=1&f=G&l=50&d=PALL&RefSrch=yes&Query=PN/9665881 [Last accessed 20/6/2018].

18 Displaydata commissioned report (2018) Analogue to automated: retail in the connected age, *PlanetRetail RNG*, May. Available from: https://info.display-data.com/planet-retail [Last accessed 27/6/2018].

19 Official Journal of the European Communities (1998) Directive 98/6/EC of the European Parliament and of the Council on consumer protection in the indication of the prices of products offered to consumers, *EUR-Lex*, 16 February. Available from: https://eur-lex.europa.eu/legal-content/EN/TXT/?uri=celex%3A31998L0006 [Last accessed 27/6/2018].

20 Official Journal of the European Communities (2011) Regulation (EU) No 1169/2011 of the European Parliament and of the Council of 25 October 2011 on the provision of food information to consumers, *EUR-Lex*, 25 October. Available from: https://eur-lex.europa.eu/eli/reg/2011/1169/oj [Last accessed 27/6/2018].

21 Profitero (2013) Profitero Price Intelligence: Amazon makes more than 2.5 million daily price changes, *Profitero*, 10 December. Available from: https://www.profitero.com/2013/12/profitero-reveals-that-amazon-com-makes-more-than-2-5-million-price-changes-every-day/ [Last accessed 27/6/2018].

22 Dastin, Jeffrey (2018) Amazon tracks repeat shoppers for line-free Seattle store – and there are many, *Reuters*, 19 March. Available from: https://ca.reuters.com/article/technologyNews/idCAKBN1GV0DK-OCATC [Last accessed 27/6/2018].

23 Liu, Richard (2018) Interview conducted by broadcaster and Plenary session moderator of World Retail Congress, Munchetty, N, Madrid, 17 April.

Store of the future: shifting from transactional to experiential

12

> 'We're in a moment of absolute transition. We all have to think about how to reinvent, react, how to win. We have to make big, powerful strategic relationships around the world… and we'll move as fast as we possibly can because we look at our friends at Amazon and if they can move that fast, why can't a company like ours…?'
> **Richard Baker, Chairman, Hudson's Bay, 2017[1]**

Previous chapters have aimed to illustrate how the instore experience will become more frictionless and hyper-personalized through technology. Addressing customer bugbears like product navigation and waiting in line at the checkout will allow retailers to take the physical store into the 21st century, achieving a level of convenience and ease that was traditionally only associated with e-commerce players.

The urgency for retailers to reinvent the physical space will be reinforced as more categories move online. Shoppers can buy literally anything online today and, thanks to Prime, usually have it delivered the very next day. Amazon has taken every effort out of shopping. In the future, this will go one step further as certain household products move towards simplified and auto-replenishment. As our homes get smarter, shoppers' lives will get easier. The average adult currently makes a whopping 35,000 decisions every day,[2] but in the future our connected homes will do all the low-level, mundane re-ordering of household products, freeing up time to focus on more enjoyable tasks. Shoppers will no longer have to traipse down supermarket aisles when they run out of bleach or toilet paper. They will spend less of their valuable time buying the essentials and we believe the impact on the physical store will be immense; retailers today should be rethinking store layout, trip drivers and the broader purpose of the store.

In the future, we will see a greater divergence between functional and fun shopping. No one does functional like Amazon, so competitors must focus on the fun element. Winning in retail today means excelling where Amazon cannot, and therefore focusing less on product and more on experience, services and expertise.

WACD – What Amazon Can't Do – has become a recognized acronym in the retail industry as competitors desperately seek ways to survive in the age of Amazon. Even the very terminology – words like 'retailer' and 'store' – must be reconsidered: Apple want their outlets to be called 'town squares' and cycling chain Rapha, 'clubhouses'. In a similar vein, many shopping malls are actually ditching the m-word in favour of phrases like 'village', 'town centre' and 'shoppes'.[3] Others have taken the notion of experiential retail to the extreme – UK department store retailer John Lewis lets shoppers stay overnight in an instore apartment while US home furnishings retailer West Elm has branched out into running hotels.

Not all retailers will have the means or incentive to go to such extremes, but one thing is clear – stores must be repositioned as genuine destinations. It can no longer be just about product; instead, retailers must tap into community and leisure, providing an experience that is compelling enough to ditch our screens for. Angela Ahrendts, Apple's SVP of Retail, observed in 2017 that 'while people are more digitally connected than ever, many feel more isolated and alone.' The physical store is well-positioned to cater to a growing consumer desire for social connectedness in today's digital age.

We've already talked extensively of the trend towards a more blended retail experience as online and offline continue to merge. But bricks and mortar retailing will also become more blended in the sense that retail space won't just be about retail. The future, particularly for malls and larger formats like department stores, is mixed-use development, which will open doors for collaboration with all kinds of unconventional partners. These aren't entirely new concepts: retailtainment (or retail theatre) and positioning retail as a leisure activity have featured in retailers' playbooks for the past century. Mr Harry Gordon Selfridge himself once said that 'a store should be a social centre, not merely a place for shopping.'[4]

This is sound advice for retailers today. For all its perks, shopping on Amazon is still a very utilitarian experience. This presents an opportunity for competitors to distance themselves by injecting some personality and soul into their stores, which will further blur the lines between retail, hospitality and lifestyle.

We believe the store of the future won't just be a place to buy things but also a place to eat, play, discover, and even work. It will be a place to borrow and to learn, but also, crucially, a place for retailers to appease the 'on-my-terms' shopper through instore collection and returns, as well as same-day delivery. In an increasingly digital world, the role of the physical shop will have no choice but to move from transactional to experiential.

From shop to lifestyle centre: ensuring brand values align

For those willing to embrace change, this is a fantastically exciting time for retail. By becoming more experience- and service-led, retailers can add a social dimension to their brand, enabling them to simultaneously tap into consumer spending shifts and differentiate from online rivals.

However, it's vital that such diversification is aligned with the retailer's own brand. It might sound obvious, but you only need to cast your mind back to 2012 when Tesco began filling its stores with artisan cafés, restaurants, upmarket bakeries, yoga studios and even gyms. By 2016, they had sold off all the companies they had begun investing in just a few years earlier: Harris + Hoole, Giraffe and Euphorium.

There were various reasons for the 180 in strategy: a new CEO with very different priorities to his predecessor; the need to rationalize non-core assets in order to turn around the core grocery business; plus these concessions were largely loss-making. We would argue that the strategy was fundamentally flawed in that the partner brands' aspirational stance was misaligned with Tesco's own values as a low-priced, mass-appeal grocer. After buying a freshly ground piccolo macchiato, shoppers would turn to face a swathe of red and yellow signs shouting about 3-for-2 deals.

Tesco might have failed to reinvent the superstore concept at the time, but they certainly learned a great deal through the experimentation. Today, they've successfully filled excess space by partnering with other retailers such as Holland & Barrett, Arcadia Group (Dorothy Perkins, Evans and Burton), Dixons Carphone (Currys PC World) and Next. Sure, there is some overlap in product categories – Dorothy Perkins concessions tend to be co-located with Tesco's own label F+F ranges – but the concessions create a point of differentiation for Tesco while the brands benefit from the supermarket's regular footfall.

A decade ago, Tesco wouldn't have dreamed of teaming up with competitors but today they have a shared enemy in Amazon. Co-opetition allows them to better serve the customer and jointly fend off the Seattle behemoth. Despite the previous branding misalignment, Tesco's intentions to turn its stores into an under-one-roof shopping, leisure and foodservice destination were not far off the mark. They were perhaps just a few years too early with such a radical reinvention plan.

A place to eat

Food: fashionable footfall driver

'Whilst a screen will deliver products, ultimately people will still want to try things on, feel the fabric and experience a service which is unique to the shop, and there is no better way to bring people into shop than food.'
Richard Collasse, president of Chanel Japan[5]

Today, retailers are fighting for their survival and scrambling to redefine the retail space. A tried-and-tested method of driving footfall and increasing dwell time is through the addition of cafés and restaurants. From McDonalds in Walmart stores to the glitzy KaDeWe food halls of Berlin, foodservice has always been a natural extension of retail. This is particularly true for department stores and other big-box concepts such as Ikea, for example, whose Swedish cuisine has become as famous as its Billy bookcase.

'We've always called the meatballs "the best sofa-seller",' says Gerd Diewald, head of Ikea's US food operations, 'because it's hard to do business with hungry customers. When you feed them, they stay longer, they can talk about their [potential] purchases, and they make a decision without leaving the store.'[6]

So what's new? The roster of retailers is growing and so is the breadth of their offering.

Earlier in the book, we discussed how fashion retailers have been hit hardest by the rise in experiential spending as shoppers increasingly prioritize a meal out or a cinema trip over a new pair of jeans. Plus, they're under constant pressure from more nimble online fashion chains. ASOS alone adds 5,000 new products each week. What high street retailer can compete with that?

It's no surprise then that many fashion chains are now turning to food and drink experiences as a way to differentiate from their online rivals and entice shoppers through the doors. Millennial favourite Urban Outfitters pioneered this trend back in 2015 when it acquired the Philadelphia-based Vetri Family group of restaurants. The unprecedented move raised eyebrows at the time but since the deal, more and more clothing retailers around the globe have added dining options to their stores. Uniqlo shoppers in Manhattan and Chicago can grab a Starbucks coffee instore. In the UK, Next is adding pizza and prosecco bars to its stores. Meanwhile, even fast fashion chains are jumping on the bandwagon – H&M's Flax & Kale à Porter restaurant in Barcelona features a variety of organic and vegetarian food.

> 'Until they invent actual replicators like on Star Trek, e-commerce is not a threat to the restaurant business.'
> **Jeff Benjamin, co-founder of Vetri Family (restaurant chain sold to Urban Outfitters)**[7]

Luxury retailers have also tapped into this trend by extending their own brands or aligning with like-minded restaurants – Nobu, for example. Gucci and Armani now have cafés and restaurants around the world. In 2016, Burberry opened its first ever café, Thomas's, in its London flagship store. The menu reflects the luxury brand's quintessentially British stance, from cream tea to lobster and chips. Similarly, Ralph's Coffee & Bar from Polo Ralph Lauren plays up to its American heritage with oysters, club sandwiches and cheesecake.

> 'We wanted to create a space where our customers can spend time relaxing and enjoying the world of Burberry in a more social environment.'
> **Former Burberry CEO Christopher Bailey**[8]

Department stores are also upping their game in this area. Saks Fifth Avenue is planning to open a version of French eatery and celebrity magnet L'Avenue in its renovated flagship store, while competitor Neiman Marcus partnered with celebrity chef Matthew Kenney to open a vegan café in 2016. 'In the past, the restaurants were developed to keep customers in the store longer and spend more', said Marc Metrick, president of Saks Fifth Avenue. 'Now restaurants are a way to attract people into store.'[9]

Food: beyond fashion

Looking beyond fashion now, we believe that incorporating food and drink experiences will also be a powerful tool (and logical extension) for supermarkets. Grocery retailers around the world should be taking inspiration from the likes of Eataly and Whole Foods Market, flexing their fresh credentials with food emporiums, cookery classes and grow-your-own initiatives. In China, online giants are redefining the physical supermarket for today's modern shopper with tech-infused stores that place a strong emphasis on freshness and experience. For example, Alibaba's Hema chain allows customers to select their own live seafood and have it prepared by instore chefs, while instore dining accounts for around half of rival JD.com's 7Fresh supermarket's sales.[10]

Meanwhile, in Italy, Co-op's 'store of the future' features a restaurant that cooks only with their own-label products, reinforcing both quality and provenance. More upmarket supermarkets like Waitrose and Publix have long capitalized on their higher-end positioning and reputation for instore experience with cookery classes. Meanwhile, Germany-based Metro became the first retailer in Europe to implement instore farming and Whole Foods Market has experimented with rooftop greenhouses.

The Markt Halle concept from Real, also owned by Metro, is a fantastic example of how large hypermarkets and superstores can distance themselves from both their online and discounter rivals through a greater focus on fresh foods and hospitality. The aim of the store is to convey the atmosphere of a traditional market hall and as such, the food/non-food split has gone from 60/40 per cent to 70/30 per cent. An internal dining area and winter garden can host nearly 200 people and customers can enjoy seasonal food that is freshly prepared in front of them. Some foods like pasta are made instore and shoppers can also take part in culinary-related activities like sushi workshops. USB-enabled device-charging points are also offered, encouraging shoppers to spend more time instore, whether that's socializing, shopping or even working.

A place to work

Retail isn't the only sector being redefined by technology. The workplace is evolving rapidly as increased connectivity liberates employees from the traditional 9–5 office-based routine. By 2020, there are expected to be more than 26,000 shared office spaces in the US, hosting 3.8 million people – which is phenomenal considering the trend was virtually unheard of as recently as 2007.[11]

> 'In cities, we have been paying particular attention to the new ways space and time are used, which are radically changing consumer behaviours. The lines between work, culture and fun are being blurred, creating a new way of living.'
> **Jean Paul Mochet, CEO of convenience banners at Casino Group, 2018[12]**

The rise in remote working, co-working spaces, hot-desking and third spaces is transforming consumers' lives – and creating opportunities for retailers in the process. As with the Real example, major European food retailers have been becoming more hospitable in a bid to increase dwell time, offering free Wi-Fi and device-charging points while enhancing their foodservice options. In 2017, Carrefour Italy took this a step further by introducing a new store concept in Milan – Carrefour Urban Life – that featured co-working space for the first time. Carrefour describes the store, which also features a meeting room and lounge bar serving more than 200 Italian and international beers, as an innovative solution for busy city dwellers 'who seek more than ever to combine pleasure, work and socialization'.[13]

In the future, we believe hybrid store concepts like Carrefour's will become a common sight in urban areas around the globe. According to the UN, two-thirds of the world's population will live in cities by 2050,[14] and in the US today, many cities are growing faster than their suburbs as millennials forgo the white picket fence dream in favour of a no-strings-attached urban lifestyle.

As urbanization takes hold, physical spaces must adapt by becoming smaller, more convenient and multi-dimensional. 'The trend of urbanization is something we must all recognize and understand', says Adam Neumann, CEO and co-founder of shared office space provider WeWork. 'People from every walk of life are seeking spaces in big cities that allow for human connections. There is no reason why retail space should not be part of that movement.'[15]

WeWork: a lifeline for department stores?

Collaboration with shared office providers like WeWork will especially help to bring department stores into the 21st century. As discussed earlier in the book, the biggest challenge for these large stores today is making use of surplus space as spending shifts online. In a bid to cut costs, most department stores today are now looking to rationalize store portfolios or shrink the size of their outlets – Macy, Kohl's, Nordstrom, Debenhams, M&S, House of Fraser, the list goes on.

According to real estate service company JLL, 30 per cent of corporate real estate holdings will be flexible office spaces by 2030 – compared to less than 5 per cent in 2017.[16] WeWork is now central London's biggest office occupier. In just eight years, the company has earned a $20 billion valuation and opened more than 200 locations around the world. They have picked at the carcasses of ailing department stores but are also proving to be a lifeline for those brands that are willing to partner with them by downsizing and broadening their scope.

Converting dead department store space into co-working areas is a no-brainer. Not only does it provide an alternative source of income, but it drives traffic, increases dwell time and, as is the case with other services like click & collect, there is a very good chance of additional spend once instore. Plus, shared office space is a natural extension of services found in most department stores – cafés and free Wi-Fi.

WeWork has already been linked to Debenhams in the UK (John Lewis too is exploring the option of co-working space) and in Paris they have opened in the former headquarters of French department store retailer Galeries Lafayette. But it was their $850 million acquisition of the iconic Lord & Taylor building in Manhattan that will have quashed any doubt that co-working is part of the future of retail. The deal, announced in 2017, will see the 5th Avenue store shrink to about a quarter of its size in the 660,000-square-foot building. The upper floors will be occupied by WeWork – both as its headquarters and office space.

As part of the agreement, WeWork will lease space in parent Hudson's Bay's department stores around the world, starting with stores in Vancouver and Toronto and Galeria Kauhof in Frankfurt. 'In those three locations we'll lease them the top two floors, and they'll pay market rent for floors that no one thought had value', said Richard Baker, executive chairman of Hudson's Bay. '…We will drive those millennials through our entrances and create excitement and interest around our locations… We've been focused on reinventing the old, tired stores we bought, and one of the ways to do that is to bring new uses into the stores.'[17]

A place to play

Hudson's Bay may be looking to co-working space to breathe new life into its department stores – but they understand that this is just one small cog in a very big wheel. Perhaps inspired by experiential marketing strategies of fitness brands like Lululemon and Sweaty Betty, department stores are now also looking to instore fitness as a way to crank up the leisure factor.

In 2017, Hudson's Bay converted 16,000 square feet of a Saks store into The Wellery, an upscale fitness centre with two workout studios, salt rooms and even a vegan nail salon. Across the pond, Debenhams has also been experimenting with instore gyms with specialist Sweat! in a bid to provide a 'credible leisure experience'. Never failing to impress, Selfridges launched the world's first boxing gym within a department store. Meanwhile, now-defunct department stores (BHS sites, for example) are being reincarnated not only as fitness centres but also bowling alleys, crazy golf centres, cinemas and even an art gallery.

And if Elon Musk has his way, his Tesla supercharger stations across the US will feature upmarket convenience stores alongside climbing walls, outdoor cinemas and 1950s-style drive-in restaurants with waiting staff on roller skates – giving customers something to do during the 30 minutes it takes to recharge their vehicles.[18] It's not quite colonizing Mars, but it's certainly blurring the lines between retail and entertainment.

Meanwhile, some retail companies are turning to virtual reality to create playful and immersive instore experiences. North Face ran a campaign allowing its shoppers to don a virtual headset and tour Yosemite National Park and the Moab desert alongside professional athletes and, in 2017, Topshop turned its store windows into an interactive pool scene and let shoppers ride a virtual water slide around Oxford Street.

Shopping malls too are looking to rather unconventional ways to fill space such as hotels, entertainment (from laser tag to full-scale concert arenas) and kid-oriented experiences like KidZania or the Crayola Experience. Some are even positioning themselves as resort-style destinations where shoppers can spend a day out with their family. Rushden Lakes, for example, is the UK's first shopping centre combined with a nature reserve. The Northamptonshire centre, which opened in 2017, features a first-of-its-kind lakeside setting where shoppers can go canoeing or explore the adjacent nature trails by foot or bike. 'We genuinely believe we are redefining the UK retail landscape – where else can you come to shop by canoe?' said Paul Rich, centre manager of Rushden Lakes. In 2019, the centre will add more leisure activities including golf, trampolining and indoor climbing.

Across the pond, Miami is set to become home to the nation's largest shopping mall. Spanning 6 million square feet, the 'American Dream' complex will feature a water park with a giant indoor pool, ice climbing wall, artificial ski slope, 'submarine' rides, 2,000 hotel rooms and up to 1,200 stores.

Meanwhile, in Canada, the circus is coming to shopping centres. Cirque du Soleil's new concept CREACTIVE will allow shoppers to engage in a range of acrobatic, artistic and other Cirque du Soleil-inspired recreational activities such as bungee jumping, aerial parkour, wire and trampolines, mask design, juggling, circus track activities and dance. The first will open in late 2019 in the Greater Toronto area.

Also opening in 2019 in Las Vegas is Area15, another new shopping mall concept that is being billed as a '21st-century immersive bazaar'. The 126,000-square-foot hybrid retail-entertainment complex is expected to offer attractions like escape rooms and virtual reality, art installations, festivals, themed events and live events (everything from concerts to Ted talks).

Catering to pint-sized customers

No one is better positioned to embrace the fun factor than high street toy retailers. The problem is these are few and far between these days. Over the past decade, we've seen the famous FAO Schwarz store close on 5th Avenue, in addition to the demise of entire chains like KB Toys and, more recently, the iconic brand Toys R Us. Meanwhile, baby goods and toy retailer Mothercare has nearly halved its store numbers in recent years.[19]

It would be easy to blame others for the toy specialists' problems (cue the Amazon Effect). Supermarkets and big-box retailers have been chipping away at the specialists' business for decades; today Hasbro and Mattel each generate nearly a third of their sales from Walmart and Target.[20] Meanwhile, in the UK a newly combined Asda-Sainsburys-Argos will create a toy retailing powerhouse – which will help them to fend off the growing threat of Amazon which, prior to the merger, had been on track to overtake Argos as the country's largest toy seller.[21]

The internet, of course, lends itself to toy retailing. It's a commodity category where, like books and DVDs, shoppers generally know what they're getting without having to see the product in person. A Hatchimal is a Hatchimal regardless of where you buy it. What is more, the use of augmented reality is helping to instil even greater confidence in online shoppers – for example, the Argos app allows shoppers to see full-scale versions of select Lego toys before buying them. It's no surprise then that the toy category has one of the highest online penetration rates – and it continues to grow. By 2021, Kantar predicts that 28 per cent of all US toy sales will take place online, up from 19 per cent in 2016.[22]

When you factor in the growing trend towards same-day delivery, bricks and mortar retailers lose their one remaining USP – immediacy. In toy retailing today, you need to be cheap, convenient or fun. Online and mass retailers may deliver on the first two, but there is still very much a place for specialists to inject some fun into the offering.

This was where Toys R Us went wrong. In the fast-moving sector, they fell behind in delivering on each of these areas, leaving them stuck in a retail no man's land. As a specialist, the Toys R Us experience had high potential to be a magical one with instore events, dedicated play areas and product demonstrations. The reality was a soulless shed with very little innovation or technology to draw shoppers in. Private equity ownership was a big factor here – saddled with debt, they were simply unable to adapt to a changing retail environment. It's also worth mentioning, as this is a book on Amazon after all, that another pitfall of Toys R Us was outsourcing their e-commerce business to Amazon in the early days, giving one of their biggest competitors an incredible insight into their customers' toy buying habits. Co-opetition isn't always good for business.

The demise of Toys R Us should serve as a stark reminder of the dangers of complacency. Department stores like JCPenney in the US and Marks & Spencer in the UK – neither of which are short of their own problems – have since begun adding toy sections to their stores in a bid to capture a share of lost revenue from Toys R Us in their respective markets.

We believe there is an opportunity to put the joy and magic back into toy stores – or any type of retail geared towards children and families. This seems like common sense retailing. Why doesn't Mothercare offer soft play for toddlers? Why doesn't Tesco offer mum and baby classes in its large superstores? Why didn't Toys R Us roll out play zones to let kids interact with the toys their parents were going to buy? In fairness, they did begin testing this in 2015 but sadly it was too little, too late.

In the US, Disney is redesigning its stores to make shoppers feel like they're on vacation – daily parades at Disneyland in California and Walt Disney World in Florida are being streamed live to cinema-sized screens instore. During the parades, customers can sit on mats and purchase cotton candy and light-up Mickey Mouse ears, as if they were in the theme park themselves.

In the UK, The Entertainer regularly holds events where children can meet famous characters like Poppy and Branch from Trolls, while another toy retailer Smyths offers Magformers demonstrations and Barbie dress-up days. Hamleys runs a mini theme park in its Moscow store, while Lego famously lets both pint-sized and grown-up customers build instore, offering imaginative and creative spaces that cannot be replicated in a digital setting.

Meanwhile, in Canada, Nations Experience is an innovative new concept described as part supermarket, part quick-service restaurant and part amusement park. Its Toronto store, which opened in a former Target site in 2017, features over 10,000 square feet of entertainment space including a 4,000-square-foot, kids-only playground, 135 arcade games and five party rooms that can be rented out.

CASE STUDY   Westfield's Destination 2028

The shopping centres of the future will be 'hyper-connected micro cities' driven by social interaction and community, according to Westfield.

In 2018, the leading shopping centre laid out its vision for the future of retail with a concept called Destination 2028. AI-infused walkways and hanging sensory gardens feature in an environment designed to cater to the growing importance consumers will place on experience, leisure, wellness and community. New technologies, from AI to drones, will blend seamlessly with back-to-basic concepts such as 'classroom retail'. The makers and process behind any product will take centre stage – from craftspeople creating a masterpiece in front of a live crowd to resident artists painting in the live gallery. New stage areas will host a series of showpiece interactive activities and events.

Technology will enable the shopping centre of the future to become more frictionless and personalized. Dubbed 'extra-perience' by Westfield, eye scanners will bring up information on entry about a visitor's previous purchases and recommend personalized fast lanes around the shopping centre. Magic mirrors and smart changing rooms will allow shoppers to see a virtual reflection of themselves wearing new garments while other innovations, like smart toilets that can detect hydration levels and nutritional needs, will enhance the overall experience.

Wellness is a key theme of Destination 2028. A 'betterment zone' allows customers to reflect in a mindfulness workshop, while reading rooms will be available for shoppers to unwind and tranquil green space will be featured both indoors and outside. The addition of allotments and farms gives shoppers the opportunity to select their own produce for their meal, while a network of waterways will not only offer an alternative route around the shopping centre but also access to watersports – one of the many leisure activities available.

Westfield's 'Destination 2028' concept also highlights the rise of the sharing economy, with 'rental retail' expected to become the norm for post-millennials seeking to rent everything from clothes to exercise gear. Pop-ups, temporary retail, and co-working spaces are also likely to emerge in the future of retail, according to Westfield.

A place to discover, a place to learn

Retailers must not overlook the importance of discovery as they aim to create a more meaningful connection with shoppers. The need to surprise and delight shoppers instore has never been greater, whether through conventional methods like a Costco-style treasure hunt or more high-tech measures such as augmented and virtual reality.

One brand that has ditched traditional retail norms and embraced the art of discovery is New York City-based Story, which describes itself as 'the store that has the point of view of a magazine, changes like a gallery, and sells things like a store'. As its name implies, the focus is on stories – not products. Every six to eight weeks, the 2,000-square-foot store gets a makeover with a new design, curated range and fresh marketing messages. 'If time is the ultimate luxury and people want a higher return on investment of their time, you need to give them a reason to be in a physical space', said Story Founder Rachel Shechtman.[23] The concept is simple, refreshing and entirely relevant for today's modern shopper who wants to do more than just transact when coming into a physical store. In 2018, Story was acquired by Macy's.

Personal shopping and merchandise-free stores

An increasingly popular way to tap into the art of discovery is through personal stylists. Once reserved for elite shoppers, personal shopping has become democratized both on- and offline. The rise of online styling services like Stitch Fix and Trunk Club have led major retailers like Amazon and ASOS to create their own versions of 'trying before you buy'. Amazon and ASOS' iterations currently lack the personal styling element – they are arguably more about instilling confidence in buying clothes online – but this would be a logical future move for both retailers.

Instore, everyone from H&M to Agent Provocateur now offers personal styling; however, some retailers have gone to the extreme of getting rid of products altogether in order to focus on the experience and customer service.

Men's fashion brand Bonobos, previously a pure-play online retailer, wanted to allow its online shoppers to try before they came up with the concept of 'guideshops'. Here's how it works: shoppers come in for a personalized visit where they are fitted and provided with individual measurements. They can try anything on instore – Bonobos keeps all sizes, colours, fits and fabrics in stock at all times (only one of each item variation) – but they can't walk out with any merchandise. Shoppers can either pay for clothes instore and have them shipped, or order online when they get home.

Bonobos has been so successful that it was acquired by Walmart in 2017. The same year, Nordstrom launched an equally revolutionary concept – Nordstrom Local. At just 3,000 square feet, the stores do not carry their own inventory, though you can get items from nearby full-line stores within hours. What the Nordstrom Local stores lack in merchandise, they certainly make up for in amenities – personal styling consultations, clothing alterations, manicures and a bar serving beer, wine and pressed juice. The stores are also intended to serve as a convenient hub for online collection and returns, which will be critical for Nordstrom as it prepares for online to account for half of its sales by 2022.

The no-inventory model sounds wacky, but there is certainly some merit to it. Without massive piles of stock, these showrooms can trade from a significantly smaller footprint – which means a significantly lower rent bill. And without any shelves to restock, employees can devote more attention to the customer with the ultimate aim of driving sales and decreasing the likelihood of returns. The customer meanwhile gets the perfect fit and doesn't have to worry about carrying clothes home.

Education, guidance and inspiration

'How could our stores, Apple's largest product, do more to enrich lives? This became our dream – that our stores would become vital hubs where everyone could connect, learn, and create.'
Angela Ahrendts, SVP of Apple Retail[24]

When we think of retailers as educators, Apple workshops immediately spring to mind. Apple was doing experiential retail well before it went mainstream; however, even they are upping their game in this area. Remember the town square concept? Apple's blueprint for the future of retail places an even greater emphasis on experience and education, as boss Angela Ahrendts believes that shopping centres of the future will be 80 per cent experience and 20 per cent shopping. Apple stores now offer coding lessons to kids and host additional educational workshops and events, such as sessions for photography, music, gaming and app development.

In 2018, John Lewis opened its very first 'discovery room' in its London Westfield store where shoppers can learn new skills or get advice on a variety of topics – how to choose the right camera, how to light a room, improve their garden or how to get a perfect night's sleep. The same store also features a 700-square-foot studio where shoppers can have one-to-one or group style consultations, receive beauty and makeup advice and also indulge in afternoon tea.

In Paris, Casino Group partnered with L'Oreal in 2018 to open '…le drugstore parisien', an innovative new concept positioned as 'the urban store for beauty from within, practical treats and serendipity [the art of making unexpected discoveries].'[25] The store ranges from beauty and well-being to over-the-counter pharmaceutical products, sewing kits, and healthy snacks and treats. With the urban consumer in mind, the store also features a number of amenities such as free Wi-Fi, mobile phone charging points, hairdressers, dry cleaning, parcel pick-up points, light therapy areas, key exchange and one-hour Glovo delivery for certain products.

Ethical beauty retailer Lush, meanwhile, creates a completely sensory experience through its use of smell and colour, while the lack of packaging allows shoppers to engage directly with the products. Demonstrations are a core feature of the instore experience as staff are encouraged to show how products work (and justify the $14 price tag that comes with a bottle of shampoo).

Beyond the famous bath bomb demos, Lush employees are trained to recognize and respond to individual customer behaviours, allowing them to deliver a superior, tailored customer experience. For example, if a customer seems inquisitive, staff will spend the time getting to know their needs, explaining the product origins and demonstrating how they work; however, staff are also expected to identify and efficiently serve those who want to get in and out quickly. It might sound straightforward, but the ability to distinguish between two very different customer types in a discovery-led setting is vital.

Known for going the extra mile, Lush employees are also empowered to make their own decisions to better connect with the customer, whether that's giving away a free sample or changing the merchandising mix to reflect the weather (ie putting out more colourful, cheery products on a rainy day). The result is a more meaningful, more memorable experience – and certainly one that goes beyond the transaction.

A place to borrow

Last but not least, we believe that the store of the future will be a place to borrow. The sharing economy has already disrupted transportation and tourism but has yet to make its mark on the retail sector – shops naturally want to sell, rather than lend, to their customers. Well, the times are a-changing.

We are entering an age where access will trump ownership. This is due to the combination of a growing population, unprecedented connectivity and shifts in consumer values and priorities. We are no longer defined by our material possessions; instead we're opting to spend less on stuff and more on experiences. This is particularly pertinent among Millennials and younger generations who are increasingly – though not necessarily willingly – forgoing ownership of homes, cars, bicycles, music, books, DVDs, clothes and even pets. The World Economic Forum predicts that by 2030 products will become services and the notion of shopping will become a 'distant memory'.[26]

> 'We have an ownership society now, but we're moving toward an access society, where you're not defined by the things you own but by the experiences you have.'
> **Airbnb co-founder and CEO Brian Chesky[27]**

How is this impacting retail? Sites like *Rent the Runway* and *Bag, Borrow or Steal* give shoppers today access to luxury items without having to fork out $2,500 for an Anya Hindmarch bag. In the UK, Westfield launched the first ever standalone rental retail pop-up Style Trial in 2017. According to a study from the shopping centre group, nearly half of 25–34-year-olds are interested in renting fashion and around one-fifth would be willing to spend £200 or more per month on unlimited clothing rental subscriptions.[28]

Outside of fashion, electricals retailer Dixons Carphone has talked of a membership scheme where shoppers would pay for access to a washing machine, for example, including installation and repairs – but without actually owning it.

In the future, it will be essential to create deeper relationships with customers as the focus shifts from product to service. This explains why a retailer like Ikea acquired TaskRabbit in 2018. The online marketplace connects 60,000 freelance 'taskers' with consumers looking to hire someone to do chores such as furniture assembly. Now you can buy a Stuva wardrobe without the anxiety of putting it together.

Similarly, Walmart has joined forces with Handy for installation and assembly services for televisions and furniture. This is how retailers can survive in the age of Amazon – removing friction and establishing a meaningful customer relationship that transcends the physical store. (Side note: Amazon is expanding its own home services division, which it has been rolling out across the US since 2015, and was expanded to the UK in 2018.)

We believe there's an opportunity for hypermarkets and superstores, as a large store format with regular footfall, to consider library-style concessions where shoppers could borrow select items. This would be well suited to products that are expensive to buy outright, infrequently used and/or difficult to store – for example, sewing machines, tents, drills.

In southeast London, the Library of Things is a 'borrowing space' social enterprise that stocks everything from kitchenware to wetsuits. It's free to join and members can borrow up to five items each week, most of which can be rented for less than £4.[29] An instore 'library of things' could be part of the solution for those retailers who are struggling to fill dead space. Not only would it drive traffic to stores, but more importantly it would allow retailers to tap into the local community and develop a much deeper bond with customers.

In summary

Today, retail really is everywhere – in stores, our phones, our homes, in objects, even in media.

Online retailers like Amazon may have given shoppers unrivalled accessibility and near-instant gratification but, in doing so, they've taken the touch and feel out of shopping. Bricks and mortar retail must evolve to serve a purpose beyond just shifting product. Stores need to become special and fulfilling again. They need to tell a story, and to appease a growing desire for human connection in an increasingly digital world. Stores need to be focused on the community and provide a sensory, immersive and memorable experience that cannot be replicated online. The aim should be to make the physical space so compelling that shoppers might even be willing to pay an admission fee, as they do when going to an amusement park or the theatre.

The sector will also become more collaborative as retailers recognize the importance of working together to stand apart. But not every single store needs to become an all-singing, all-dancing version of its previous self. There will still be a place for those retailers who can genuinely offer the best value for money, convenience or have a unique product assortment. Aldi and Primark, for example, will not look very different in 10 years' time.

For most retailers, however, evolution is necessary for survival. Retailers must think of their stores as assets and not liabilities. They must break down silos and change their metrics – same-store sales growth and sales per square foot are no longer valid measures of success. Such KPIs inherently measure the physical store *against* e-commerce. Retailers are changing gears to measure the success of the physical store *alongside* e-commerce, with KPIs such as brand impression, digital purchase intent, percentage of online orders fulfilled by the store, inspiration per square foot, return on friction, convenience for associates and customer experience. Now, let's move on to explore how the store of the future is also evolving to become a hub for fulfilment.

Notes

1 Kestenbaum, Richard (2017) HBC's Richard Baker on WeWork-Lord & Taylor deal: 'This is a moment of transition', *Forbes*, 24 October. Available from: https://www.forbes.com/sites/richardkestenbaum/2017/10/24/richard-baker-of-hudsons-bay-talks-about-we-work-lord-taylor-deal/#2ca653d23487 [Last accessed 30/6/2018].

2 Microsoft Office 365 (2017) Introducing Microsoft To-Do, now in Preview (online video). Available from: https://www.youtube.com/watch?v=6k3_T84z5Ds [Last accessed 1/7/2018].

3 Thomas, Lauren (2017) Malls ditch the 'M word' as they spend big bucks on renovations, *CNBC*, 24 October. Available from: https://www.cnbc.com/2017/10/24/malls-ditch-the-m-word-as-they-spend-big-bucks-on-renovations.html [Last accessed 29/3/2018].

4 Selfridges (nd) Selfridges loves: the secrets behind our house. Available from: http://www.selfridges.com/US/en/features/articles/selfridges-loves/selfridges-lovesourhousesecrets [Last accessed 6/9/2018].

5 Abrams, Melanie (2017) Come for the shopping, stay for the food, *New York Times*, 26 October. Available from: https://www.nytimes.com/2017/10/26/travel/shopping-in-store-restaurants.html [Last accessed 30/6/2018].

6 Ringen, Jonathan (2017) Ikea's big bet on meatballs, *Fast Company*. Available from: https://www.fastcompany.com/40400784/Ikeas-big-bet-on-meatballs. [Last accessed 12/9/2018].

7 Henninger, Danya (2015) Vetri to sell restaurants to Urban Outfitters, *Philly*, 16 November. Available from: http://www.philly.com/philly/food/Vetri_to_sell_restaurants_to_Urban_Outfitters.html [Last accessed 30/6/2018].

8 Prynn, Jonathan (2015) Burberry invites customers to check out its all-day cafe in the flagship Regent Street store, *Evening Standard*, 12 June. Available from: https://www.standard.co.uk/fashion-0/burberry-invites-customers-to-check-out-its-all-day-cafe-in-the-flagship-regent-street-store-10315921.html [Last accessed 30/6/2018].

9 Abrams, Melanie (2017) Come for the shopping, stay for the food, *New York Times*, 26 October. Available from: https://www.nytimes.com/2017/10/26/travel/shopping-in-store-restaurants.html [Last accessed 30/6/2018].

10 Ryan, John (2018) In pictures: how China's ecommerce giants Alibaba and JD.com have reinvented stores, *Retail Week*, 5 June. Available from: https://www.retail-week.com/stores/in-pictures-chinas-alibaba-and-jdcom-reinvent-stores/7029203.article?authent=1 [Last accessed 30/6/2018].

11 Alton, Larry (2018) Why more millennials are flocking to shared office spaces, *Forbes*, 9 May. Available from: https://www.forbes.com/sites/larryalton/2017/05/09/why-more-millennials-are-flocking-to-shared-office-spaces/#3ec317ee69e8 [Last accessed 30/6/2018].

12 Casino Group and L'Oreal (2018) The Casino Group and L'Oréal France unveil '…le drugstore parisien', 22 June. Available from: https://www.groupe-casino.fr/en/wp-content/uploads/sites/2/2018/06/2018-06-22-The-Casino-Group-and-LOreal-France-unveil-le-drugstore-parisien.pdf [Last accessed 6/9/2018].

13 Translated from French.

14 Anonymous (2018) Two-thirds of world population will live in cities by 2050, says UN, *Guardian*, 17 May. Available from: https://www.theguardian.com/world/2018/may/17/two-thirds-of-world-population-will-live-in-cities-by-2050-says-un [Last accessed 30/6/2018].

15 Sharf, Samantha (2017) WeWork's acquisition of flagship Lord & Taylor is a sign of the changing real estate times, *Forbes*, 24 October. Available from: https://www.forbes.com/sites/samanthasharf/2017/10/24/in-a-sign-of-the-time-wework-acquiring-lord--taylors-manhattan-flagship/#16255ee326ad [Last accessed 30/6/2018].

16 JLL (2017) bracing for the flexible space revolution. Available from: http://www.jll.com/Documents/research/pdf/Flexible-Space-2017.pdf [Last accessed 30/6/2018].

17 Kestenbaum, Richard (2017) HBC's Richard Baker on WeWork-Lord & Taylor deal: 'this is a moment of transition', *Forbes*, 24 October. Available from: https://www.forbes.com/sites/richardkestenbaum/2017/10/24/richard-baker-of-hudsons-bay-talks-about-we-work-lord-taylor-deal/#2ca653d23487 [Last accessed 30/6/2018].

18 Taylor, Kate (2018) Tesla may have just picked a spot for Elon Musk's dream 'roller skates & rock restaurant' – here's everything we know about the old-school drive in, *Business Insider*, 13 March. Available from: http://uk.businessinsider.com/elon-musk-tesla-restaurant-los-angeles-2018-3 [Last accessed 1/7/2018].

19 Anonymous (2018) Mothercare confirms 50 store closures, *BBC*, 17 May. Available from: http://www.bbc.co.uk/news/business-44148937 [Last accessed 1/7/2018].

20 La Monica, Paul (2018) The death of the big toy store, *CNN*, 13 March. Available from: http://money.cnn.com/2018/03/15/investing/toys-r-us-toy-retailers-dead/index.html [Last accessed 1/7/2018].

21 GlobalData Retail (2017) Press release: 46.2% of toys & games will be sold online by 2022, *GlobalData*, 17 October. Available from: https://www.globaldata.com/46-2-of-toys-games-will-be-sold-online-by-2022/ [Last accessed 1/7/2018].

22 Anonymous (2017) The challenge of selling toys in an increasingly digital world, *eMarketer*, 19 September. Available from: https://retail.emarketer.com/article/challenge-of-selling-toys-increasingly-digital-world/59c169efebd4000a7823ab1c [Last accessed 19/6/2018].

23 Hoand, Limei (2016) 7 Lessons for retail in the age of e-commerce, *Business of Fashion*, 13 September. Available from: https://www.businessoffashion.com/articles/intelligence/concept-store-story-rachel-shechtman-seven-retail-lessons [Last accessed 1/7/2018].

24 Ahrendts, Angela (2017) Another exciting chapter, *LinkedIn*, 27 December. Available from: https://www.linkedin.com/pulse/another-exciting-chapter-angela-ahrendts/?trk=mp-reader-card&irgwc=1 [Last accessed 1/7/2018].

25 Casino Group and L'Oreal (2018) The Casino Group and L'Oréal France unveil '…le drugstore parisien', 22 June. Available from: https://www.groupe-casino.fr/en/wp-content/uploads/sites/2/2018/06/2018-06-22-The-Casino-Group-and-LOreal-France-unveil-le-drugstore-parisien.pdf [Last accessed 1/7/2018].

26 Parker, Ceri (2016) 8 predictions for the world in 2030, *World Economic Forum*, 12 November. Available from: https://www.weforum.org/agenda/2016/11/8-predictions-for-the-world-in-2030/ [Last accessed 1/7/2018].

27 Taylor, Colleen (2011) Airbnb CEO: The future is about access, not ownership, *Gigaom*, 10 November. Available from https://gigaom.com/2011/11/10/airbnb-roadmap-2011/ [Last accessed 12/9/2018].

28 Westfield (2017) Press release: Westfield launches style trial pop-up – rent this season's looks, November. Available from: https://uk.westfield.com/content/dam/westfield-corp/uk/Style-Trial-Press-Release.pdf [Last accessed 1/7/2018]

29 Balch, Oliver (2016) Is the Library of Things an answer to our peak stuff problem? *Guardian*, 23 August. Available from: https://www.theguardian.com/sustainable-business/2016/aug/23/library-of-things-peak-stuff-sharing-economy-consumerism-uber [Last accessed 1/7/2018].

Retail fulfilment: winning the customer over the final mile

13

'You do not want to give Amazon a seven-year head start.'
Warren Buffett, US business magnate[1]

In Chapters 11 and 12, we saw how the store of the future will have to evolve to simultaneously reduce friction and become more experiential. The influence of digital on the shopping journey has also increasingly seen the role of the store develop as an online fulfilment hub. Before e-commerce, the only supply chain logistics a retailer had to worry about were getting products from suppliers to the distribution and fulfilment centres, and then into their stores.

The promise to deliver

In the early e-commerce days, retail executives recalled exasperated calls from store managers demanding to know if online returns they had to accept instore would 'come off their targets'. It was then that established bricks and mortar retailers making their first forays online began to realize the true impact of e-commerce on their stores. They recognized that they could turn the fact that they had not foreseen online returns impacting their bricks and clicks presence into an advantage over the likes of then-pure-play Amazon by managing both the fulfilment process and the returns instore. They were happy to embrace this new store role if it meant shoppers assuming the delivery costs when they came in to pick up, which the retailers themselves would otherwise incur, particularly when they had to reschedule missed deliveries. This is a particular challenge for e-commerce operators when you consider return rates can be as high as 40 per cent in sectors such as fashion, and one study found that 1 per cent or more of all revenue can be lost due to delivery fraud alone.[2] Little did they know how popular these so-called 'click & collect' services would become.

Many European countries were first to see the widespread adoption of click & collect. This is due to a number of factors: prohibitively high e-commerce delivery charges; the geographic density of its populations, where they were never far from a retail chain's store; high internet broadband and mobile access; and consumers' relatively mature acceptance of alternatives to cash payment, with card-not-present and cash-on-delivery transactions facilitating the remote shopping model of e-commerce in the first place. The click & collect operations of French grocers and other retailers give 80 per cent of the population access within 10 minutes to some 4,000 pickup points. Known as 'click and drive', the fulfilment method already accounts for 5 per cent of grocery sales in France and is expected to reach 10 per cent in the next decade.[3] UK consumers are also enthusiastic click & collectors; a study forecast that click & collect sales will account for 13.9 per cent of total online spend in the UK by 2022.[4]

On Amazon's home turf in the US, the impact of click & collect fulfilment on the store has developed using drive-through additions to existing large formats, as it has in France. Target, Walmart and Kroger have expanded or plan to expand their click & collect 'Drive Up', curbside pickup and ClickList locations respectively to 1,000 each through to 2019. The introduction of automated 'kiosks' by Walmart for grocery order fulfilment takes this development to its most sophisticated incarnation. The US giant has employed learnings from its UK subsidiary Asda, which uses similar kiosk concepts, in support of reducing the extra operational overheads associated with e-commerce delivery. These larger kiosks are designed to fulfil grocery orders over $35, which are picked and packed by store staff. The 160-square-foot buildings are located in Walmart supercentre parking areas.

Like all click & collect services, Walmart's kiosks also serve to balance its e-commerce growth by incentivizing store visits and potential additional footfall. Retailers have found that click & collect customers can drive instore footfall and incremental spend through increased instore conversion rates and basket sizes. A 2015 UPS European shopper survey found 47 per cent of its respondents had used an instore collection service and, of these, 30 per cent had made additional purchases during their click & collect store visit.[5]

By comparison, before it could even think about acquiring a physical grocery chain, Amazon made its first foray into click & collect via lockers.

The first Amazon Lockers appeared in Amazon's home town of Seattle, as well as New York and London, in 2011. Customers can choose any locker location for their delivery and receive a unique pickup code via e-mail or text message to retrieve their orders, which they enter on the touchscreen of their assigned locker to open its door. Amazon has scaled its locker service by partnering with retail property owners to place the lockers in shopping malls, and in the stores of retailers such as 7-Eleven and Spar, as well as Co-op and Morrisons in the UK. Amazon Lockers can also be found Canada, France, Germany and Italy, while the company is not opposed to using less traditional locker locations, including public libraries[6] and urban apartment complexes, with its locker-based Amazon Hub service.[7] As of 2018, Amazon Lockers were currently located in more than 50 cities, across over 2,000 locations.

Remote pickup convenience

The beauty of lockers is that they eliminate specific last-mile fulfilment issues, such as theft, missed deliveries and the need for redelivery, as well as the associated added costs. Customers can also return unwanted goods using the system. But not every third-party Amazon seller can make use of the locker option if the carrier they use relies on a system that requires a signature to confirm receipt of delivery (although Amazon Hub delivery lockers accept parcels from all carriers). There is also the fact that Amazon Lockers are also unsuitable for perishable goods. With a larger online grocery market, Europe has led in the development of temperature-controlled click & collect lockers. Here, emmasbox is worthy of note. The Munich, Germany-based start-up supplies its refrigerated pickup stations for online food order fulfilment to the country's public transport authority, Deutsche Bahn, as well as other transit locations such as Munich Airport and grocery retailers Edeka and Migros. French retailer Auchan introduced 250 temperature-controlled click & collect lockers for groceries in the Saint-Etienne area in 2017 shortly after discounter Lidl also installed three pickup points for online grocery orders in Belgium. Other models, such DHL/Deutsche Post's Packstation in Germany, La Poste's Cityssimo in France and ByBox in the UK, are based on the provision of full-blown pickup locations in or near transport hubs or other high-traffic footfall urban areas, rivalling the role of the traditional post office or FedEx and UPS retail outlets. Even Amazon UK customers can pick up their parcels from Doddle's 200-plus locations, for example.

When it comes to targets, many retailers now measure the impact of e-commerce by factoring the order location into store-based or regional sales. This is why industry consensus still credits between 80 and 90 per cent of global retail sales as being 'completed' in a store. A customer may order and pay for a product online, but then choose to collect it from a local store or third-party location at a time that's more convenient for them, while also often allowing them to forgo the premium of a delivery charge. When it comes to delivery charges, Amazon was one of the first to use free delivery as a lure for more customers in 2002. It introduced its Super Saver shipping offer, lowering the threshold from $100 to $25. Outside of its Prime membership scheme, Amazon today offers free shipping on orders of $35 or more of eligible merchandise.

So, the retail industry has had to become increasingly obsessed over the 'last mile' since internet access became ubiquitous and interfaces pervasive, and as demand for near-instant fulfilment has soared. Traditionally a term used by telecommunications network providers to refer to the infrastructure that physically reaches the end-user's premises, the 'last mile' has been adopted by retail to refer to the last stage in the product or service fulfilment process. Replenishment to store, home delivery, or a hybrid of the two: fulfil-to-store for click & collect, or lockers on third-party premises, for example. Research we conducted while at PlanetRetail RNG in fact revealed that there are over 2,500 permutations of the retail fulfilment process today (see Figure 13.1).

This is when you consider the proliferation of options the consumer now has, alongside the traditional shopping trip, where the customer picks, packs and receives their own goods in a store. Supply chain capabilities have had to rapidly evolve beyond traditional hub-and-spoke, distribution and fulfilment centres to store networks to enable shoppers to access products however, wherever and whenever they want them. The 'terms', as we have referred to them in this book, of the 'on-my-terms' shopper are dictated by the order (Figure 13.2).

Figure 13.1 New fulfilment options driving heightened complexity in retail supply chains

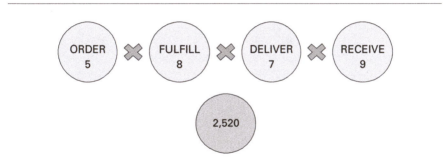

Figure 13.2 The growing complexity of fulfilling e-commerce customer orders

Order

Selected (and/or scanned) by Customer instore

OR

Telephone

Mobile – site/app

Desktop

Handsfree (voice)

Fulfil – Pick & Pack

By Customer instore

OR

Instore by retailer for collection or shipping

Dark Store

Hybrid Store

Centralized – FC/ Hybrid DC

3rd Party

Drive

Wholesaler

Manufacturer

Fulfil – The last mile

By Customer instore

OR

(pick-up)

3rd Party – on-demand, 'drop ship'

National/Global Couriers

National Parcel Post (local or express)

Retailer Own Transportation Fleet

Retailer Own – store employees deliver

Cross-Border Facilitator

Receive

By Customer instore

OR

Instore Click & Collect Desk

Curbside

Locker/Kiosk

Drive

Proximity Retail

Post Office

Non-Store/Public Space

Home

Discovery, List Mgmt & Order | Pick & Pack | Ship | Fulfil

With the consumer in control, the variations of the traditional supply chain are multiplying rapidly. These variations are driving heightened complexity in retail and manufacturing supply chains. But historically the supply chain has been considered a cost centre for many organizations. When considering the 'Amazon Effect', now more than ever, supply chain models – which dictate where an order will be picked, packed and fulfilled over the last mile, in support of new paths to purchase – will be one of the most critical growth enablers for both retailer and manufacturer organizations. This is because Amazon has already been winning over the last mile for some time now.

Developing the last mile

Winning the last mile increasingly dictates who wins the overall race to reach the consumer – success means also beating the competition on frequency, as well as relevancy, and, ultimately, loyalty. Amazon's fulfilment infrastructure is its competitive engine, in service of the speed and convenience that powers its flywheel. Without it, its two biggest supply chain-based growth generators – Prime and Fulfilment by Amazon (FBA) – could not be successful. In winning the last mile, Amazon is well known for wanting same-day and, in some areas, one-hour delivery to be the norm, where its customer proposition also makes it just as easy to order whatever you want. In that, it is a genuine disruptor.

Take, for example, YouTuber Rob Bliss, who decided to use Amazon's Prime Now to deliver goods to the homeless community around New York City. He asked each person what they needed and ordered them. Donations included socks, shoes, sleeping bags, long johns, and other hygienic items. Within hours, the items were delivered, while his videos and idea went viral.[8]

In Chapter 6 we saw how much of its last-mile strategy has also been built on the foundations it is using to gain ground in the grocery market. But it's worth restating how its massive AWS computing capability powers the complex algorithms that orchestrate its massive logistics capability and manage the complexity of getting an order processed, picked, shipped and packed to a street corner in downtown Manhattan within a matter of minutes. The AWS pillar underpins Amazon's delivery mechanisms in the most literal sense.

If you look at the final part of the shopping process in isolation, it starts from the time that the customer decides to buy an item and place an order online. This is whether they are using their own device to place the order and complete the purchase or one belonging to the retailer instore, including checkouts with e-commerce integration, kiosks, or other 'endless aisle' applications. Here, we've already seen how Amazon has enticed Prime members into its book stores with preferential pricing. It also highlights the ease of using their existing online accounts to speed payment, just as it set the standard for 1-click purchasing, which simplifies the most laborious parts of the online checkout process – filling in delivery and payment information. As we acknowledged earlier in the book, Amazon directly influenced the widespread adoption of this feature with its 1-click patent; while its Dash Buttons and Wand simple auto-replenishment, as well as its Alexa voice assistant embedded in its technology hardware range, can all perform the search, browse and discovery stages of the online shopping process hands free, right through to the order and putting items in the customer's basket for checkout.

When it comes to checkout, Amazon has also built a major play. Amazon Payments, the online payments gateway gives Amazon.com customers the option to pay with their Amazon accounts on external merchant websites. Just like its rivals Google Checkout and PayPal, Amazon Payments effectively enables customers to use one account from a trusted provider for all their online payments, while merchants are charged a percentage of the transaction and a transaction fee. One of the reasons third-party merchants like Amazon Pay is that its customers never leave the merchant's website during the checkout process and can pay using any method supported by Amazon. It is also device agnostic and merchants receive a customer's name and verified e-mail at check-in. It has also built API integrations to some of the e-commerce platforms that are popular with mid-sized merchants, such as BigCommerce, Magento and Shopify, so their users can activate a free plug-in to add the Amazon Payment option to their checkouts.

In the race for the online payments space, however, Amazon Payments cannot claim market dominance, although its client base makes it a major player. It can access 300 million-plus active customer accounts, while payments gateway rival PayPal has some 200 million. But Apple last publicly stated in 2014 that it had 800 million iTunes accounts, which require payment information, while industry estimates put Google Play accounts at around the same number. Meanwhile, the competition from social media is mounting. Facebook said at the beginning of 2018 that it had over 1.45 billion daily active users and, although its payments processing revenue is a tiny proportion of its earnings in comparison to its advertising revenues, it declared $711 million in payments and other fees in 2017 from sources including in Facebook Payments and Marketplace.[9] But you need not necessarily register payment details in order to use the social network, unlike some of the others. Despite this, while most of the others – with the exception of PayPal – have larger user bases, Amazon is the only retailer with this extended capability (though Apple has retail stores to sell its own consumer electronics products and services, and also offers Apple Pay). The only real online rival in both size, scale and sector in this regard is Alibaba subsidiary AliPay, which had 520 million registered users as of 2018.

Checkout to go

The main reason for considering purchase as part of the fulfilment process and its influence over the last mile is to put the Amazon Go store concept into its proper context here. Completely eliminating the need for checkout and payment points the way towards store of the future concepts that are more focused on fulfilment. The previous two chapters focused on how retailers can look to reduce friction at every stage of the shopping journey – from search and browsing to discovery. But, in terms of those processes that may discourage conversion instore, checkout and payment loom front and centre; retailers should take a tip from Amazon and see stores as a way of letting customers get hold of the products they want with as little effort and inconvenience as possible.

UK grocer Waitrose has trialled a cashless store in its 'little Waitrose' format, while Walmart and Kroger certainly heeded the Amazon Go threat in the US, with both developing checkout-less shopping services but with differing fortunes. In 2014, Walmart initially tested its 'Scan & Go' mobile app that allowed customers to scan the barcodes of selected products and then check them out without having to complete an additional stop at a checkout – although those customers did have a dedicated Express lane to exit the store with their purchases, for security purposes. Then, just before the Amazon Go store opened to the public in Seattle at the beginning of 2018, Walmart announced that it was expanding its 25-store trial to 100 stores across the US after successfully implementing a similar service at its wholesale chain, Sam's Club. But, just as suddenly as it made its announcement, six months later it said it was abandoning the trials at Walmart stores due to low uptake. Some in the industry said customers found it difficult to manage their device, the product they were scanning, and their basket, trolley or shopping bag; that theft was also an issue. Walmart said it will continue to offer its Scan & Go service using proprietary handheld scanning guns, with no risk of them running out of battery life, and dedicated trolley holders. Kroger has fared slightly better, rolling out a similar mobile app and handheld scanner-based service it calls 'Scan, Bag, Go', to 400 stores in 2018, having first trialled the concept a year before. One last point of note here is that Waitrose was first to roll out proprietary handheld scanning guns... in 2002!

So, Amazon's checkout and payment strategy certainly ensures it has a role to play in the ordering and payment processes of other retailers as it continues to revolutionize this part of the shopping journey from a physical perspective too. Although it does not include these services in its third-party Marketplace financials, let's not forget this part of the flywheel in our consideration of Amazon's role in the order, pay and fulfilment process, where Amazon provides the entire e-commerce front-end, online shopping service for third-party merchants.

Where every part of the Amazon infrastructure, offering and ecosystem reinforces its core aim, to sell 'more stuff', its last-mile proposition very much reinforces the core values of its offer: choice, convenience and speed. The multi-track Amazon last mile extends from auto-replenishment to Prime and its free, unlimited two-day delivery offer, or same day depending on the delivery location.

It's worth considering how well Amazon fares in using the mechanics of subscription to drive increased sales among members. Certainly, led by Amazon's example with Prime, subscription services have been growing in popularity for a while. For example, a recent survey found British consumers were spending on average over £2 billion ($2.6 billion) annually on delivery subscriptions.[10] Of course, the most popular subscription service was Amazon Prime, with 61.4 per cent of those who took part in the survey signed up to benefit from the service. Other popular subscriptions revealed by the poll were: healthy snacks company Graze (12.3 per cent), fashion and homewares retailer nextunlimited (9.7 per cent), fast fashion pureplay ASOS Premier (8.8 per cent), Pact Coffee (8.5 per cent) and beauty provider Glossybox (7.8 per cent). Respondents also said both convenience (45 per cent) and value for money (60 per cent) were the key drivers behind them signing up, while almost half (48.9 per cent) admitted to buying items they wouldn't have otherwise bought if they hadn't had the subscription service. It's easy to see why Unilever was willing to pay $1 billion for Dollar Shave Club in 2017.[11] The direct-to-consumer (D2C) acquisition gave the brand giant a recurring revenue source and predictable demand from a loyal customer base.

Recurring revenues

Melanie Darvall, director of marketing and communications at Whistl, the UK postal delivery company that sponsored the subscription survey, commented that the key to launching a successful subscription service is finding the right balance to make the offering beneficial for both parties – the retailer and consumer. 'Ensuring the quality of product or value of discount is high enough to make your customer base loyal and consider spending money outside of what is essentially a monthly "taster" service can certainly be a challenge, but once you've cracked that side of things, you'll reap the rewards and hopefully retain a happy customer base', she commented.[12] To Darvall's point, a recent Amazon advertising campaign used the slogan 'Amazon Prime Delivers More', in reference to the free video and music streaming Prime members have access to, alongside free delivery, among its many other benefits.

Amazon also raised the order fulfilment stakes with the introduction of Prime Now, which, as previously discussed, introduced one-hour delivery for subscribers in eligible urban shipping areas. Prime Now serves as a potent example of the behemoth's ability to build on its innovations, but also of how potent a force its speed to market can be. Now Amazon's growing Prime subscriber base is driving its fulfilment capacity demands.

So, in the rest of this and the next chapter, we'll look at how it is building out its last-mile fulfilment logistics proposition, including current and future innovation through Prime Now, lockers and ultra-rapid delivery by drone, as well as FBA, but also how its supply chain strategy is evolving to encompass added online-to-offline (O2O) capabilities in a growing array of other sectors, including fashion and, of course, grocery too.

Building out the last mile

Amazon was actually a relative latecomer to the instant delivery space. At launch, industry watchers questioned whether Amazon could afford to dump money into a war with the rash of on-demand start-ups springing up to challenge traditional retail fulfilment models in response to consumers' insatiable appetite for instant gratification. Others suggested it had no choice but to go head-to-head with the Postmates, Shipts, Instacarts and Delivs of this world, where these competitors own no products and fulfil customer orders on behalf of their retailer clients who are also playing catch-up to Amazon on same-day delivery, including the Walmart-to-Go initiative and Tesco's one-hour delivery tie-up with Quiqup in London.

Direct competitors also responded quickly: eBay, for example, differentiated its same-day delivery service by adding 80 small businesses in Brooklyn to the eBay Local programme. This was seen as an acknowledgment of the fact Amazon was potentially cutting its Marketplace merchants out of its new last-mile development by using Prime and Prime Now selections to favour its nascent private label ranges, which include nappies and other everyday essentials. But it does highlight some local retailer partnerships, such as with Spirited Wines, Morrisons and Booths in the UK and regional US grocer New Seasons Market, for example.

eBay had, in fact, bought the start-up responsible for the world's fastest e-commerce delivery – Shutl – for an undisclosed sum in 2013, a year before Prime Now launched. Shutl expanded its deliveries for purchases made via the e-commerce sites of major retailers', including Argos and B&Q Tradepoint, as well as fashion brands like Karen Millen, Oasis, Coast and Warehouse, in as little as 90 minutes across 11 cities way back in 2011. Making its first delivery in 2010, Shutl claims its fastest was completed in 15 minutes, making it an early developer of the algorithms required to match local independent, third-party couriers with orders and pickup points based on cost, location and capacity. Yet eBay took three years to fully incorporate the start-up into its operations, launching a new delivery service for its UK sellers in 2017 based on a platform built from scratch by Shutl. Merchants weren't happy that there was no option to opt out of using its express delivery services. One posted on a merchant noticeboard: 'Shutl could be an asset if they redesign it and make it work efficiently, it's another example of eBay launching a service before it is fully ready. It is of course just a booking agent like P2Go, basically a middle man between seller and postal carrier. One label per sheet of paper, lack of choice, compensation limited, all are problems at the moment.'

Competitive context

Google, in comparison to eBay, was quicker to launch a same-day and overnight delivery service from local and national US retailers in 2013 with Google Shopping Express, which was later shortened to Google Express. Delivery is carried out via branded vehicles and third-party courier firms and customers must have a Google Play account. Although the retailers can add delivery surcharges, deliveries are charged at $5 per stop, and delivery windows come nowhere near those of Prime Now, with a three- to five-hour window. But it has seen gradual expansion, in part because its voice assistant integration offers retailers a capable alternative to Amazon's Alexa, signing deals with Walmart, Costco, Target and Carrefour.

Given rivals Google and eBay's apparent lack of speed to market or ability to rapidly scale their rapid fulfilment efforts, it's easier to understand

Amazon's relatively measured entry into express delivery with Prime Now in 2014. At its launch, CNET senior editor, Dan Ackerman, pointed to the huge expense of servicing and expanding Prime Now. He pointed to 'the manpower, the infrastructure to not just put something in a box and mail it but to actually put it on the back of a bike messenger in a city and send it out.'[13] In that same year the free shipping (and rapid Prime delivery) that Amazon uses to delight its customers and best the competition cost more than $4.2 billion or nearly 5 per cent of net sales. Stephenie Landry, Amazon Prime Now vice president, addressed questions about the cost of Prime Now at an industry event in 2017.[14] 'Ultra-fast shopping is an expensive proposition', she admitted. 'It isn't easy to do but the only way to learn about it is to be in the game.' But, in the true spirit of living the Amazon Leadership Principles, Landry added, 'As leader of this business, I don't spend much of my time thinking about delivery costs; I really think about customer love – how do I make a customer love this product? I would take a cost problem over a customer love problem any day.'[15]

Food takeaway expansion

In addition to consolidating the wider benefits of Prime within Amazon's ecosystem – feeding the flywheel – Amazon also added restaurant delivery to the services available with Prime Now. Launched in the summer of 2015, offering free two-hour delivery and one-hour delivery for $7.99, Amazon Restaurants is an online food ordering service available in 20 urban areas throughout the US and London, England. As of 2018, the service had over 7,600 restaurants offering delivery through the Prime Now service. As well as independent restaurants, the service includes chains such as Red Robin, Applebee's, Olive Garden and P.F. Chang's. Amazon Restaurants is available on the Prime Now mobile app and on Amazon's website. One-hour delivery is free once users meet a certain spending amount, determined by the restaurant using a comparable business model to those of Just Eat, Delivery Hero, foodpanda, foodora and a whole host of other restaurant food delivery intermediaries. Interestingly, arguably the king of fast food giants, McDonalds, has been operating its McDelivery service in 25 countries; it first launched in the US in 1993, predating the rapid food delivery gold rush. The latest McDelivery development, however, shows just how disruptive third-party delivery intermediaries have become, rolling out in the UK via Uber Eats in 2018.

Deliveroo is worth a mention here, not only for the fact it shares similarities in its rapid restaurant food delivery model with the Just Eats of this world, but that it has also taken on some of the food production as well. Founded in London in 2013, its fleet of independent but branded couriers deliver both sole trading and chain restaurant fare in 200 cities across 12 countries. But Deliveroo has gone on to launch its pop-up Editions 'dark' kitchens in its home market in 2017. The so-called 'RooBox' takeaway-only kitchens prepare branded food from the likes of Thai chain Busaba Eathai, US-style MeatLiquor diners and Franco Manca pizza parlours, from locations like industrial estates and disused car parks, to reduce the set-up costs in comparison to a full-service restaurant.

Also, like Deliveroo, Instacart has been learning from the clients it serves. Brittain Ladd, industry consultant and former Amazon executive, wrote:

> Instacart is given complete and unfettered access to every detail and costs of the retailers who signed them. Instacart has been actively increasing the amount of capital they raise so that they can become a grocery retailer, wholesaler, and manufacturer of private label products. The grocery retailers who viewed Instacart as being their saviour taught Instacart their business, including their strengths and weaknesses. As Instacart expands their business model, they'll be able to use their knowledge of their grocery customers to their advantage.[16]

Driving last-mile demand

So, we can see how expansion of services, including Amazon Restaurants, AmazonFresh and Pantry, respond to growing sector opportunities through the mechanisms of Prime Now. They may have Amazon's scale behind them to add significant momentum to its flywheel, but they must compete against increasingly diverse rivals.

One area where Amazon has sought to stay ahead of the competition when it comes to the differentiation of Prime Now is, of course, the actual online shopping experience. A good example of this is the tracking capability first introduced in the US with a soft launch in 2017, and which Amazon began quietly ramping up the following year. It gives customers a real-time map of their delivery's journey, as well as how many other stops or deliveries your courier will make before yours. But early reports suggest that the system is only compatible with parcels fulfilled by its own logistics network and not those handled by the US Postal Service, UPS or FedEx. However, the fact that the tracking capability also eliminates missed deliveries and fraud, means it is a system Amazon is likely going to want to roll out to more Prime users in future.

Notes

1 Video (2017) 'You do not want to give Jeff Bezos a seven-year head start,' *CNBC*, 8 May. Available from: https://www.cnbc.com/video/2017/05/08/ buffett-you-do-not-want-to-give-jeff-bezos-a-seven-year-head-start.html [Last accessed 5/11/2018].

2 Lexis Nexis (2014) Annual Report: True cost of fraud study: post-recession revenue growth hampered by fraud as all merchants face higher costs, *LexisNexis*, August. Available from: https://www.lexisnexis.com/risk/ downloads/assets/true-cost-fraud-2014.pdf [Last accessed 7/6/2018].

3 Wells, Jeff (2017) Report: France's drive is a growth model for U.S. grocery e-commerce, *RetailDive*, 20 July. Available from: https://www.fooddive.com/ news/grocery–report-frances-drive-is-a-growth-model-for-us-grocery-e-com-merce/447522/ [Last accessed 6/6/2018].

4 Global Data (2017) Click & Collect in the UK, 2017–2022, *GlobalData*, December. Available from: https://www.globaldata.com/store/report/ vr0104ch–click-collect-in-the-uk-2017-2022/ [Last accessed 6/6/2018].

5 IMRG (2016) IMRG Collect+ UK Click & Collect Review, *IMRG*, 14 June. Available from: https://www.imrg.org/data-and-reports/imrg-reports/imrg-collect-plus-uk-click-and-connect-review-2016/ [Last accessed 6/6/2018].

6 Gov.uk (2016) Case study: Amazon lockers in libraries, *Gov.uk*, 5 January. Available from: https://www.gov.uk/government/case-studies/amazon-lockers-in-libraries [Last accessed 7/6/2018].

7 Schlosser, Kurt (2017) Amazon's new 'Hub' delivery locker system is already a hit in San Francisco apartment building, *GeekWire*, 25 August. Available from: https://www.geekwire.com/2017/amazons-new-hub-delivery-locker-system-already-hit-san-francisco-apartment-building/ [Last accessed 7/6/2018].

8 Lang, Cady (2017) How you can use Amazon Prime to help people in need this holiday season, *Time*, 12 December. Available from: http://time.com/5061792/ amazon-prime-charity/ [Last accessed 2/6/2018].

9 Facebook (2018) Facebook Quarterly Earnings Slides Q1 2018, page 4, *Facebook Investor Relations*, 25 April. Available from: https://investor.fb.com/ investor-events/event-details/2018/Facebook-Q1-2018-Earnings/default.aspx [Last accessed 6/6/2018].

10 Whistl (2018) Press release: Brits spending over £2bn on average a year on delivery subscriptions, *Whistl*, 25 May. Available from: http://www.whistl. co.uk/news/subscription-services-a-whistl-survey/ [Last accessed 6/6/2018].

11 Primack, Dan (2017) Unilever buys Dollar Shave Club for $1 Billion, *Fortune*, 20 July. Available from: http://fortune.com/2016/07/19/unilever-buys-dollar-shave-club-for-1-billion/ [Last accessed 24/4/2018].

12 Morrell, Liz (2018) British consumers spending more than £2 billion a year on delivery subscriptions, edelivery, 14 May. Available from: https://edelivery. net/2018/05/british-consumers-spending-2-billion-year-delivery-subscriptions/ [Last accessed 13/9/2018].

13 Staff writer (2014) Instant gratification: Amazon launches 1-hour shipping in Manhattan, *CNBC*, 18 December. Available from: https://www.cbsnews. com/news/amazon-launches-1-hour-shipping-in-manhattan/ [Last accessed 6/6/2018].

14 Wienbren, Emma (2017) Two-hour deliveries will be normal, says Amazon Prime Now VP, *The Grocer*, 20 March. Available from: https://www.thegrocer. co.uk/channels/online/two-hour-deliveries-will-be-normal-says-amazon-prime-now-vp/550248.article?rtnurl=/# [Last accessed 6/6/2018].

15 Galloway, Scott (2015) The future of retail looks Like Macy's, not Amazon, *Gartner L2*, 1 May. Available from: https://www.l2inc.com/daily-insights/the-future-of-retail-looks-like-macys-not-amazon [Last accessed 7/6/2018].

16 Ladd, Brittain (2018) The Trojan Horse: Instacart's covert operation against grocery retailers, *LinkedIn*, 18 March. Available from: https://www.linkedin. com/pulse/trojan-horse-instacarts-covert-operation-grocery-retailing-ladd/ [Last accessed 4/9/2018].

The last-mile infrastructure

14

'Amazon makes money differently from a conventional publisher. It is an infrastructure player.'
Nick Harkaway, novelist[1]

Having seen how Prime and Prime Now expand Amazon's reach across categories and act as a conduit for the introduction of new services to strengthen its flywheel effect and fuel its rapid growth, it is important to think about how the cost of satisfying such impatient and varied demand impacts Amazon's broader fulfilment logistics strategy. Consider for instance that Amazon's first Prime Now fulfilment centre (FC) was in midtown Manhattan, opposite the Empire State building, and dedicated Prime Now teams work to fulfil orders via a variety of methods. 'We are taking our operational expertise that we've developed at our more than 100 fulfilment centres around the globe and bringing it to New York to fuel this service', declared Kelly Cheeseman, Amazon communications spokesperson, at its launch. 'Delivery associates will walk, take public transportation, bike or drive to deliver to customers.'

The Prime Now FC locations are miniature 'Hubs', rather than full-blown Amazon FCs. They are smaller: for example, the Prime Now Kenosha, Milwaukee hub covers 25,000 square feet, which is equivalent to around twice the size of an average urban grocery store. Compare this in size to its mega 1 million-square-foot FC in Dunfermline, Scotland or the 1.27 million-square-foot FC in Phoenix, Arizona, which is large enough to fit 28 football pitches. In the absence of a substantial physical store network in a given location, these FC hubs shorten the last-mile fulfilment costs in densely populated urban areas, where transit times can be severely impacted by traffic. More importantly, they also serve as Amazon's next-best means of competing with the instant gratification of a local retail store visit, with the advantage of your purchases being brought to you. According to Cooper

Smith, an analyst at research firm Gartner L2, Amazon 'now has warehouses within 20 miles of half the US population'.[2] This closes the last-mile gap to the densest urban populations but is still comparatively further than the average distance of a US consumer to a Walmart, which is 6.7 miles.[3]

The Prime Now 'pickers', so-called in the logistics industry because they pick and pack orders in FCs, use mobile handheld barcode-reading devices to locate items. Space is saved by using a 'random stow' system, instead of designated stock areas that more automated warehouse management systems require. While this can lead to some incongruous items being stored alongside each other, where items are put on the aisles of shelving is left down to the pickers to maximize use of space. An Amazon spokesperson reported that random stow enhances picking accuracy; it might be easier to make a mistake if many different versions of the same item were stored in the same location.

The Prime Now FCs also feature easily accessible 'high-velocity pallets' for frequently ordered items, such as toilet paper and bananas, and walk-in refrigerator and freezer units for chilled and frozen goods that might also be ordered through via AmazonFresh and Pantry household and grocery services. After picking, orders are prepared for dispatch via what Amazon calls its 'SLAM' line, which is an acronym for 'scan, label, apply, manifest'. Orders are then fulfilled using a number of delivery methods; the company's bike courier experiments in Manhattan received a lot of publicity and fuelled rumours of a move into express delivery in the weeks before Prime Now's launch.

Last-mile labour

From the perspective of last-mile labour costs, Prime Now differs to the rest of Amazon's fulfilment infrastructure in its intensive use of pickers, as well as its random stow system. This makes it more reliant on more human labour than in its larger FCs, where its Kiva warehouse robotic sortation systems take on more of the traditional picking and packing tasks. Its use of express courier services to deliver Prime Now orders is also another extra labour-intensive expense Amazon must absorb for the price of having the fastest and most extensive last mile. This is why it also quickly followed up on its initial launch of Prime Now with the introduction of Amazon Flex, a platform for independent contractors to provide delivery services, towards the end of 2015. The platform capitalizes on the expanding gig economy popularized by Uber and other express delivery rivals to first meet the demand for Prime Now, but it now manages regular Amazon deliveries too.[4] In the same way as Uber matches drivers with what it calls 'riders' and Instacart matches customers with 'shoppers', the Amazon Flex Android-based app directs 'Flexers' to delivery locations within a radius local to them.

Flex is interesting for two main reasons: the first is that its entry into the 'gig economy' by employing independent contractors over its last mile hasn't exactly proved the most customer-centric solution to last-mile express delivery Amazon might have hoped for. True, it gives Amazon end-to-end control, where it can share its last-mile visibility with customers through its delivery tracking app feature. But the fact that Flexers use their own vehicles and initially wore nothing that identified them as working for Amazon, led to an initial backlash by worried neighbourhood watch activists, who were 'creeped out' by these strangers coming to their door.[5] Like Uber, Amazon has also had to defend contractor lawsuits brought by ex-Flexers, who argued that they took home less than minimum wage after costs associated with running their own vehicles. Some plaintiffs who were sub-contracted by Amazon.com via Amazon Logistics and local courier firms, claimed Amazon should pay them as full-time employees because they worked out of its warehouses and were highly supervised by Amazon, who also provided their customer service training.[6]

Perhaps staff working for its Whole Foods acquisition could carry out deliveries after work to lessen the litigious risk from gig economy-based models, just like Walmart said it was testing in 2017. In yet another attempt to cut e-commerce fulfilment costs, Walmart can exploit not only its extensive store estate to promote click & collect, but also began looking to its large store staff base to carry out home deliveries. The retailer was offering to pay staff extra to use an app that could direct them to deliver up to 10 customer orders per commute. 'It just makes sense', said Marc Lore, Walmart US e-commerce president and CEO, in a blog post. 'We already have trucks moving orders from fulfilment centres to stores for pickup. Those same trucks could be used to bring ship-to-home orders to a store close to their final destination, where a participating employee can sign up to deliver them to the customer's house.'[7]

Third-party carrier custom

The second reason for singling out Flex is that Amazon's gig-based initiative reveals a fulfilment logistics strategy that seeks to lessen its reliance on the US Postal Service, FedEx and UPS's third-party parcel delivery services. Bear in mind that 20 different partners currently ship some 600 million Amazon parcels a year, with the US Postal Service, FedEx and UPS moving the most. Cost management is an obvious priority, where Amazon can realize efficiencies by gaining end-to-end visibility over its entire supply chain. Entrusting the last mile to third parties cedes control over the most visible customer-facing part of that chain and is at odds with its customer-driven ethos. Its US Postal Service custom has also recently been in the firing line of Donald Trump's peripatetic Twitter rants in what some have seen as thinly veiled attacks on Jeff Bezos and his ownership of the *Washington Post* newspaper, which has been critical of the US President's threats against journalists who provide coverage he deems unfavourable. In what Trump has termed Amazon's 'Post Office scam', he tweeted, 'It is reported that the US Post Office will lose $1.50 on average for each package it delivers for Amazon.'[8] While this and the taxes Amazon pays have been criticized by Trump and may end up becoming part of a wider antitrust move by the Republican president, industry consensus puts the US Postal Service's woes down to reasons that have little to do with Amazon. Some estimates show that the US Postal Service is charging below market rate for package delivery, where Amazon undoubtedly has the scale to negotiate the best possible price; but its falling revenues are actually attributable to the slowdown in direct mail demand rather than package deliveries.[9] Amazon has also had spats with FedEx and UPS over how much business it puts through their US Postal Service rival. But they have, in turn, also been critical of the amount of fixed costs they are required by law[10] to cover with revenue from their competitive parcel business – FedEx and UPS argue that at least 5.5 per cent is not enough, when its competitive business now accounts for 30 per cent of its total revenue, up from 11 per cent a decade ago.

Other competitive challenges of note have come from direct retail rivals, Walmart and Target. Reports surfaced at the end of 2017 that Walmart had told a number of its contracted carriers that it may choose not to do business with them if they were also doing business with Amazon,[11] such is the demand for third-party fulfilment capacity driven by US e-commerce sales growth. Walmart took a similar stance with those suppliers using AWS. Target's acquisition of grocery marketplace and same-day delivery platform Shipt for $550 million at the end of 2017 was seen as a direct challenge to Amazon's ability to fulfil same-day deliveries, while also giving the retail chain a greater capability to overcome inventory challenges associated with click & collect. In a company blog about its purchase, John Mulligan, Target's chief operating officer, cited the acquisition as part of a series of measures aimed at 'making shopping at Target easier, more reliable and more convenient' for its customers, which included expanding ship-from-store capabilities to more than 1,400 stores nationwide, launching its next-day essentials delivery service Target Restock and Drive Up in-car fulfilment service, and acquiring last-mile transportation technology company Grand Junction.[12] Target's declared aim was to bring same-day delivery to about half of Target stores in early 2018.

> 'I have 1,800 mini warehouses across the country. 460 feature backrooms converted into online order fulfilment centres. Employees who are cross-trained to work the sales floor and the backrooms pick online orders from stores' shelves or inventory and pack them at the store. UPS picks up the orders and delivers them to hub-and-spoke distribution centres.'
> **Brian Cornell, Target CEO, 2018**[13]

We've seen how Prime and Prime Now power the flywheel, and how new additions like Amazon Prime Pantry, AmazonFresh and Amazon Wardrobe add scale and breadth to the wider Amazon ecosystem. But we've also begun to explore how these new additions also put increased pressure on its supply chain and fulfilment logistics. All of this expansion must be fed by an ever-growing distribution and fulfilment network.

Amazon laid the foundations for Prime with a traditional FC and logistics network model, using third-party carriers as already discussed. But it has continued to innovate, using its substantial AWS computing power to boost the ability to orchestrate its huge logistics network so it can yield greater levels of automation, efficiency and productivity. It started its business with two FCs in Seattle and Delaware and over the next two decades grew this estate to over 250 million square feet of data centre and FC space around the globe.

Growing IT infrastructure

Looking at its data centre estate, this vast computing resource is rarely discussed, as it is the Amazon business, developer toolset and internet traffic running on top that people care about. With some of the world's biggest media and social networks, streaming services, publishers and retailers all running on the AWS cloud, it's very difficult to estimate how much of the world's internet traffic flows across it. An estimate by DeepField Networks put the proportion at a third of the world's internet traffic – and that was back in 2012.[14] Amazon is also particularly tight-lipped about its AWS data centre infrastructure, never offering tours of any of its facilities. Its website only displays rough approximations of the locations of their data centres, divided into 'regions', each region containing at minimum two 'availability zones' which are home to a handful of data centres. It locates these data centres as near as possible to internet exchange points, which transfer content traffic, and builds its own accompanying electric substations, each of which can generate as much as 100 megawatts or more – enough to power tens of thousands of the densest servers per site, or millions globally. Having set up its first AWS data centre in northern Virginia, US in 2006, as the centre of this infrastructure, by 2018 it had 50 availability zones across the world. It operates much of this estate through a subsidiary company, Vadata Inc.

The rise of Amazon Logistics

In much the same way as it has built its AWS services by rapidly scaling its global data centre infrastructure, Amazon has used similar blitz tactics to build out and support its physical last-mile fulfilment network through its Amazon Logistics operations. While its first two FCs were established in 1997, it has been ramping up its supply chain and logistics footprint aggressively since 2005 and the launch of Prime, and now over 80 per cent of its total global real estate is dedicated to data centres and some 750 warehouse facilities. Its North American FC roll-out strategy between 2008 and 2010 can be tracked against those states that offer the most tax-friendly breaks for retail sales.

But, by 2013, as each state started to implement tax fairness policies, Amazon had moved its focus to serving more urban areas to minimize transportation costs over its last mile and nurture its Prime Now ambitions. Marc Wulfraat, President and Founder of supply chain, logistics, and distribution consulting firm MWPVL International Inc., commented in an e-mail to the authors, 'If you sort the US metro population in descending sequence, you can see that Amazon clearly started to build out FCs close to major metro markets.' It operates a variety of different types of fulfilment and distribution centres, including those that handle small sortable, large sortable, large nonsortable, speciality apparel, footwear and small parts, and return items, as well as its third-party logistics outsourced facilities. It also has a network of ambient and cold-storage grocery DCs to serve its Amazon Pantry and AmazonFresh operations.[15]

Also in 2013, Amazon and many other retailers in the US competing for last-minute Christmas spending were unable to deliver packages on time due to the fact that many pushed order deadlines back to as late as 11pm on 23 December, and were overwhelmed by a surge in demand that amounted to a 37 per cent year-on-year increase in orders placed during the last week-end before the holiday.[16] Many blamed UPS, which was responsible for the last-mile delivery of a fair proportion of the approximately 7.75 million packages it shipped through its air network on the Monday before that Christmas.

Amazon's leasing patterns have also emphasized last-mile warehouses driving proximity to the consumer in the latest phase of its warehouse network expansion in response to the learnings from 2013 and subsequent demand for Prime Now. Amazon now splits its logistics warehouse invest-ment between four types of facility:

- Fulfilment Centre (FC): A large warehouse (typically of approximately 1 million square feet) that receives items in bulk, stores them and ships them out individually.

- Inbound and Outbound Sortation Centres (SCs): After the shipping debacle of 2013, Amazon started adding SCs that pre-sort packages for carriers, such as UPS and FedEx, as well as its Saturday and Sunday US Postal Service deliveries. (The SCs are usually adjacent and/or connected via conveyor belt to an FC.) These facilities sort packages by area code for delivery to the carrier responsible for the final delivery of indi-vidual packages. From there, the carrier performs last-mile delivery to the customer. Sortation centres also ship packages to Amazon's exten-sive Delivery Station Network, which represents the final node in the Amazon distribution network. Sortation centres can handle packages for a regional area on behalf of one or more fulfilment centres.

- Redistribution Fulfilment Centre (RFC) or the Inbound Cross Dock (IXD) Network: Amazon has in some regions opened B2B facilities to feed into a network of individual FCs. For example, the warehouse known as 'ONT8' in California – Amazon names its facilities using nearby airport codes and the numerical order in which they're built – is an RFC for the other ONT and California FCs. These facilities are located near major ports to minimize inbound ground transportation expense from the port to the facility.

- Prime Now Hubs and the Delivery Station Network: Sometimes an FC is close enough to a metro to support Prime Now (eg Atlanta, Georgia). In other regions, Amazon opens a specific Prime Now Hub (eg Chicago, Illinois). The Hubs also complement an additional subset of metro

Delivery Station facilities to service a Delivery Station Network. These smaller, 100-square-foot locations are for the sorting and dispatching of packages via local courier firms and Amazon Flex couriers.

The introduction of regional SCs in 2014 across the US increased control over the outbound transportation of packages within its own distribution network. Experts recognize these buildings are key enablers to moving away from its reliance on UPS and FedEx, so packages can be delivered by the US Postal Service, local couriers and Amazon.

Real estate demand

The rise of e-commerce, bolstered by Amazon's inexorable expansion in the US and Europe in particular (and which is now spreading to Asia and the Indian subcontinent), is heating up the industrial real estate market. The Urban Land Institute's Emerging Trends Report for 2018 listed fulfilment centres and warehouses as the top two sectors with investment potential, and their average size has increased from 24 to 34 feet in height to cater for e-commerce fulfilment. Amazon has said its warehouses can ship more than 1 million items a day during busy holiday seasons and that a typical Amazon delivery requires just one minute of human labour.[17] That said, Amazon has also come under fire for working conditions in its warehouses such as onerous screening and tracking procedures, long hours and distances travelled per shift with highly regulated bathroom and work breaks, and relatively low levels of remuneration. So much so that in 2013, German unions called for strikes over Amazon warehouse workers' pay rates.[18]

> 'The factory [or warehouse] of the future will have only two employees: a man and a dog. The man will be there to feed the dog. The dog will be there to keep the man from touching the equipment.'
> **Warren Bennis**[19]

Let's not forget, as referenced in our exploration of automation development, Amazon bought Kiva Systems, the company that manufactures the robots, for $775 million in 2012. Following the acquisition, to cover itself for the 2014 holiday season, it added about 15,000 Kiva robots to 10 US fulfilment centres. Current estimates suggest they now make up one-fifth of the Amazon workforce and also reduce warehouse operating costs by 20 per cent. The robots are responsible for moving proprietary shelving 'pods' along a predefined grid to workstations where Amazon picking staff pick, pack and prepare the items for shipment, loading them onto a network of conveyor belts that can handle some 400-odd orders per second. Its warehouse management software matches the right sized box with each order and handles the application of shipping labels.

The parts of the process managed by the Amazon Robotics system are claimed to be five to six times more productive than manual picking and eliminate the need for human-scale aisles, taking up half as much space as a traditional, non-automated warehouse. Their flexibility also means they can be used to constantly reconfigure the warehouse space based on sales data, so high-velocity items can be retrieved more quickly. The robots, however, can only handle relatively small items that fit in the pods they transport, in comparison to traditional retail and wholesale warehouses which rely on carrying and stacking most of the inventory on pallets with fork-lift trucks. For larger items, large robotic arms known as 'robo-stows' (manufactured by Thiele Technologies) handle these, moving and packing boxes at Amazon's larger FCs. Another warehouse technology feature is the vision system that can unload and receipt an entire trailer of stock in as little as 30 minutes, while in 2017, the company created a team to guide its use of driverless-vehicle technology, for the deployment of self-driving forklifts, trucks and other such vehicles that can build on its existing automation efforts.

With such a huge supply chain and fulfilment logistics network, and a constant drive to improve performance and cut delivery cost and time, it was perhaps inevitable that Amazon would also enter the transportation market. Indeed, transportation and logistics could be the next billion-dollar opportunity for e-commerce companies, according to industry research.[20] The global shipping market, including ocean, air, and truck freight, is worth $2.1 trillion, according to figures from the World Bank, Boeing and Golden Valley Company. With so much at stake, legacy shipping companies, which have been able to capitalize on the boom in parcel delivery as e-commerce spending has risen, are under increasing pressure from Amazon and the likes of Alibaba, JD.com and Walmart. Amazon and its rivals have to date focused on building out last-mile logistics fulfilment capabilities but are increasingly going after the middle and first mile of the fulfilment supply chain.

Amazon started by offering outsourced consolidation for international sellers in 2014, leveraging bulk discounts for cheaper US import rates. Towards the end of 2015, it emerged in rapid succession that it had been negotiating to lease 20 Boeing 767 jets for its own air-delivery service, had registered to provide ocean freight services in China, and had purchased thousands of truck trailers to ship merchandise between distribution facilities.[21] Amazon China then registered to provide ocean freight services, essentially pushing Chinese sellers to use its services for shipping to Amazon US customers and giving it control over the significant trading routes between China and the US. Amazon Maritime, Inc. holds a US Federal Maritime Commission operating licence, as a non-vessel-owning common carrier (NVOCC).

Amazon as a carrier

In 2016, Amazon received options to purchase up to 19.9 per cent of Air Transport International's stock and began scheduled operations with 20 Boeing 767 aircraft. A year later, it unveiled its first branded cargo plane and announced that Amazon Air would make Cincinnati/Northern Kentucky International Airport its principal hub. It also received tax breaks to the tune of $40 million for the construction of a 920-acre facility with a 3-million-square-foot sorting facility and parking space for over 100 cargo aircraft at an estimated total cost of $1.5 billion. According to plans filed for an onsite sorting facility, 440 acres is scheduled for completion in 2020, while the remaining 479 acres will be developed by 2025–2027 during a second phase, by which time it is planned to handle freight from 100 aircraft based at the hub and operate over 200 flights daily. This move also complements the set of cargo-handling facilities built out at smaller airports to enable connectivity between its Air Sortation Centre in Hebron, Kentucky and major cities with FCs. MWPVL International Inc. refers to these as 'air sortation hubs'. They are positioned close to airport runways for the purpose of handling and receiving freight packages being shipped to the Hebron Air Hub.

In addition to its disruptive moves with same-day and one-hour delivery, managing its own fleet of couriers, trucks cargo ships and planes, and reducing its reliance on third-party providers, in 2017 Amazon also introduced its first app for truck drivers, designed to make it easier to pick up and drop off packages at Amazon warehouses.[22] Giving Amazon direct access to millions of truck drivers across the country, it is also thought to be working on a similar app that would match truck drivers with cargo. Another, slightly more leftfield innovation is the patent Amazon filed in 2015 for delivery trucks equipped with 3D printers that would enable them to manufacture products on the way to the customer destination.[23] It filed a further 3D patent in 2018, covering the eventuality of cutting the manufacturer out of the equation altogether by taking custom orders for 3D-printed items to get them made and have them delivered to or collected by the customer.[24]

Fulfilment by Amazon

If Amazon really is looking to cut the middleman out of the fulfilment process and take end-to-end control of its supply chain, it is impossible to view any moves to expand its global logistics footprint as anything other than an extension of its 'Fulfilment by Amazon' service, which stores, picks, packs and ships products and handles returns sold by third-party merchants on the Amazon.com marketplace, and also includes Amazon Pay. The service is sold as the best way to optimize the end customer's buying experience, but it can also serve to meet their strict shipping and delivery timelines, and consideration for listing among Prime-eligible products. Notable FBA expansion included roll-outs to Germany in 2010, Canada in 2012, Spain in 2013, India in 2015 and, most recently, Australia in 2018.

Boosted in part by ever-increasing speed and scale that Amazon has dedicated to its last mile with Prime Now, the number of merchants actively selling via the Marketplace and using FBA rose by 70 per cent between 2015 and 2016, although it does not disclose the revenue it generates from its Fulfilment by Amazon service. Meanwhile, the number of items Amazon sold on behalf of third-party sellers doubled during the same period. From a B2B perspective, we should also consider the impact of Amazon Business (known as AmazonSupply from its launch in 2012 until it was renamed in 2015). This competitive marketplace for B2B products on Amazon.com serves procurement business needs across a variety of product categories, such as laptops, computers, printers, office supplies, office furniture, hand tools, power tools, safety equipment, office kitchen essentials and cleaning supplies. A year later, the company revealed that Amazon Business had generated $1 billion in revenue, serving 400,000 business customers. From this perspective, given the sheer volume of products handled by both FBA and Amazon Business and, taken with its most recent moves into air cargo, ground transportation and ocean freight, Amazon is already a major global logistics player.

Even here, though, Amazon has experimented with services to make products available for rapid delivery directly from merchants to avoid overwhelming its own warehouses with additional inventory. The service, called Stellar Flex at its 2017 launch, was tested in India and on the US West coast and takes Amazon's logistical reach beyond its FCs to those of its merchants. The latest iteration, FBA Onsite, which emerged in 2018, gives Amazon greater flexibility and control over the last mile, while saving money through volume discounts and avoiding FC congestion. This comes after some industry insiders hinted that Amazon was a victim of its own and FBA's success, reducing orders through the end of 2017 due to capacity issues. At the same time, some estimates have suggested the cost savings of having sellers hold merchandise in their own facilities could be as high as 70 per cent. So, extending FBA into sellers' facilities could be another way of adding both capacity and scale to its growing logistics demands.

Amazon has also experimented with the returns process, which we referenced earlier as having a significant impact on all e-commerce players' bottom lines. Industry estimates suggest as much as 30 per cent of all products purchased online are returned. In a pilot programme announced late in 2017, Amazon partnered with Kohl's, for the US department store to sell Amazon hardware devices, but also to accept Amazon returns from customers. The retailer's store staff pack and ship eligible items back to an Amazon fulfilment centre for free.[25] Kohl's Chairman, President and CEO Kevin Mansell, commented a few months into the partnership: 'One thing is for sure: the experience is amazing, and people are using the service. If the customer responds, they think it's a great experience, they use the service, but very importantly, it drives incremental traffic, then we're going to look to expand it.'[26]

Race for the last mile

By comparison, Walmart's expanding transportation and logistics operations are driven largely by cost savings, required to balance the rising cost of fulfilling its e-commerce business with its vast, global store network. The grocer has begun leasing shipping containers to transport manufactured goods from China and is making greater use of lockers and instore pickup options mentioned earlier to cut down on delivery costs. In 2017, Cristy Brooks, Walmart US Innovations Development Director, outlined how the company is also tackling on-shelf availability in its larger stores. Out-of-stocks have been an issue the retailer has been urgently addressing in recent years. Its so-called Top Stock system stores inventory on the top shelves of the sales floor. This, Walmart claims, enables it to maintain 'fuller shelves while keeping a better in-the-moment read on inventory'. Benefits include a reduction in Walmart's use of rented temporary inventory trailers and the freeing up of back-room space, which has allowed the retailer to also integrate services like online grocery pickup, according to Brooks. This free space is also being used to provide staff training. Brooks cites its Morrisville, NC store as reducing its back-room inventory by 75 per cent in two months after implementing Top Stock and using the new space to open an associate training academy.[27] It also stole a march on Amazon and its Kohl's returns programme by updating its own online returns process in its stores via an update to the Walmart app late in 2017. The update meant some of its items for sale online, such as health and beauty products, were available for instant refunds without the need to visit a store.[28]

Amazon already offers instant refunds on some first-party and third-party purchases, and items below a certain value do not need to be physically returned. But Walmart has sought to keep pace in the fulfilment stakes with this returns initiative, which builds on its online grocery pickup, pickup towers, and free two-day shipping services – the latter of which it notably stresses is available without a membership fee.

Alibaba has begun leasing containers on ships, similar to Amazon's ocean freight initiative. This means that Alibaba Logistics can now facilitate first-mile shipping for third-party merchants on its marketplace. It is worth comparing the Alibaba logistics model with Amazon's. In 2003, Alibaba jointly launched the China Smart Logistic Network, also known as Cainiao, with eight other financial services and logistics companies. Today the Cainiao logistics network is made up of more than 15 major 3PL or logistics companies, while Alibaba took a controlling stake, increasing its share in the company from 47 to 51 per cent in 2017 with an $807 million investment. The Chinese giant said at the time that it was going to invest 100 billion yuan ($15 billion) in its global logistical capabilities over the next five years. It aims to build this capability using drones and robotics technology to deliver anywhere in China within 24 hours and anywhere in the world within 72 hours.

Considering Cainiao fulfils 57 million deliveries a day, the sheer dominance of Alibaba in its home market means it can wield significant power over the region's logistics network. Much like Amazon, it bases this power on technology investments that provide the supply chain visibility and data integration required to efficiently orchestrate fulfilment processes across this network. Despite the US, as the world's largest consumer economy, providing a base to its global operations, Amazon's market share is a fraction of the already mature US e-commerce market. By comparison, Alibaba's market share in China is over 60 per cent, where traditional trade still accounts for over 78 per cent of the world's second-largest and most rapidly growing consumer economy.

Alibaba rival JD.com has also been busy building out its own logistics network. Following a model similar to that used by Amazon, by the end of 2017 it had created a network of seven fulfilment centres and 486 warehouses across China and thousands of local delivery and pickup locations. JD.com has also reportedly been considering opening an FC in Los Angeles as an outpost for a US logistics expansion. Most notably for JD.com, in the spring of 2018, it launched a Europe–China freight train to carry goods that it can market to its domestic customers as soon as they are logged and on board. The first China Railway Express train, which travels 10,000 kilometres from Hamburg, Germany to Xi'an, the capital of central China's Shaanxi province, where JD operates one of its most important distribution hubs for cross-border imports, took 35 fewer days than ocean freight alternatives at a cost 80 per cent cheaper than air transport.

Liu Han, General Manager of International Supply chain at JD Logistics, said in a statement at the time, 'Through our use of a train from Germany to China fully dedicated to carrying goods destined for JD.com, we are dramatically reducing the time to market for European retailers and suppliers and providing our consumers with even more product choices at cheaper prices. With demand for imported European products soaring on JD, we expect to launch a regular service later this year, and we look forward to seeing this train make many more trips in the months and years ahead.'

Whole Foods and the future

Having examined the effect of express delivery and its impact on fulfilment demand and capacities on different continents, we come to the final major area of Amazon's fulfilment strategy, and it takes us back to where we started this chapter – where Amazon did not have a significant physical retail presence outside of its bookstore network, and so could not offer extensive online-to-offline services, such as click & collect, like its US rivals Walmart and Target or others across Europe and Asia. That was until the 2017 acquisition of Whole Foods Market and, by extension, not just its 450+ stores but also Whole Foods' retail grocery distribution network that serves them.

> 'When you think about [stores] doubling as warehouses, they're already profitable, they're already there, product is getting to them in full truckload quantities. It's the most efficient way to get product forward deployed.'
> **Mark Lore, Walmart US e-commerce division CEO**[29]

As discussed in Chapter 7, the acquisition of Whole Foods' distribution network, which is largely focused on perishables merchandise for its retail stores in each major market region served, will support the fulfilment of more third-party and own-label ranges while its store network will give it direct exposure to more urban retail locations. Some reports, however, highlighted how existing customers were unhappy that some stores' parking had been allocated to Prime Now delivery vehicles and that workers picking orders on the shop floor were competing for products and space with customers.

It's worth mentioning here that, at the time of writing, Whole Foods still fulfils orders through Instacart. At the time of the acquisition, Whole Foods accounted for nearly 10 per cent of Instacart's business and also owned a minority stake in the third-party delivery provider. But with Whole Foods now a subsidiary of Instacart's biggest rival, one wonders whether Amazon will sell Whole Foods' stake in Instacart, or just perhaps acquire it too? Given the initial online-to-offline success it has enjoyed with this acquisition, plus the last-mile distribution and fulfilment advantages that came with it, it is no wonder that speculation is also rife that it may be on the lookout for a similar acquisition in Europe that would provide it with another 1,300 stores 'doubling as warehouses', as Marc Lore might put it. Speculation is further fuelled by the fulfilment deals it has struck with a number of European retailers, including Casino banner Monoprix in France, Morrisons and Celesio pharmacies in the UK, Dia in Spain, and the Rossmann drugstore chain in Germany.

But with its current supply chain and store network strategy, moves to grow an ever greater supply of goods through it that includes fashion and grocery, and the means to drive demand with auto-replenishment and Alexa, what's next for Amazon fulfilment? One thing is for sure, it is likely to continue innovating in order to keep breaking records over the last mile, shrinking delivery windows and delighting customers by delivering their purchases to them ever faster.

Remote innovation

We haven't mentioned them yet but, having now explored Amazon's last-mile ambitions, we can now think about other interesting areas of development around not just fulfilment but also instant gratification outside of the traditional store format. The Amazon Treasure Truck gives Amazon app users access to daily discounts and exclusive products by registering to be notified when it is nearby. It was launched in Seattle in February 2016 and has since expanded to 30 major cities in the US and UK. Two other express fulfilment initiatives launched in 2017, AmazonFresh Pickup and Amazon Instant Pickup, can also now be understood in their full context. The first of these promises to have orders ready in as little as 15 minutes for people who pay an extra $15 per month for the 'Fresh Add-on' to their annual Amazon Prime subscription, as discussed in Chapter 7. The latter initiative raises the stakes even higher by making available items ready for collection from an Amazon Locker location within two minutes of placing an order. Again, customers must be Prime members who can refresh their app near an Amazon Instant Pickup location to see available items. These include small essentials, such as phone chargers, drinks and snacks, and Amazon products, including the Kindle and Echo, which are placed in an Amazon locker by an Amazon employee within two minutes of an order being placed. The first of these Instant Pickup lockers were placed near college campuses to cater to their constant turnover of visitors. In both of these cases, Amazon's anticipatory shipping patent – discussed earlier in the book as an example of Amazon's AI development – could prove crucial to their success, especially when combined with Amazon's developing metro-based Prime Now Hub and Delivery Station Network.

Also, in 2017, Amazon introduced in-home and in-car deliveries with Amazon Key. It gives Prime members in 37 eligible US urban areas the option to have Amazon Flex contractors drop deliveries off in their homes using a one-time entry code. At launch, customers were required to have specific manufacturers' smart locks and a capable version of Amazon's Cloud Cam security camera. To confirm delivery and protect against potential claims of fraud, the camera records as the courier uses the entry code to gain entry and until they exit, sending an image of the activity to the customer's smartphone. The Amazon Key app also enables remote door locking and unlocking, as well as for its users to issue virtual keys. But in 2018, Amazon ramped up its commitment in this and the wider Connected Home space with the acquisition of smart camera and doorbell manufacturer, Ring, for $1 billion. The investment is likely to accelerate efforts to increase the reach of its in-home delivery initiative, in a bid to one day perhaps consign missed deliveries to the history books and link the camera and audio equipment in Ring's doorbells to its proliferating Alexa voice-enabled Connected Home ecosystem.

Amazon Key In-Car allows owners of compatible vehicles to get packages delivered in their vehicle's trunk, as long as they are in the same areas served by Amazon Key's in-home delivery. Customers must park their cars in a publicly accessible area but they require no additional hardware. Like the in-home delivery, customers are given a four-hour delivery window.[30] It remains to be seen whether either in-home or in-car delivery proves popular enough to overcome any privacy and security concerns. But, as an extension of the locker concept and its last-mile advantages, Amazon has been developing the requisite technology for several years and can exploit a first-mover advantage. Future developments could see it capitalize on alliances it may forge to embed its Alexa voice assistant into car operating systems.

The final frontier, as far as Amazon's journey to fulfil orders ever faster is concerned, is drone technology. Jeff Bezos revealed plans to commercialize drone delivery at the end of 2013. By the end of 2016, Amazon announced that Prime Air had completed its first fully autonomous drone delivery. Flying from a Prime Air fulfilment centre in the Cambridge area with no pilot, it took 13 minutes from click to delivery.[31] Eligible items must be less than five pounds in weight, small enough to fit into the drone's cargo box and be delivered to within 10 miles of a participating FC. In addition to the Cambridge centre in the UK, the company has development centres in the US, Austria, France and Israel. The plans reveal the scale of Amazon's fulfilment ambitions, but are currently still only a concept, as the likely regulatory obstacles are still unknown.

In the meantime, Alibaba's own food delivery app Ele.me recently started using drones for food deliveries in China, while JD.com is well on its way to exploiting the vast continent's geographical scale to ramp up its use of drones too. In 2017, JD announced it was planning to build 150 airports for unmanned aerial deliveries, representing a significant strategic commitment to the technology. Its drones can currently carry up to 50 kilograms, although it is said to be working on drones that can carry 500kg. However, the investment will only support its limited application in the remote, mountainous Sichuan Province where long-range, radio-controlled communications are most effective. Battery life has also improved enough now for drones to fly almost continuously. But, practically speaking, the most advanced drones designed for commercial use today can fly for, on average, up to about 100 minutes with a flight range of some 35km. Even with such limitations, it is easy to see why JD.com is forging ahead with drone delivery, given its aim for this fulfilment method is to help cut freight costs by 70 per cent.

Whoever wins the race to mass drone deployment, one thing's for certain – it won't be the last innovation in the race to own the cheapest and fastest last mile.

Notes

1 Harkaway, Nick (2012) Amazon aren't destroying publishing, they're reshaping it, *Guardian*, 26 April. Available from: https://www.theguardian.com/books/2012/apr/26/amazon-publishing-destroying [Last accessed 5/11/2018].

2 Sisson, Patrick (2017) How Amazon's 'invisible' hand can shape your city, *Curbed*, 2 May. Available from: https://www.curbed.com/2017/5/2/15509316/amazon-prime-retail-urban-planning [Last accessed 6/6/2018].

3 Holmes, Thomas J (2005) The diffusion of Wal-Mart and economies of density, *Semantic Scholar*, November. Available from: https://pdfs.semantic-scholar.org/947c/d95a37c55eefb84ccab56896b4037f5c2acd.pdf [Last accessed 6/6/2018].

4 Machkovech, Sam (2015) Amazon Flex will pay you '$18-25 per hour' to deliver Prime Now packages, *Arstechnica*, 29 September. Available from: https://arstechnica.com/information-technology/2015/09/amazon-flex-will-pay-you-18-25-per-hour-to-deliver-prime-now-packages/ [Last accessed 17/5/2018].

5 Consumerist (2016) Amazon Flex Drivers are kind of freaking customers out, *ConsumerReports*, 7 October. Available from: https://www.consumerreports.org/consumerist/amazon-flex-drivers-are-kind-of-freaking-customers-out/ [Last accessed 7/6/2018].

6 Bhattacharya, Ananya (2015) Amazon sued by delivery drivers, *CNN Tech*, 29 October. Available from: http://money.cnn.com/2015/10/29/technology/amazon-sued-prime-now-delivery-drivers/ [Last accessed 7/6/2018].

7 Lore, Marc (2017) Serving customers in new ways: Walmart begins testing associate delivery, *Walmart Today* (Blog), 1 June. Available from: https://blog.walmart.com/innovation/20170601/serving-customers-in-new-ways-walmart-begins-testing-associate-delivery [Last accessed 7/6/2018].

8 Trump, Donald (2018) Amazon US Postal Service tweet, @realDonaldTrump, 31 March. Available from: https://twitter.com/realDonaldTrump/status/980063581592047617 [Last accessed 7/6/2018].

9 Gold, Michael and Rogers, Katie (2018) The facts behind Trump's tweets on Amazon, taxes and the postal service, *New York Times*, 29 March. Available from: https://www.nytimes.com/2018/03/29/us/politics/trump-amazon-post-office-fact-check.html [Last accessed 7/6/2018].

10 US Postal Accountability and Enhancement Act 2006.

11 Jaillet, James (2017) Walmart pressures its carriers against doing business with Amazon, *ccjdigital*, 17 July. Available from: https://www.ccjdigital.com/walmart-pressures-its-carriers-against-doing-business-with-amazon/ [Last accessed 17/5/2018].

12   Target (2017) Here's how acquiring Shipt will bring same-day delivery to about half of Target stores in early 2018, a bullseye view (Blog), 13 December. Available from: https://corporate.target.com/article/2017/12/target-acquires-shipt [Last accessed 7/6/2018].

13   Waldron, J (2016) Bullseye! The Power of Target's Fulfilment Strategy, *eTail*, 20 June. Available from: https://etaileast.wbresearch.com/bullseye-the-power-of-targets-fulfillment-strategy [Last accessed 8 October 2018].

14   Deepfield Networks (2012) How big is Amazon's Cloud? *DeepField Networks*, 18 April. Available from: https://blogdeepfield.wordpress.com/2012/04/18/how-big-is-amazons-cloud/ [Last accessed 10/6/2018].

15   Wulfraat, Marc (2018) Amazon Global Fulfilment Centre Network, *MWPVL International Inc.*, June. Available from: http://www.mwpvl.com/html/amazon_com.html [Last accessed 19/6/2018].

16   Finley, Klint (2013) Christmas delivery fiasco shows why Amazon wants its own UPS, *Wired*, 30 December. Available from: https://www.wired.com/2013/12/amazon-ups/ [Last accessed 10/6/2018].

17   Sisson, Patrick (2017) 9 facts about Amazon's unprecedented warehouse empire, *Curbed*, 21 November. Available from: https://www.curbed.com/2017/11/21/16686150/amazons-warehouse-fulfillment-black-friday [Last accessed 9/9/2018].

18   Edwards, Jim (2013) Brutal conditions in Amazon's warehouses threaten to ruin the company's image, *Business Insider UK*, 5 August. Available from: http://www.businessinsider.com/brutal-conditions-in-amazons-warehouses-2013-8?IR=T [Last accessed 10/6/2018].

19   Wikiquote (nd) Warren Bennis. Available from: https://en.wikiquote.org/wiki/Warren_Bennis [Last accessed 23/9/2018].

20   Smith, Cooper (2016) The Future of Shipping Report: Why big ecommerce companies are going after the legacy shipping industry, *Morgan Stanley*, June. Available from: https://read.bi/2JxXJMc [Last accessed 6/6/2018].

21   Greene, Jay and Gates, Dominic (2015) Amazon in talks to lease Boeing jets to launch its own air-cargo business, *Seattle Times*, 17 December. Available from: https://www.seattletimes.com/business/amazon/amazon-in-talks-to-lease-20-jets-to-launch-air-cargo-business/ [Last accessed 10/6/2018].

22   Kim, Eugene (2017) Amazon quietly launched an app called Relay to go after truck drivers, *CNBC*, 16 November. Available from: https://www.cnbc.com/2017/11/16/amazon-quietly-launched-an-app-called-relay-to-go-after-truck-drivers.html [Last accessed 17/6/2018].

23   Amazon Technologies, Inc. US Patent Application (2013) Providing services related to item delivery via 3D manufacturing on demand, US Patent & Trademark Office, 8 November. Available from: https://bit.ly/1aQfBvU [Last accessed 10/6/2018].

24 Amazon Technologies, Inc. US Patent Application (2018) Vendor interface for item delivery via 3D manufacturing on demand, US Patent & Trademark Office, 2 January. Available from: http://pdfpiw.uspto.gov/. piw?Docid=09858604 [Last accessed 10/6/2018].

25 Amazon has also rolled the same service out at Whole Foods to Amazon.com customers since its acquisition.

26 Gurdus, Elizabeth (2018) Kohl's CEO says 'big idea' behind Amazon partnership is driving traffic, *CNBC.com*, 27 March. Available from: https://www.cnbc.com/2018/03/27/kohls-ceo-big-idea-behind-amazon-partnership-is-driving-traffic.html [Last accessed 20/6/2018].

27 Brooks, Cristy (2017) Why smarter inventory means better customer service, *Walmart Today*, 16 August. Available from: https://blog.walmart.com/ business/20170816/why-smarter-inventory-means-better-customer-service [Last accessed 20/6/2018].

28 Walmart (2017) Walmart reinvents the returns process (blog post), *Walmart*, 9 October. Available from: https://news.walmart.com/2017/10/09/walmart-reinvents-the-returns-process [Last accessed 20/6/2018].

29 Nusca, Andrew (2017) 5 moves Walmart is making to compete with Amazon and Target, *Fortune*, 27 September. Available from: http://fortune. com/2017/09/27/5-moves-walmart-is-making-to-compete-with-amazon-and-target/ [Last accessed 13/9/2018].

30 Amazon (2018) Press release: Buckle up, Prime members: Amazon launches in-car delivery, *Amazon*, 24 April. Available from: http://phx.corporate-ir.net/ phoenix.zhtml?c=176060&p=irol-newsArticle&ID=2344122 [Last accessed 10/6/2018].

31 Amazon (2016) First Prime Air delivery (video). Available from: https://www.amazon.com/Amazon-Prime-Air/b?ie=UTF8&node=8037720011 [Last accessed 9/9/2018].

Conclusion: peak Amazon? 15

'Amazon is now a large corporation and I expect us to be scrutinized.'
Jeff Bezos, 2018[1]

Since Day 1, Amazon's relentless mission to put the customer at the centre of everything it does has also led to it offering its customers almost everything. Amazon has capitalized on the advent of pervasive tech interfaces, ubiquitous connectivity and autonomous computing embraced by the on-my-terms shopper to become one of the most dominant retail forces the world has ever seen.

Our examination of Amazon's flywheel model and digital ecosystem has demonstrated the central role it has had to play in exposing its rival incumbent retail leaders' deficiencies. Overspaced, underperforming and digitally barren store estates with poorly integrated e-commerce channels will continue to weed out the winners from the losers, only feeding Amazon's competitive ambitions.

But Amazon's astronomical growth to date certainly hasn't gone unnoticed in Washington, where the topic of the retailer's dominance is getting increasingly more airtime. Even Bezos himself recognizes that it's only normal that a sprawling empire like his attracts greater government scrutiny.

According to Lina Khan, author of the highly influential paper 'Amazon's Antitrust Paradox', published in the *Yale Law Journal* in 2017, Amazon has previously evaded such attention from lawmakers because current antitrust law 'assesses competition largely with an eye to the short-term interests of consumers, not producers or the health of the market as a whole; antitrust doctrine views low consumer prices, alone, to be evidence of sound competition.'[2]

With Amazon, it's difficult to demonstrate any harm done to consumers in the form of higher prices or lower quality. Ripping shoppers off is hardly conducive to Amazon's mission to become Earth's most customer-centric company. Such a strategy wouldn't have supported its growth to become worth over two and a half times more than its biggest brick-and-mortar counterpart, Walmart, in 2018. The difference in market valuation comes in spite of Walmart generating approximately three times Amazon's annual revenue and net income in 2017. 'It is as if Bezos charted the company's growth by first drawing a map of antitrust laws, and then devising routes to smoothly bypass them. With its missionary zeal for consumers, Amazon has marched toward monopoly by singing the tune of contemporary antitrust', said Khan.

Amazon's dominance has come at a cost – one that most normal retailers could not bear – and now there are growing calls for existing legislation to be rewritten for the digital age. Trump's tweets may get all the publicity, but Amazon is now facing bipartisan backlash. On the far right, former Trump advisor Steve Bannon has called for tech giants to be regulated like public utilities since they have become so essential to 21st-century life; while Democratic Party leaders pushed for a wider antitrust crackdown in 2018 as part of their 'Better Deal' economic platform. 'We're seeing this incredibly large company getting involved in almost every area of commerce and I think it is important to look at the power and influence Amazon has', said Democratic Senator Bernie Sanders in 2018.[3]

Khan argues that predatory pricing and vertical integration are highly relevant to analysing Amazon's path to dominance – and that current doctrine underappreciates the risk of such practices. The playing field has been tilted since day one, from the moment that Bezos convinced his early investors that a growth-over-profits strategy would yield results in the long run. Amazon has always played by its own set of rules. The result today? It is uncatchable.

Its competitive advantage only deepens as Amazon relentlessly diversifies into new services and upends entire sectors. This is, after all, the whole premise of Amazon's flywheel. But how much is too much? Not just for regulators, but also consumers. No other retailer has so successfully embedded itself into the consumer's life and physical home. Amazon has become ubiquitous. Through its ecosystem, Amazon is an indispensable resource, a way of life for many shoppers – but as Amazon moves into new consumer-facing sectors like grocery, fashion, healthcare and banking, its brand elasticity will be tested. Consumers will sacrifice many things for convenience (price and privacy, for example), but we believe that sentiment would quickly change if Amazon became too powerful, too pervasive. Are we perhaps nearing peak Amazon?

At the same time, Amazon's platform has become a dominant e-commerce enabler. Amazon is the world's largest product search engine. Its algorithms promote its own products. Its various devices – from Echo speakers to Dash Buttons – seamlessly funnel purchases through to its platform. Amazon has access to data unlike any other retailer in the world. For decades, it wasn't subject to the same tax laws as its bricks and mortar counterparts. Its retail business is subsidized by higher-margin segments like AWS and, in the future, advertising will continue to grow to become another highly profitable revenue stream. You don't need to be an antitrust guru to recognize that Amazon has reaped the rewards of an uneven playing field.

So, what happens next? Could Amazon be broken up? Could it spin off its AWS division to appease both regulators and competing retailers (a growing number of which refuse to dance with the devil)? In our opinion, the prospect of antitrust activity represents one of the only current credible threats to Amazon's growth. But its flywheel business model has also in-built resilience: founded on the tech-based concept of a service-oriented architecture, each component or module shares core internal services provided by the three pillars. This is one of the reasons why we predict Amazon's services revenue will soon outstrip that of its retail business.

We can count on one hand the number of retailers that can genuinely give Amazon a run for its money (hint: they're all based in Asia). Amazon is and will always be a technology company first, retailer second. But understanding where it applies its technology expertise to remove friction from the most functional shopping experiences can help rivals keep pace. We believe retailers can co-exist with Amazon if they stick to these five basic principles:

1 Curate: don't try to out-Amazon Amazon.

2 Differentiate: go (way) beyond selling.

3 Innovate: think of your stores as assets and not liabilities.

4 Don't go it alone.

5 Move quickly.

This is not to say that there won't be some short-term pain along the way. We must brace ourselves for further rounds of store closures, bankruptcies, redundancies and consolidation as the sector reconfigures for the digital age. Time is of the essence – there will be no second chances for retailers that fail to adapt, as the climate is simply too unforgiving. Ultimately, the retailers that survive digital transformation will be those that follow the customer, ensuring they remain relevant in the age of Amazon.

Notes

1 Kumar, Kavita (2018) Amazon's Bezos calls Best Buy turnaround 'remarkable' as unveils new TV partnership, *Star Tribune*, 19 April. Available from: http://www.startribune.com/best-buy-and-amazon-partner-up-in-exclusive-deal-to-sell-new-tvs/480059943/ [Last accessed 2/11/2018].

2 Khan, Lina (2017) Amazon's antitrust paradox, *Yale Law Journal*, 3 January. Available from: http://digitalcommons.law.yale.edu/cgi/viewcontent.cgi?article=5785&context=ylj [Last accessed 7/7/2018].

3 CNN (2018) Sen. Bernie Sanders: Amazon has gotten too big, *YouTube*, 1 April. Available from: https://www.youtube.com/watch?v=-AxDWoR_zaQ&feature=share [Last accessed 8/7/2018].

INDEX

Note: Chapter notes are indexed as such page numbers in *italic* indicate figures or tables